The Royal Navy and the

By the same author

GUNBOAT DIPLOMACY
(Chatto and Windus, 1971)

The Royal Navy

&

the Siege of Bilbao

JAMES CABLE

CAMBRIDGE UNIVERSITY PRESS

CAMBRIDGE

LONDON   NEW YORK   NEW ROCHELLE
MELBOURNE   SYDNEY

Published by the Press Syndicate of the University of Cambridge
The Pitt Building, Trumpington Street, Cambridge CB2 1RP
32 East 57th Street, New York, NY 10022, USA
296 Beaconsfield Parade, Middle Park, Melbourne 3206, Australia

© Cambridge University Press 1979

First published 1979

Printed and bound in Great Britain by
T. & A. Constable Ltd, Edinburgh

Library of Congress Cataloguing in Publication Data
Cable, James, 1920-
The Royal Navy and the Siege of Bilbao.
Bibliography: p.
Includes index.
1. Bilbao, Spain—Siege, 1937. 2. Spain—History—
Civil War, 1936-1939—Foreign participation—British.
3. Spain—History—Civil War, 1936-1939—Hospitals,
charities, etc. 4. Spain—History—Civil War, 1936-
1939—Children. 5. Spain—History—Civil War, 1936-
1939—Refugees. 6. Great Britain—History, Naval—
20th century. I. Title.
DP269.27.B5C32   946.081   78.73238
ISBN 0 521 22516 7

For Viveca as always

For the Thracian ships and the foreign faces
The tongueless vigil, and all the pain

Swinburne

Contents

Acknowledgments

Transcripts of Crown-copyright records in the Public Record Office appear by kind permission of the Controller of H.M. Stationery Office and references to a manuscript in the National Maritime Museum at Greenwich, as well as the photograph on the dust jacket, by that of the Trustees. Individual references to these documents as well as to the sources, whether written or oral, of other statements in the text will be found in the footnotes and need not be repeated here.

This is, however, the appropriate place to record the author's gratitude to all the people who helped him with information and advice, as well as to all the writers whose books he has consulted or quoted. Vice-Admiral Clifford Caslon, Vice-Admiral Sir Ian McGeoch (who kindly permitted quotation from articles in the *Naval Review*), Vice-Admiral Sir Peter Gretton, Mr and Mrs Bautista Lopez, Mr Angus Malcolm, Dame Leah Manning, Rear-Admiral W. J. Munn, Mr Angel de Ojanguren, Miss Pilar Ortiz de Zarate, Professor A. Temple Patterson, Mr Marcel Segurola and Miss J. Stevenson patiently answered innumerable questions and, in many cases, read and commented on portions of the text. Professor Bryan McL. Ranft, formerly of the Royal Naval College at Greenwich, has always been a helpful guide and many other naval officers, officials, librarians and learned men and women have smoothed the author's path for him. None of these bears any responsibility for the opinions expressed in this book or for its errors.

JAMES CABLE

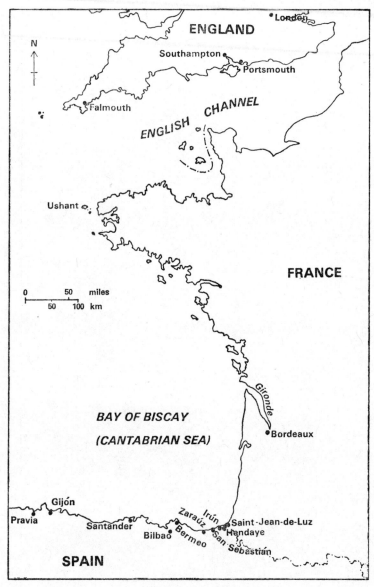

Map 1 showing the general area of naval operations.

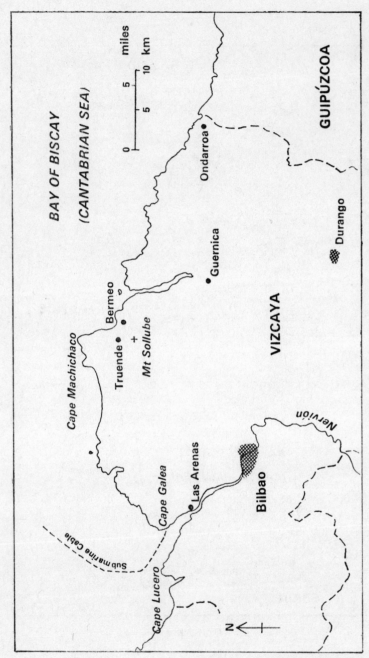

Map 2 showing the scene of the war in the north.

Introduction

―――――

> What was the explanation of this
> curious incident in the history of
> British shipping?
>
> Thomas[1]

This is the story of an episode in the Spanish Civil War, but
that conflict will be treated as no more than the background,
vast, sombre and luridly flickering, to the minor drama of
British naval diplomacy on the north coast of Spain during the
spring of 1937. The central theme is the use of British warships
to protect Spanish children in their flight across the Bay of
Biscay. Introduced by an account of the origins and motives of
British intervention, it will find its final resolution in a discussion of the consequences. To employ a musical metaphor, the
central theme will be expounded and elaborated in the key of
British public opinion, of the controversies that divided
British officials and the doubts that assailed British Ministers.
The incidents described would never have occurred, and their
exposition would be incomplete, without the wider context
of the convulsion that for three bitter years held all Spain in its
frantic grip. But the agonies and the animosities of Spaniards
are not the subject of this book, which tells an essentially
British tale and from a standpoint that is deliberately insular.

The Spanish setting may thus be simplified to the barest
framework of time and place. General Franco's right-wing
revolt against the left-wing government of the Spanish Republic
began on 18 July 1936; by September he had established his
authority over that part of the country north and west of Madrid

―――――

[1] Hugh Thomas, *The Spanish Civil War* (Eyre and Spottiswoode, 1961),
p. 411.

except for a strip of the Biscayan coast 150 miles long; in the following March his troops launched an offensive against this enclave and, by mid-June, had captured Bilbao, principal city and port of northern Spain and capital of the ephemeral Basque Autonomous Republic. This offensive, however, was supplemented by efforts to exercise a maritime blockade of the Spanish ports on the Bay of Biscay and it is the resulting encounters between Spanish and British warships, together with the contortions these introduced into British policy, that give this spring its special relevance in these pages.

The events of those few months, their antecedents and their results, offer a twofold interest. Their analysis presents an instance of the recent employment of an ancient, yet still valid, expedient of governments: the use of limited naval force, otherwise than as an act of war, to promote the objectives of foreign policy.[1] As we follow the evolutions of warships, consider the results of their actions and compare these with the motives of those issuing the orders, we may hope to reach conclusions on the utility and nature of the techniques involved. But this story is also a revealing anecdote from a vanished era, an illustration of British attitudes in those last, now almost inconceivable, years when Britain still asserted her claim, already challenged and even then sometimes hesitantly advanced, to the proud independence of a Great Power. This is how even a weak, reluctant, timorous British Government could once impose their presence and enforce their wishes upon the international scene.

The significance, in the larger perspectives of world history, of the conduct of the British Government is a question neither posed nor answered in these pages. Nor has much attempt been made to assess the moral or the political merits of the considerations that influenced those concerned. This artificially isolated drama is developed in terms of the contemporary motives of its actors, who are praised or blamed in the light of the objectives they had themselves selected. This is a study of technique, but

[1] For a more extended discussion of this concept, see James Cable, *Gunboat Diplomacy* (Chatto and Windus, 1971).

it is also a story of human beings and of their confused, uncertain, sometimes impulsive, reactions to situations as emotionally provocative as they were often morally and politically ambiguous.

This approach, with its British bias and its attempt to depict Spanish problems as glimpsed through naval binoculars or interpreted by diplomats and consuls, has also dictated the choice of sources. These are primarily the telegrams and despatches of British representatives in Spain, the reports of naval officers off-shore, the records of ministerial and official deliberations in London. They fill many volumes in the archives, now preserved in the Public Record Office, of the Admiralty, the Cabinet and the Foreign Office. Many more, alas, are missing, a few because they are still withheld from public scrutiny, most because they have been irretrievably destroyed. The gaps are most tantalising in the records of the Admiralty, who had the odd habit of filing the instructions they issued in isolation from the reports of action taken. Moreover that Department destroyed its archives with a wanton hand. No less than twenty-four large volumes, all of them apparently bearing on this particular episode and probably containing most of the orders issued by the Admiralty, together with the minutes which led up to their decisions, were peremptorily pulped.

Fortunately many of the holes can be plugged from the records of the Cabinet and the Foreign Office, who preserved communications from the Admiralty and copies of their signals more carefully than did the originators. The copious Reports of Proceedings compiled by naval officers on the spot also often include the text or a digest of the orders on which they acted. Some gaps remain, however, and have necessarily been filled by conjecture. If this guess-work, which is always indicated as such, occasionally does less than justice to the Admiralty of those days, then the officials who preserved the log of ROYAL OAK, yet destroyed the instructions issued to the Admiral whose flag she flew, must bear the consequences of their own heedlessness of history.

However critically interpreted, therefore, this account is in the main drawn from British official sources and reflects events in a single, and somewhat partial, perspective. Nevertheless, some attempt has been made to enliven, and even to correct, the picture seen at the time by bureaucratic eyes. Contemporary newspapers, for instance, though often factually inaccurate, add local colour and reflect the attitudes and impressions prevailing at the time. So does Hansard and the author has had access to some useful private letters composed when the events they described were still fresh in the minds of the writers. For memory is fallible, a truism vividly impressed on the author by his interviews with survivors of these events. His gratitude to them is separately and individually recorded. Their remembered impressions were valuable; the naval officers among them, in particular, were often able to explain much that might other-wise have remained obscure to a landsman; they were all generous in the time they devoted to answering questions. But some had altogether forgotten the incidents in which they had been concerned and the recollections of others could not be reconciled with what they had themselves recorded when it happened. Their information has been sparingly and cautiously employed.

Better sources are to be found in books, articles and pamph-lets published at the time. Even when these are marked by the strong bias characteristic of most writings on the Spanish Civil War, a little evidence can usually be winnowed from the chaff of propaganda. When many pages are devoted to explaining an incident away, then the likelihood that something of the sort actually took place is at least worth exploring.

Books written from memory alone lose evidential value with every year that divides them from the events they describe. Most of them are useful only to indicate the prejudices of their authors, which linger for years after facts are forgotten. The works of historians, on the other hand, labour under an oppo-site disability. Anything published before 1969 was necessarily written without the advantage – for which every historian should gratefully salute Sir Harold Wilson – of access under the 'thirty year rule' to the relevant official records. Nevertheless the author is deeply indebted to the work of many historians whose diligence and professional abilities put his to shame.

The most efficacious corrective, however, to the insidious attractions of the official view was provided by a remarkable book, now regrettably out of print: *The Tree of Gernika: A Field Study of Modern War* published in January 1938 by Hodder and Stoughton. Its author, George Lowther Steer, was described in the obituary which *The Times* published after his tragically wasted death in a motor accident on Christmas Day 1944 as the son of a South African newspaper proprietor. Born in the town of East London in 1909 he was educated at Winchester (where he edited the school magazine) and Christ Church, began his journalistic career in South Africa and joined *The Times* in 1935 as their special correspondent in Abyssinia, whence he was expelled by the Italians. He was subsequently sent by *The Times* to Spain, where he concentrated much of his efforts on observing and reporting those events in the northern sector with which this book is particularly concerned. His account of the destruction of Guernica was accorded great prominence in his newspaper, attracted much attention and exercised considerable influence.

Having severed his connection with *The Times* – in circumstances not specified in his obituary – Steer then wrote a book about the short-lived autonomous Basque Republic and its destruction in the Civil War. This was a work of passionate engagement, a vivid, moving, exciting justification of Basque nationalism, a shrewd, if slanted, analysis of the circumstances and causes of their defeat, an urgent warning to his own countrymen of the wrath to come. Steer was something of an artist and his book has a quality rare in the productions of even the most brilliant journalists. The historians who have followed his version of events, however, had more than the seduction of his style to excuse their choice. Steer had seen for himself much of what he described and, as a brave man driven to desperation by the recent loss of his first wife, he saw more than most, being particularly fascinated by the detailed conduct of military operations.

Of course, he also had the faults of his professional virtues. He was a journalist, not a historian, and he affected the omniscience of his trade, too often blurring the distinction between observation and deduction, evidence and hearsay. His facts are not always reliable, his judgments are occasionally hasty, his dates are slapdash.

Nevertheless, anyone who takes the trouble to compare Steer's guesses with the evidence of the documents is continually astonished, not at his inevitable errors, but at the frequency with which his assumptions were correct. Written in the incandescence of 1937 Steer's interpretation of the motives of his countrymen hit the mark more often than it went astray. He had the advantage of being an outsider educated in the bosom of the Establishment: his outlook and his ideas were intensely individual, but he understood those of the orthodox. The special value of his account, however, resides in its very bias. The prudential considerations – of British national interests and British domestic politics – which influenced the conduct of British Ministers and officials were alien to Steer, even if he understood and analysed them. As a romantic he had surrendered himself to the lost cause of Basque Nationalism; as an idealist, a visionary, he was utterly convinced that General Franco represented the enemy, not only of Britain, but of the hopes of humanity. He devoted himself to exposing the shams and hypocrisies of British policy primarily as the partisan of a different and incompatible purpose. But he also had a healthy hatred of humbug and this occasionally bursts out in unexpected places.

He is thus the natural *advocatus diaboli* of the present work and excerpts from his narrative will appear throughout these pages, both as counterpoint to the official melody and on their own merits as the first-hand impressions of an exceptionally literate reporter. If his words are sometimes introduced only to be refuted, this is because enthusiasm occasionally betrayed him into injustice. His account remains one which no student of the period can afford to neglect: a constant and necessary irritant to investigation.

6

Introduction

It is naturally not a book which can be recommended to anyone in quest of an objective and impartial description of the Spanish background – the storm-wrack projected on the cyclorama behind the selectively illuminated actors of these pages. These men and women, playing their minor and incidental parts, have been depicted with such dispassion and understanding as the author can command. But there may be readers impatient at so restricted a perspective, anxious to judge British actions in a wider context than the immediate and interested preoccupations of those Britons who were officially or politically or emotionally involved. Finding no guidance in these pages such readers may wish to be directed to the book, or books, that will illuminate the Spanish background, set this little drama on a greater stage, reveal the larger truth or, at least, identify the prejudices of the author.

There are hundreds, perhaps thousands, of books on the Spanish Civil War: broad treatments, microscopic investigations, tracts and reminiscences. They are written in most languages and cater for every prejudice. The student will find a few of the more directly relevant listed in the bibliography of the present work. But the reader wanting no more than a sense of the moral climate of the war and an indication of the author's particular bias need study only one. It is conveniently compact – a mere eighty-five pages – it is easily understood and its authority is beyond dispute. It is called *Los Desastres de la Guerra* by Francisco Goya and it is not a book for the squeamish.

CHAPTER I

The encounter

algún buque grande, de esos que
nosotros vimos en el már al venir
hacia aqui.

The children's letter[1]

There was little warmth in the darkness at four o'clock (British
Summer Time) in the morning, when the watch was relieved
on board H.M.S. ROYAL OAK. Admittedly it was spring –
Thursday 6 May 1937 – and the battleship was steaming slowly,
creeping obliquely towards the coast of Spain through a moderate sea and a breeze that was no more than brisk. But this was
the Bay of Biscay, not the Mediterranean, and at 50° Fahrenheit
the air was as cool as the water.[2] Sunrise, at 0545, left the
thermometer unmoved, but the spreading light did at least
reveal H.M.S. FAULKNOR, leader of the Sixth Destroyer Flotilla,
breasting the waves in company after her return from the
vicinity of Bilbao where she had earlier hove to just outside
territorial waters and sent Mr Consul Stevenson, whom she
had brought from Saint-Jean-de-Luz, ashore by boat.[3] A less
familiar sight at this early hour was the arrival, not merely of
Captain Drew, but of Rear-Admiral Ramsey, irreverently
nick-named 'The Ocean Swell',[4] whose flag ROYAL OAK was
flying in his capacity as Rear-Admiral Second Battle Squadron.

[1] 'Some big boat, one of those we saw in the sea on our way here.' Letter of
19 June 1937 from the Basque children at North Stoneham Camp, Hampshire, to Mr Neville Chamberlain, Prime Minister of Great Britain, File
FO 371 21372 in Public Record Office, London. All subsequent manuscript references are to documents in the Public Record Office, unless
otherwise stated.
[2] Log of ROYAL OAK, ADM 53/105586.
[3] FO 371 21292.
[4] Sir Geoffrey Thompson, *Front Line Diplomat* (Hutchinson, 1959), ch. 10.

And, as if to illustrate the inevitable consequences of disturbing an admiral at dawn, sharp on the hour of six sleep was shattered for all on board by the sounding of Action Stations. The helm was put over, speed was slightly increased and, now ready for anything, ROYAL OAK and FAULKNOR headed for Bilbao. To be precise, they were making for a point 4 miles off that port, where H.M.S. FORTUNE, still 12 miles away and out of sight, was waiting. Also waiting, but over the northern horizon, were ROYAL OAK's sister ship, H.M.S. RESOLUTION and her two accompanying destroyers.[1]

The cause of all this naval activity was not immediately apparent. Only FORTUNE was even in sight of the green hills of Vizcaya, where tired Basques and their Spanish Republican allies had another two hours to await the renewed onslaught of German bombers, Spanish Nationalist and Italian infantry, and Spanish artillery. And that battle would be no concern of the British Navy's. Unlike the eager representative of *The Times* – 2 miles inland at that moment and striding south from Truende on his inspection of the front – whose passionate commitment to the defenders still burns from his vivid pages,[2] Admiral Ramsey was obliged by British policy to regard the progress of General Mola's offensive with complete detachment. The doctrine of Non-Intervention, of scrupulous British abstention from assistance to either side in the Spanish Civil War, had been impressed on the Navy for nearly a year now and, although there might be occasional variations, even differences of opinion, in its interpretation and practical application, it probably commanded general support as well as obedience. The Navy would take no hand in that day's struggle for Cape Machichaco or Mount Sollube – would not even know how the issue had been decided, until the B.B.C., or *The Times*, should tell them.

In any case, nobody was looking that way. For the moment the focus of attention was a plume of smoke approaching from

[1] ADM 116 3516.
[2] G. L. Steer, *The Tree of Gernika* (Hodder and Stoughton, 1938), pp. 268–9.

the eastern horizon – visibility was 8 miles – and it was already identifiable, with the aid of a good pair of binoculars, as the Spanish Nationalist cruiser ALMIRANTE CERVERA, a long, low, elegant ship, Spanish built to a British design.[1] At 0624 a signal winked out from the flagship and FAULKNOR surged off in the spectacularly accelerating curve that is the special privilege and delight of destroyers. She had a message to deliver. Almost simultaneously, at 0633, a signal came in from FORTUNE, still patrolling four miles off the entrance to the outer harbour of Bilbao: the Spanish liner HABANA and the steam yacht GOIZEKO-IZARRA were just emerging. All the characters were now on stage and preparing to gather off Galea Point: it was time for the play to begin.

Though technically the correct description, the word 'liner' could give a misleading impression of HABANA. With a top speed of 16 knots, this 10,000 tonner had never been in the Cunarder class, but now she was fourteen years old and a trifle shabby. Moreover, she had been crammed with passengers till these seemed bound to burst over the rails that crowned her rusty, black sides: three thousand of them, two thirds children, filling every cabin, packing the public rooms, pushing and shoving through every corridor, thronging the open deck. Even the little GOIZEKO-IZARRA, a rich man's toy, with the gold leaf still enlivening her flaking white paint, had 300 children to admire her buff funnel, her two raked masts, her clipper bow. Both ships were supposed to have been flying the Saint George's Cross, but this detail of an elaborate plan, nearly all of which had survived weeks of aerial bombardment and diplomatic and political argument, had somehow escaped attention. Flag or no flag, however, everyone knew that these were two shiploads of Republican refugees seeking safety in France, where the Confédération Générale du Travail had offered hospitality, from the Nationalist bombing and the blockade of Bilbao.[2]

ALMIRANTE CERVERA, in particular, had by now been told by FAULKNOR that the Royal Navy had orders to protect HABANA

---

[1] *Jane's Fighting Ships* (Sampson Low, Marston, 1937/8).
[2] ADM 116 3516; Steer, *Tree of Gernika*, pp. 261-2.

and GOIZEKO-IZARRA once these had passed the 3 mile limit. This happened before 0700, the responsibility of identifying the exact moment being laid upon the destroyer FORTUNE, who then hoisted the international signal for 'follow me' and simultaneously informed ROYAL OAK, who flashed the message on to ALMIRANTE CERVERA, by now at the convenient distance of 1 mile north of the British flagship.

The cruiser's captain – the Royal Navy thought he was the Duke of Santo Maura[1] but he was actually Capitán de Navío don Manuel Moreu[2] – did not at first seem disposed to draw the appropriate conclusions from the information thus communicated. Indeed, having closely observed ALMIRANTE CERVERA's movements, FAULKNOR felt constrained to send Admiral Ramsey a reassuring message at 0710: the cruiser's starboard torpedo tubes were not loaded. Nevertheless the cruiser's course – and she had nearly twice the speed of ROYAL OAK[3] – was clearly designed to intercept the two refugee ships. At 0715 Captain Moreu decided to remove all doubts and signalled to ROYAL OAK:

I got orders from my Government to stop any Spanish Ship leaving Bilbao. I protest if you stop me in the exercise of my rights.

Admiral Ramsey allowed himself a few minutes to compose a careful answer, which was sent at 0732:

These ships are carrying non-combatant refugees certified by British Consul. I have orders from my Government to protect these ships on the High Seas. I have noted your protest and will inform my Government.

---

[1] ADM 116 3518.

[2] Almirante Juan Cervera Valderrama, *Memorias de Guerra* (Editora Nacional, Madrid, 1968), p. 135. The cruiser was not named after this officer, then Chief of Staff of General Franco's Navy, but after one of his ancestors, the Cerveras having for generations contributed a disproportionate number of Admirals to the Spanish Navy. This author quotes a slightly different wording for some of the signals exchanged on 6 May 1937, but the sense is the same.

[3] So Admiral Ramsey thought at the time, but Vice-Admiral Sir Peter Gretton has obligingly pointed out to the author that ALMIRANTE CERVERA then had condenser trouble and was not nearly capable of her designed speed.

ROYAL OAK, whose speed never exceeded 14 knots that morning, ploughed ponderously on, her 29,000 tons cleaving the waves on a course of 030° towards the distant mouth of the Gironde. She had previously been steering S.W. to close FORTUNE and the refugee ships, but, once they were near enough, had reversed her course, in order to escort them towards France and safety. At this moment ROYAL OAK was probably ahead of the convoy (still steaming north) and steering an obliquely closing course. ALMIRANTE CERVERA, not yet ready to take 'no' for an answer, profited by her superior speed to cross ROYAL OAK's bows at a distance of about 4 cables (4/10 of a nautical mile), thus allowing Admiral Ramsey to observe that her guns were manned and to deduce that she intended (she was steering east) to place herself between the battleship and the two Spanish vessels – escorted by FORTUNE – which were by now well outside territorial waters. But the cruiser had been manoeuvred onto an outer circle and, while she described a surging arc towards her objective, ROYAL OAK's slower turn to starboard preserved the British ship's interposing stance.

Her manoeuvre foiled, ALMIRANTE CERVERA reverted to argument. At 0740 she signalled:

Non-combatants should be conducted to National Port where they will be assisted by my Government.

'Assist' – according to the Spanish account the word employed was 'atendidos', which means 'attended to'[1] – can sometimes be an ambiguous verb, but there was no need for Admiral Ramsey to ponder its subtleties or to recall those unfortunate occasions when offers of quarter – from both sides in this bitter war – had been unexpectedly interpreted. His reply at 0745 could be, had to be, simple and straightforward:

My Government order me to conduct these ships to a French port.[2]

In 1937 a battleship was still a superior ship, particularly when she had contrived to keep herself in the interposing position and was rather unfairly accompanied by two destroyers

---

[1] Cervera, *Memorias de Guerra.*   [2] ADM 116 3516.

capable of outpacing even a light cruiser. ALMIRANTE CERVERA's gun crews (she had only 6 inch guns and ROYAL OAK 15 inch) were observed to fall out and, at 0757, as H.M. ships, together with the two Spanish vessels they were escorting, altered course to 030° once more, the cruiser sheered off and headed towards Bilbao. Even before the watch could again be changed at 0800 the whole episode was over, probably before the Spanish Ambassadress in London – a Republican Ambassadress naturally – whose gown of green mousseline, train of Granada point lace, pearl tiara and pearls had been noted at the Court held by the King and Queen at Buckingham Palace the night before, had even had time to taste her morning chocolate.[1] Some hours would pass before Stevenson called on President Aguirre in Bilbao and listened, with sad surprise, to His Excellency's optimistic account of the battle raging in the eastern hills,[2] or before Sir Henry Chilton, the British Ambassador to Spain, now more conveniently accommodated in the French town of Hendaye, would read General Franco's anticipatory description of the morning's maritime events as 'an attack upon the prestige of its navy and upon the sovereignty of Spain'.[3] It was still rather early, but not too early for the Junkers and Heinkels which, at this precise moment of eight o'clock – just as, one hopes, the Admiral was contemplating the prospect of a peaceful and well-earned breakfast – began, along the armed mountain ridge that still barred the road to Bilbao, to unleash the first bombs of the day on the fathers and husbands and brothers of HABANA's passengers.[4]

Few of these – and probably still fewer on GOIZEKO-IZARRA – are likely to have been capable of savouring these naval manoeuvres or guessing at the course of diplomatic and military events. Even a moderate Biscayan swell must have been distracting to unaccustomed stomachs and to nerves already tormented by the agony of parting from everyone and everything known and dear. There was more than homesickness to suffer as the little armada continued towards the coast of France.

---

[1] *The Times*, 6 May 1937.   [2] FO 371 21291.
[3] FO 425 414.   [4] Steer, *Tree of Gernika*, p. 269.

The Royal Navy and the siege of Bilbao

Aboard ROYAL OAK, however, nothing now prevented the day from resuming its familiar pattern: at 0930 Divisions were held, followed by Physical Training and, at 1012, the hands were employed in holystoning the deck.[1] One more of the innumerable, the unpredictable, the often incomprehensible tasks imposed on the Royal Navy by the exigencies of the Spanish Civil War and the vagaries of British policy had been successfully discharged. Without firing a shot, without even an explicit threat of force, the presence at the appropriate point on the ocean of a superior man-of-war had once again enabled the views of His Britannic Majesty's Government to prevail. Some 3,300 women and children, escaping from the bombardment, the blockade, the siege of Bilbao, had been allowed to continue unmolested their journey to sanctuary in France.

This 90 minute operation had been preceded–and was to be followed – by weeks of argument, recrimination and misunderstanding. The actual protection of Basque children by a British battleship had been a simple and smoothly executed manoeuvre: it will take us the rest of the book to unravel the tangle of events and the peculiar conflict of motives that resulted in Admiral Ramsey being ordered to the rescue.

[1] Log of ROYAL OAK, ADM 53/105586.

CHAPTER 2

The British theme

We live under the shadow of the last
war and its memories still sicken us.
Baldwin[1]

The past has few perspectives harder to grasp than those which
just exceed the span of a generation. Four out of every five
Britons living today are too young to have any vivid recollection
of the world on which the Spanish Civil War erupted. They were
not born, or they were at school or they were only starting a
tentative involvement in the strange complexities of the adult
environment. The stories of their elders fall on uncomprehending ears. It all happened too long ago to be the subject of
personal concern. Yet the interval has been too short for the
era to become part of conventional history, the history that is
taught in schools or romanticised by the cinema, by television
or by popular fiction. The middle thirties, for most of those now
alive, are obscure foot hills on the farther side of that daunting
mountain range: the Second World War. Those years are no
longer a memory and they are not yet a period.

Yet the flavour of the times must somehow be recaptured if
this story is to be understood. All the principal participants
were concerned with the reactions of British public opinion.
Some tried to influence it, others appealed to it, many were
afraid of it, a few despised it. This public opinion was the
background to their actions, the environment in which they
took their decisions. And those of them who were British were
also susceptible, however much they prided themselves on
superior knowledge or judgment, to the same underlying

---

[1] Words spoken by Stanley Baldwin on 31 October 1935 quoted in G. M.
Young, *Stanley Baldwin* (Hart-Davis, 1952), p. 214.

currents of feeling, to similar instinctive assumptions. Ministers, officials, naval officers: none of them were immune to the political climate of their times.

This was different from ours. People were not so dissimilar, but the things they took for granted were. Those British men and women whose intermittent interest in political affairs justified their inclusion in the ranks of public opinion lived in a different world from ours, or at least in a world which they regarded differently. About a quarter of it, for instance, was coloured red on the map. This was the British Empire. Few British newspaper readers could have named half of the dominions and colonies, the dependencies and protectorates, that comprised this vast constellation, larger then than it had ever been before. It existed, it had been there a long time, and it would, so it was generally assumed, continue indefinitely to revolve around Britain, the natural centre of the world. Even to those who disapproved of some of its features, who thought that Indians, for instance, might eventually govern themselves, or that Africans were sometimes exploited, the Empire was an immense responsibility. It invested the conduct of the British Government with added significance, gave the ordinary British newspaper reader a special conception of the world, a heightened awareness of his country's position in the international firmament.

But this beneficent girdle, where peace and order still prevailed, only encircled the globe: it did not fill it. Beyond its borders, as the British were uneasily conscious, war had for years savagely flickered in the vast turbulence of China. The imminent menace of Japan was all too visible over the horizon. Behind closely guarded frontiers lay the great enigma of the Soviet Union, a bogey to one minority, the hope of the future to another, a withdrawn and sullen giant to most. The United States was more attractive – recovering its reputation for riches after the dark years of the Great Depression – but equally remote and aloof. Neither country figured prominently in British headlines.

That disagreeable distinction was reserved for the countries of Europe, then generally known as 'the Continent'. Most British people knew this part of the world – Britain did not belong to it, of course – primarily as the theatre of the most terrible war in British history, a war that was still called 'The Great War' and that remained a burning memory. The annual celebration of Armistice Day still reminded most British families of a father or an uncle, a cousin or a friend, who had died in Europe. Only a minority actually visited the continent – holidays abroad were still the privilege of the prosperous few – but it was widely known as the source of trouble, a region whose inhabitants were politically unreliable, often bellicose, usually unfriendly.

This distaste had been sharpened into apprehension by the crescendo of violence that began on 27 February 1933 with the burning of the Reichstag in Berlin and was shortly followed by the inauguration of Adolf Hitler as the first Chancellor of the Third German Reich. The domestic brutality of the new régime was matched by vigorously expressed discontent with the shape of Europe as this had emerged from the Treaty of Versailles. German withdrawal from the League of Nations, the published increases in the military budget, the bloody purge of June 1934, the murder of the Austrian Chancellor a month later, the introduction of conscription in March 1935, the revival of the German Air Force, the occupation of the Rhineland in March 1936: one blow succeeded another to emphasise the warlike language of German propaganda, indeed, to exaggerate its significance.

And these alarms were echoed from Italy, where words were equally strident and, in 1935, matched by actual assault upon Abyssinia. The spectre of a new war in Europe was as obvious to the British public as it was utterly repugnant. The impact was curious. Only a minority saw Britain as directly threatened: to most the danger lay in Britain becoming involved in the quarrels of others. There was little sense of solidarity even with such potential allies as France, widely regarded as both unreliable and provocative. The British people wanted their government to steer clear of trouble, hoped that the war-clouds would eventually blow over, and shrank from gestures of defiance.

Yet this irresolute and profoundly pacific mood was far from defeatist. The reluctance displayed by the British of the thirties, either to solve the problems of others or to recognise their own, has been perhaps unduly censured by critics, whether these were foreign contemporaries or their own descendants, ill qualified to cast any stone. There was no disposition then to renounce Britain's right to a voice in the world's affairs, little acceptance that her stature and dignity had been in any way diminished. The British people still believed their nation to be a Great Power, still regarded their government as capable of commanding respect abroad. Their apprehensions were astonishingly and, to the rest of the world, irritatingly combined with complacency, even with arrogance. The habits of the past remained as potent an influence as any fear of the future. Mr Churchill, then a private Member of Parliament, was accurate as well as prescient, when he told the German Ambassador in 1937, 'You must not underrate England. She is a curious country, and few foreigners can understand her mind. Do not judge by the attitude of the present Administration. Once a great cause is presented to the people, all kinds of unexpected actions might be taken by this very Government and by the British nation.'[1]

This ambivalence was reflected in the attitudes of the Conservative and Labour parties, each pursuing policies of which they failed to accept the implications. The Conservative Government, uneasily conscious of British military deficiencies, wished to conciliate Germany and Italy, to evade causes of dispute, to gain time. But they were unwilling either to sacrifice specifically British interests or to match the pace of German military preparations. The Labour Opposition regarded this prudence as mere indulgence for Fascism, preached the doctrine of collective resistance to aggressive dictators, but were even more opposed to effective rearmament. Each party was

[1] Winston S. Churchill, *The Gathering Storm* (Cassell, 1948), p. 175.

sensitive to conflicting charges: the Conservatives to timidity in the defence of national interests; the Socialists to recklessness in the advocacy of international involvement. Both contributed more than the usual allowance of ambivalence and hypocrisy to a running debate on international issues conducted in an atmosphere of self-important illusion. Motives mattered more than results and opposing rationalisations of British policy were allowed to obscure the reality, which neither party could afford to admit, of its increasing impotence.

To the ordinary member of the British public, vaguely aware of the world's largest Empire and strongest Navy, impotence was not a credible assumption, least of all in maritime affairs. 'Rule Britannia' was still sung, often in innocent pride, sometimes for anxious reassurance. Even those who disapproved of battleships believed in the reality of their power. Bombers were feared and the long agonies of trench-warfare, but confidence in British ability to meet a challenge at sea had only been shaken, not destroyed, by ugly rumours of the Fleet's shortage of ammunition during the Abyssinian crisis. The nation expected much of its navy.

So did others. British resolution was more widely discounted abroad than the effectiveness of the Royal Navy, which had retained both its prestige and its presence in the oceans of the world. British gunboats still patrolled Chinese rivers and British warships were as familiar a sight off foreign coasts as in their own waters. The interest they showed in the safety of British shipping or in the welfare of British subjects in disturbed maritime states was not always welcomed with equal enthusiasm abroad, but it was a familiar feature of the international scene. Except in times of acute crisis, the restless movements of British warships seldom seemed provocative or alarming. They might be resented, but they were taken for granted.

If fighting had to break out in Europe, therefore, its location in Spain afforded Britain easier, though not always entirely welcome, opportunities of influencing events than anything available when the focus of trouble was situated in Austria or the Rhineland. Spain's only landward frontiers were with

Portugal, nominally Britain's oldest ally, and with France, then Britain's closest associate. The southern and eastern coast-line of Spain was conveniently adjacent to Gibraltar, then one of the bases of the substantial British Mediterranean Fleet. The northern and western coasts were accessible to the peace-time station of the Home Fleet at Portsmouth. Of the naval powers only France was closer to the scene of action and France was friendly. Moreover, the opportunities conferred by geography were matched by strategic and commercial interest: the identity of Spain's rulers could not be indifferent to the masters of Gibraltar or to a nation whose principal artery of trade and of imperial communication was flanked by well over a thousand miles of Spanish coast-line.

The reports that spurted or trickled into London at the end of the third week of July 1936 were thus neither irrelevant nor insignificant. Units of the Spanish Army and groups of right-wing sympathisers had risen in revolt in the Canary Islands, in Spanish Morocco, in mainland Andalusia. Aircraft loyal to the Spanish Government had bombed Tetuán and Ceuta, both uncomfortably close to Gibraltar. Fighting had broken out in Barcelona, in San Sebastián, in Seville. Indeed, as one diplomatic telegram and news-flash succeeded another, it became increasingly difficult to be sure of a town, or a province, of Spain that was still quiet and orderly. The crews of Spanish warships had mutinied, churches were burning in Madrid, the Spanish Government had appealed for help to the French, a country was in eruption and the peace of Europe was again threatened.

In Spain it was an agony; in Britain it was to be an increasingly grave embarrassment. The word may seem an under-statement, even an insult to the memory of thousands of Britons who cared passionately, who risked their lives, who fought, who even died, for Spanish causes. But British attitudes to the Spanish Civil War, and British conduct in the particular episode that is the subject of this book, can not be understood without emphasising the nature and extent of the purely British dilemma this conflict created. Only small minorities in Britain were whole-heartedly and unreservedly committed to either side in Spain. An instinctive desire to avoid embroilment was the middle ground of politics and influenced most of those whose preferences, whether of sentiment or of calculation, led them to adopt opposing positions. But it was pervasive rather than uniform, easier to invoke than to canalise, always susceptible of widely divergent and biassed interpretations. Even to its sincerest supporters the concept of non-involvement offered a ground for debate, not an escape from controversy. They knew what they wished to avoid, but these right-wing Socialists, those moderate Tories, the well-meaning members of all parties and of none, were divided, uncertain and changeable in their views of the policies required, in the varying circumstances of the moment, to achieve this deeply felt, but vaguely conceived, objective. The conflicting ideological inclinations, the domestic motives, the pacifist apprehensions, the humanitarianism and the patriotism of this floating and uncertain centre were played upon, incessantly and ingeniously, by the partisans of the two extremes. This exploitation of mixed motives was facilitated by the confusion and complexity both of developments in Spain and of their international repercussions.

The contestants in Spain, for instance, could be very differently regarded. The government in Madrid might be considered legitimate because it had been appointed, immediately after the revolt, by the President of the Republic. At least this view provided the convenient label, which was the most widely used, of 'Republican', though more fervent partisans preferred 'Loyalist'. Alternatively the Republican Government could be repudiated as the mere creature of a popular uprising in Madrid led by Socialists, Communists, even Anarchists. People thus inclined referred to the Republican Government and their supporters as 'the Reds'. Similarly the Junta of rebellious generals in Burgos might be described as representing the army, the royalists, the forces of order, the Church. Foreign supporters accordingly favoured the description 'Nationalist', while 'Insurgent', 'Rebel' and 'Fascist' indicated mounting degrees of disapproval. History, as enshrined in the magisterial work of

Hugh Thomas,[1] has indicated 'Republican' and 'Nationalist' as the appropriate descriptions for British writers in the seventies, but the usages and prejudices of the times will be illustrated by quotation from contemporary documents.

In 1936, and irrespective of the names used in the reports, the one thing that seemed certain to most Britons was that the conduct of both sides was appalling. Accounts of massacre, rape, torture, and every kind of cruelty and oppression flooded out of Spain. Although partisans attempted to palliate and excuse the atrocities of those whose ideology they favoured, the less committed British had every reason to regard both sides with undifferentiated horror. The extremes of Left and Right seemed to be contending with all the savagery to be expected from those of immoderate opinions.

But it was not an issue to be judged on its merits alone. In 1936 even Britain was affected by the general polarisation of European politics. Fascism was advancing and, in those countries where it had not already triumphed, was creating incongruous alliances among its diverse opponents. To a substantial minority of Britons resistance to Fascism was a cause which transcended the character of the participants. These Britons mostly deplored the excesses of Spanish Republicans, yet considered their victory desirable. They were opposed by a probably smaller minority to whom Bolshevism was the source of every atrocity in Spain and the enemy most to be feared.

These two minorities might have cancelled one another out and their views have been dismissed by the complacent centre but for another, and undeniably awkward, complication. Foreign governments were intervening in the Spanish conflict. The complicity of Portugal with the rebel generals might be passed over, but the supplies flowing to the Republicans from France and the Soviet Union, and to their opponents from Germany and Italy, were more alarming. These not only confirmed the worst fears of the ideologists (France then had a Popular Front Government supported by the Communists) but

---

[1] Hugh Thomas, *The Spanish Civil War* (Eyre and Spottiswoode, 1961).

aroused real apprehension that the conflict might spread beyond the borders of Spain or else disturb the European balance of power. The influence exerted by British partisans was thus speedily supplemented by that of advocates of British national interests.

These too were split. Some regarded Germany and Italy, particularly the former, as Britain's natural enemies, whose efforts in Spain should be actively opposed by Britain. Others wished only, from various motives, to reduce or delay the danger of European war and saw British abstention as the safest course. Many of these were also influenced by the shifting prospects of the war in Spain, arguing that Britain should be careful not to alienate the likely victors. And, in almost every advocate of the national interest, there lurked an uneasy consciousness of the difficulties of total abstention, of the risk that even inaction might imperil British interests, prestige or security.

It is scarcely surprising that no clear-cut and consistent policy emerged. The bewilderment, the contradictory impulses, the opposing calculations that divided British public opinion extended to Ministers and their officials. Admittedly these included fewer of the ideologically committed, but their preference for compromise only complicated their approach to a problem that was already sufficiently confusing. The heart of this approach was the principle of Non-Intervention, first proposed by the French Government at the beginning of August 1936, at once accepted by the British and, before the end of the month, the subject of international agreement. Although grossly, even blatantly, violated by other governments and, under the stress of particular circumstances, often infringed by the British, it remained the central dogma of British policy throughout the war. Because it commanded substantial support from the middle ground of British public opinion, this principle was as often invoked by the Opposition as by the Government and provided philosophical justification for as many incompatible proposals as any of the doctrines of Christianity. The earliest, the most lasting and the most obvious of British departures from this principle was furnished by the activities of British warships around the coasts of Spain, though these, such was the temper of the times, were not initially regarded as intervention by almost anyone in Britain. The sea was the natural domain of the Royal Navy and its uses no concern of foreigners. The chain of events that, retrospectively regarded, led inevitably to Admiral Ramsey's confrontation with ALMIRANTE CERVERA began innocently and without premeditation.

CHAPTER 3

Naval prelude

> The opportune presence of a British
> ship of war may avert a disaster.
> F.O. Memorandum of 1907[1]

Evacuation, not least of the British Army, had always been one of the traditional tasks of the Royal Navy, but the Spanish Civil War had gradually raised it to a new order of complexity. To begin with, of course, the job was straightforward enough. The military revolt on 18 July 1936 caught 2,000 British holiday-makers in Spain, a trivial total by the standards of the seventies, but then an important addition to the number of British subjects resident in that country. By 22 July fifteen British warships had been despatched to the rescue of their compatriots and by 24 July there were 'ships at every major Spanish port'.[2] It was an achievement of which the Navy were justifiably more than a little proud and one to evoke incredulous envy from any British tourist caught up in other peoples' wars thirty years later.

Curiously enough it did not earn universal approval. Mr Steer of *The Times*, always more single-minded and whole-hearted than his newspaper, saw it as another sinister right-wing manoeuvre to discredit and hamper the Spanish Republicans:

the British and French navies paid continual visits . . . and insisted that every British and French subject should be evacuated . . . they painted in colours of hell-fire the awful prospect of the Left achieving power in Bilbao . . . So the British colony in Bilbao, which was a

---

[1] F.O. Memorandum of 1907 quoted in Arthur J. Marder, *From the Dreadnought to Scapa Flow* (O.U.P., 1961), vol. 1, ch. 4.
[2] Admiralty Memorandum on 'The British Navy in the Spanish Civil War' in ADM 116 3677.

large one, was first terrified and then lifted off the shore. A few remained; but the shock to the business system of Bilbao was great.[1]

This was an early indication of the great dilemma which was to blur British policy at the time and which has since confused so many historians; any action taken by the British Government in relation to Spain was likely to have side-effects more helpful, or hurtful, to one side in the Civil War than to the other. These side-effects might be quite unforeseen by the British Government or they might simply seem irrelevant to their parochial, or their humanitarian, purposes. There were people to be rescued, Welsh blast-furnaces to be fed with ore, public opinion to be appeased. These domestic preoccupations of the British Government were never credited by the partisans of either Republicans or Nationalists, who always assumed the British to intend the natural – that is to say, the Spanish – consequences of their actions. Whereas, in Whitehall, this was just a familiar administrative problem: numbers of British subjects were potentially – some of them actually – threatened by disturbances in a foreign country. At present their evacuation might not be essential, but it was relatively easy. The longer it was delayed, the more difficult it would become and the greater would be the clamour from the British subjects themselves and their mothers, aunts, Members of Parliament and local newspapers at home. Premature evacuation – and all evacuation was voluntary – might cause inconvenience, but could at worst be regarded as an excess of zeal: leaving it too late might result in actual casualties and serious trouble for those officially concerned.

So the destroyers – they were mostly destroyers – went busily about their task: ACASTA and ARDENT, BEAGLE and BRAZEN, ECHO and ESCORT, FORESTER and FOXHOUND, HARDY and HUNTER, their flotillas ringing the changes on the alphabet as they relieved one another on duties that were not always easy or agreeable. Rescuing one's compatriots has a fine romantic ring, but the Admiralty were unlikely to take a romantic view of an officer who needlessly 'hasarded his ship' while so engaged.

[1] G. L. Steer, *The Tree of Gernika* (Hodder and Stoughton, 1938), pp. 73–4.

And, mines and bombs apart, there were the trivial accompaniments of giving up one's cabin or hammock, clearing up the mess that landsmen make on the heaving deck, sorting out the luggage, the problems, the miseries and the separations of people who were often bewildered, frightened, resentful or just very old and ill. At least the refugees themselves – those taken from Bilbao by ESK on 17 September 1936, for instance – had the joy of escaping and the luxury (as the last weeks had made it) of cocoa and sandwiches of white bread to console them for some of the inconveniences of the journey across the Bay of Biscay seated on 'mess stools and boards supported on biscuit boxes', which had been placed along the whole of one side of the ship and on which they suffered 'the unusual and lively motion of a destroyer at high speed, combined with a light shower of rain'.[1] And long after the voyage had ended and the passengers dispersed there would be the ensuing correspondence. Although many tributes from British subjects have been recorded, it was the complaints that lingered longest and, after any evacuation, the grateful were usually numbered with the silent majority.

The majority was not British. It very soon became obvious that many nationalities ardently desired to leave Spain and that H.M. ships had space to spare for foreigners. By the end of October 1936, when the first phase of naval evacuation was over, only 35% of the 11,195 people rescued by H.M. ships, which had made 220 voyages and steamed 75,724 sea-miles in doing so, had actually been British. This is all the more remarkable, when it is remembered that the French, German, Italian and United States navies were also active around the coasts of Spain and, difficult though the Admiralty found this to believe, did actually evacuate some of their own nationals. To begin with, however, relatively few Spaniards travelled on H.M. ships. Their mass evacuation from their own country was a later complication which crowned the problems of ferrying British consuls and diplomats to and fro, of delivering their

---

[1] Article in *Naval Review* of 1937.

despatches and transmitting their telegrams, of protecting British ships – there were frequent air and naval battles among Spaniards in and around the Straits of Gibraltar during July and August 1936 as well as an unsuccessful Republican attempt at blockading Insurgent ports.[1]

The Spaniards evacuated were usually those with urgent reasons for leaving a part of Spain that had suddenly become politically uncongenial, often acutely dangerous. As both sides had early begun to imprison such political opponents as they could lay hands on – often treating them as hostages – these evacuations usually had to take the form of exchanges. As early as October 1936, for instance, H.M. destroyers ESK, ESCORT and EXMOUTH had brought Basque children out of Nationalist captivity to Bilbao (the capital of the Autonomous Basque Republic and a part of Republican Spain) and taken away a number of Spanish ladies imprisoned in that city on account of their political convictions – or those of their husbands, brothers and fathers. Whenever possible these exchanges were arranged by the International Red Cross, whose representative, Dr Marcel Junod, was not only indefatigably efficient, but enabled His Majesty's Government to escape some of the odium that, in Spain, someone always managed to fasten on any exertion of humanitarianism. Not all the work, however, could be left to Dr Junod. Every British Consul had some valued friend or informant to be saved from death or worse. This occasionally demanded a degree of ingenuity. If ten naval officers came ashore to luncheon, one might have a spare uniform in his suit-case, so that eleven returned to the ship just before she sailed.[2] Regularly or irregularly, by the end of January 1937, British warships had carried 17,000 Spaniards to safety.[3]

What had begun as a simple use of warships as the most

---

[1] Admiralty Memorandum on 'The British Navy in the Spanish Civil War' in ADM 116 3677.

[2] Information given to the author in 1970 by Mr Angus Malcolm who, in 1937, was Third Secretary in the British Embassy at Hendaye (henceforth Malcolm).

[3] F.O. Memorandum of 1 March 1937 in FO 371 21368.

convenient means of evacuating endangered British subjects –
in those days a normal procedure which seldom occasioned
surprise or aroused objection – had imperceptibly developed
into a continuing and far more complex traffic of rescue and
exchange. British warships had established themselves, in the
eyes of the British Government and public opinion and with
relatively little objection from the Spaniards, as enjoying not
merely the right of access to Spanish ports but full licence to
fetch and carry, to mediate, to negotiate. They had become
privileged interlopers, whose activities were not confined to the
protection and assistance of British subjects alone. Spanish
tolerance seems sufficiently surprising in the altered international climate of the seventies, but the attitude of a British
government dedicated to the principle of Non-Intervention
can only be explained by the prevalence of two deep-rooted
convictions: that humanitarian assistance was something above
and apart from politics; and that the Royal Navy could go
where it pleased.

Even so there were constant diplomatic tangles and frequent
need for sophisticated interpretation of the basic doctrine of
Non-Intervention. There were also practical problems. These
were least important on the southern coasts of Spain, the
regular cruising grounds of British ships conveniently based at
Gibraltar. But the northern coast, where British destroyers had
been incessantly active throughout the second half of 1936 and
the early months of 1937, was devoid of British bases. There
was no fully satisfactory neutral port south of the Gironde, in
western France. H.M. ships, even when they encountered no
objection to their tasks from either of the Spanish contestants,
still required anchorages sheltered from the Biscayan storms.
Tankers had to refuel the destroyers. The men had to be given
opportunities for rest, exercise and recreation. The Reports of
Proceedings which every warship's commanding officer had to
produce in such profusion usually end by retailing the football
matches played, extolling the amusements offered by one
French town and denouncing the extortionate charges of this
hotel or the focus of venereal disease constituted by that café.

And when, rest or refuelling completed, ships resumed their missions of mercy, they sometimes found fighting Spaniards too preoccupied to recognise or respect the White Ensign. H.M.S. BLANCHE was the first to be accidentally bombed, on 17 August 1936, and she was followed by ROYAL OAK, whose captain was later wounded by anti-aircraft fire, GIPSY and HAVOCK, all in February 1937.[1] British ships took to painting large red, white and blue bands across their gun turrets.

These were naturally no protection against mines, whether lurking invisibly beneath the surface or, broken from their moorings, bobbing and lurching in the waves. There has been much criticism of the Royal Navy, mainly from landsmen of strongly partisan views, for their alleged exaggeration of the mine menace. At a later stage of our story, when the precise extent and location of the danger became a major issue of political controversy, it will be necessary to consider these arguments in greater detail. For the moment it will be enough to say that the Navy did, from the very beginning of the Civil War, tend to give more credence to stories that mines had been laid than to claims that these had been successfully swept. It was a broadcast from Burgos about the mining of Bilbao harbour, for instance, that made ESK, ECHO and ESCORT so anxious to get the last – they fondly hoped – refugees out of that city in September 1936.[2] Too many ships had blown up in past years – and would do so again in the future – in seas supposedly cleared by British minesweepers, for naval officers to place much confidence in the assurances of relatively inexperienced foreigners. Moreover, destroyers, as Vice-Admiral James pointed out to the Foreign Office on 5 March 1937, were peculiarly vulnerable to this form of attack. Unlike some aged tramp steamer, with cargo holds to take the worst of the explosion and very few men below deck, the thin hull of a destroyer enclosed a crew of 180 and half a million pounds' worth of equipment and armament.[3] He did not need to say – and he wrote his letter weeks before the argument began to rage and two months before

[1] ADM 116 3534.   [2] Article in *Naval Review* of 1937.
[3] FO 371 21368.

HUNTER hit a mine and sustained heavy damage and casualties –
that the consequences of mining a destroyer crammed with a
couple of hundred refugees over her normal complement
would be even less acceptable. Mines were a danger the Navy
would have to face in war, but which any responsible ship's
captain was expected to avoid as long as, in the words of
The Times, 'the chief concern of the Government – as it has
undoubtedly been the chief concern of the country – has been
to reduce the risk that the conflict might spread beyond the
Spanish border'.[1]

The conflict ashore and the concern this aroused in London
were the two variables which shaped the courses of British
naval activities on the southern shore of the Bay of Biscay and
it is time to survey this conflict as it appeared to naval officers –
looking inwards from the sea. At the eastern end was Saint-
Jean-de-Luz, just across the French border, the nearest peaceful anchorage (though a dangerous one in a real gale), a port for
recreation or for disembarking refugees, and the point at which
H.M. ships made contact with H.M. Ambassador to Spain.
This Ambassador, Sir Henry Chilton – known to his staff as
Sir Billy[2] – was a diplomat of the old school, appointed to
Madrid as his final post, who had moved in the normal way to
the summer capital of San Sebastián (just across the border)
and been caught there by the outbreak of civil war as Nationalist
forces drove for the sea in a successful bid to seal off that end of
the frontier. One of his staff swam out to a French warship,
where he was not (to the subsequent horror of the more
hospitable Royal Navy) restored with appropriately strong
liquor, but was allowed to send a wireless message.[3] The text
of this, tightly wrapped in a sponge bag kindly provided by the
German Chargé d'Affaires, was inside his swimming trunks.
So was another message to the German Government, which
eventually brought the German pocket battleship DEUTSCHLAND
to those waters.[4] The British destroyers VERITY and VETERAN

---

[1] First leader in *The Times* of 3 March 1937.   [2] Malcolm.
[3] Article by an officer of H.M.S. VERITY in *Naval Review* of 1936.
[4] Malcolm.

arrived on the night of 23 July 1936, the former evacuating British subjects – and some foreigners – while the latter served as a wireless link for the Embassy, who deeply impressed VERITY's officers by their efficiency and linguistic fluency. But fighting was in progress – VERITY observed with awe the precipitate departure (allowing acceleration to snap a doubtless frayed hawser there seemed no time to slip) of a bracketed Spanish warship – and destroyers could not be indefinitely immobilised to remedy the absence of normal telecommunications. So, once other British subjects had gone, the Embassy were evacuated by H.M.S. KEPPEL on the 27th,[1] and installed themselves in a grocer's shop (then untenanted) in Hendaye, a few hundred yards from the French end of the international bridge that led to Spain.

At the other end of that bridge was Irún, early occupied by Nationalist forces and seat of Major Troncoso, a cavalry officer with a disconcerting resemblance to Mussolini but a sense of humour.[2] This personal friend of General Franco was nominally the town's Military Governor but more important as the Embassy's principal link with the Nationalist administration. Contact with the Republicans was maintained by the Counsellor, who became an increasingly independent Chargé d'Affaires, first in Madrid and then in Valencia. No doubt it had originally been supposed that the Ambassador's stay in Hendaye, where he had been joined by twenty-one of his foreign colleagues from Madrid, would be brief, but the longer the fighting continued, the less apposite the moment always seemed for a return to Spain that could scarcely avoid the appearance of committing His Majesty's Government to one side or the other. So there Sir Billy stayed, taking a splendid villa (lent to the British Government by the Canadian owner)[3], and there he entertained the admirals, the captains and the commanders who called on him for information and advice. There, too, or in neighbouring Saint-Jean-de-Luz, established themselves

[1] Article by an officer of H.M.S. VERITY in *Naval Review* of 1936.
[2] Captain McGrigor's description in ADM 116 3512.
[3] Malcolm.

most of the journalists, intriguers, spies, merchants of death, profiteers and adventurers who swarmed about the Spanish honey-pot. Even the French motorists created dangerous traffic jams, in the early days of actual fighting, on the frontier road that commanded the best view of Irún.[1]

By the end of September 1936, however, all the Biscayan coast from the French frontier to the river Deva was firmly in Nationalist hands and Captain Caveda was well esconsed as captain of the port of San Sebastián. This officer soon became the naval Troncoso, the indispensable liaison between the commanders of H.M. ships and the Nationalist Navy. Courteous and agreeable, though apparently not always reliable, he was full of information about mines and capable of reasonable discussion and compromise concerning even such controversial issues as territorial waters. We shall hear more of him.

Further west the Nationalist coast-line came to an end at Ondarroa and the next 150 miles of the northern Spanish shore, as far as San Esteban de Pravia, together with a substantial hinterland, were Republican. This was a significant area of Spain, containing the major city of Bilbao and the important towns of Santander and Gijón. But it was also an area entirely enclosed on the landward side by Nationalist territory, an enclave that could only receive outside assistance by sea. This was a factor soon to assume international importance.

It was also, though this was initially less apparent to the Royal Navy, an enclave that united very diverse political attitudes under the all-embracing labels – which depended on the political outlook of the speaker – of Loyalist, Governmental, Republican, Red or Marxist. Since 7 October 1936, for instance, Bilbao – with which we shall chiefly be concerned – had been the capital of the Autonomous Basque Republic, proclaimed that day beneath the hallowed Oak of Guernica and dominated by what might not unfairly be described as the Catholic and property-owning democracy of that ancient and idiosyncratic

[1] Claude G. Bowers, *My Mission to Spain* (Gollancz, 1954).

people, very different from the Leftist Spaniards of Santander and the outright Anarchists or Communists of Gijón.[1] Even more important, however, than these ideological differences was that the Basques were one of those peoples – twenty years later the Hungarians were another – whose tragic and romantic misfortunes excited the passionate admiration and sympathy of foreigners. Mr Steer of *The Times*, whose brilliant book is one long panegyric of the Basques, may have been an extreme case, but he was by no means unique.

Naval officers, however, had only limited opportunities of meeting the Basques and appeciating their virtues. Captain Burrough, one of the first Flotilla Leaders on the northern coast was an exception – he remained strongly pro-Basque all his life[2] – and it is arguable that the Basques had more naval sympathisers than other Republicans. But many officers had rather strong initial prejudices to overcome. Even Captain McGrigor of the Fourth Destroyer Flotilla – not a man to let bias sway his independent judgment (he had accepted as his ship H.M.S. CAMPBELL, the choice of an ignorant, or a mischievous, Englishman) – had a revealing comment on his visit to President Aguirre, who had much impressed him, as a man who 'knows that the Basques, who are a clean living, religious people, are on the wrong side and have nothing in common with the Reds'. This description of the Spanish Republicans as 'Reds' and 'the wrong side' – in an official report – would probably have been echoed in March 1937 by many British naval officers.

---

[1] Steer, *Tree of Gernika*, passim, but even a Nationalist author could write that the separatist complication of Basque nationalism created 'una monstruosa complicidad' between fundamentally bourgeois groups of undoubtedly right-wing tendencies and the extremist forces of anarchism and communist Marxism – Luis Maria de Lojendio, *Operaciones Militares de la Guerra de España 1936–1938* (Montaner y Simon S.A., Barcelona, 1940).

From an opposite standpoint the Soviet Ambassador in London (and Representative on the Non-Intervention Committee) complained that 'the decisive force was the conservative and Catholic Basque National Party, in which the big bourgeois and the priests played the leading part'. Ivan Maisky, *Spanish Notebooks*, tr. Kisch (Hutchinson, 1966).

[2] Private letter from Admiral Sir Harold Burrough, communicated to the author.

Naval prelude

They had been horrified at the mass killing of Spanish naval officers by the sailors of warships declaring for the Republican Government in July 1936: one battleship, two cruisers and four destroyers. Captain McGrigor had himself just been told – and had duly reported – that only 200 out of 600 Spanish naval officers had survived.[1] These traumatic events had made a profound impression on the Royal Navy, still vividly recalled thirty-four years later by Vice-Admiral Caslon.[2] Their reaction is rather unfairly mocked by Steer, who argues – and this is not an undisputed view – that the Spanish officers had invited their fate by indicating their desire to join General Franco's revolt. He does not ask himself whether similar arguments would have reconciled him to a mass slaughter of Spanish foreign correspondents. Our sympathies are always most easily excited by those with whom we can identify. Nor did the subsequent conduct of the Republican Navy do anything to regain an esteem thus alienated. Steer himself has a horrifying description of the crew of the battleship JAIME I indulging an acquired taste for the slaughter of the unarmed, and the Basque régime were themselves forced to replace the entire crews of the destroyers J.L. DIEZ and CISCAR after these had lurked inactive for months in Bilbao harbour,[3] where the Basques, so Captain McGrigor was told, used sardonically to refer to the former as 'one of the Non-Intervention Powers'.

To the Royal Navy, therefore, the contrast was simple and compelling: on the one hand a murderous rabble of mutineers incapable of keeping their ships at sea or fighting the enemy; on the other, officers of some ability, whose conception of good manners – punctilious, elaborate, a trifle arrogant – was remarkably similar to that of the pre-war British naval officer.

---

[1] Captain McGrigor's description in ADM 116 3512.

[2] Information supplied to the author in conversation and correspondence by Vice-Admiral Caslon in 1970 (henceforth Caslon).

[3] 'He [Eguia] had only ten days earlier [3 June 1937] turned out of the 2 Government destroyers J. L. DIEZ and CISCAR most of the crews, a sorry lot of idlers, and made up the complements of these ships with Basque seamen and fishermen. These destroyers had been in Bilbao harbour for months, practically inactive.' Mr Consul Stevenson's final report in FO 425 414.

The Royal Navy and the siege of Bilbao

Joaquin Eguia, the cheerful Captain of the Port of Bilbao, who had organised a Basque auxiliary fleet from the trawlers of Vizcaya and Guipúzcoa, was personally popular with the Royal Navy, but, as professionals themselves, British naval officers could scarcely be expected to share all Steer's enthusiasm for this force, even if they admired the heroism displayed, and so notably celebrated by Steer, in their unequal combat of 5 March 1937 against the Nationalist cruiser CANARIAS. These gallant fishermen, after all, shared the general tendency of Basque artillerymen, whether ashore or afloat, to miss so enormously their Nationalist targets as occasionally to annoy those British destroyers over which their shells actually flew.[1] And, if comparisons at sea favoured the Nationalists, these were not always redressed by conduct on land, particularly during the period preceding the achievement of full Basque control of Bilbao, when refugees from that city had been allowed onto British destroyers 'with the utmost reluctance and much flourishing of shot-guns and pistols' by surly guards whom the British sailors were compelled to ply with coffee liberally laced with rum.[2]

Such sentiments did not, of course, in any way impair the Navy's readiness to obey any orders they might be given, but when an undecided government sought naval advice, it was conceivable that sympathies might sometimes colour the response. Not that this seemed likely, in the early days of March, on the northern coast of Spain, where the British Government's dual policy of non-intervention coupled with impartially humanitarian assistance had so far operated smoothly enough. Such doubts and difficulties as had arisen were essentially administrative. On 2 March, for instance, the Commander-in-Chief Home Fleet had pointed out that the impending introduction of an International Non-Intervention Naval Patrol would entail the employment of additional destroyers on the north coast, as the Ambassador at Hendaye was anxious that the Navy should still continue their contribution to the humani-

---

[1] Article on 'The Battle of Bilbao' in *Naval Review* of 1937.
[2] Article in *Naval Review* of 1937.

tarian task of evacuating Spanish political refugees from each of the combatant zones to the other. It may have been this reminder which prompted the Admiralty, in their turn, to write to the Foreign Office on the 5th, and again on the 9th, emphasising the burden placed on the Navy by the evacuation of foreigners (they seemed to have been thinking mainly of those who were neither British nor Spanish) and proposing that this should henceforth be regarded as the responsibility of the other governments concerned. They also emphasised the risk from mines which the destroyers ran whenever they entered such ports as Bilbao.[1]

These were valid points and a sympathetic Foreign Office undertook to instruct the Ambassador at Hendaye and the Consul at Bilbao accordingly. But the exploitation of British destroyers – for the evacuation of all and sundry, for the transport of important passengers in the absence of safe and reliable commercial services between the warring zones of divided Spain, even for ferrying relief supplies – was almost a standing grievance of the Admiralty's and, however often they brought it up and however sincere the promises they received in response their complaints always had to be repeated. On this occasion, for instance, the Embassy actually proposed the employment of a Spanish merchant ship for the next evacuation from Bilbao. They were confident of obtaining General Franco's agreement, so that all the Navy would have to do would be to meet the ship outside territorial waters and escort it – simply as a reassurance to the Basques providing the ship. Nevertheless, although General Franco's consent was eventually received on the 26th, circumstances had meanwhile required destroyers to carry out two more evacuations from Bilbao.[2]

The Admiralty were not, as it happened, always alone in their view that the Royal Navy were carrying a disproportionate share of the humanitarian burden. Le Courrier de Bayonne, Biarritz et du Pays Basque had devoted a remarkably laudatory article to this very subject on 25 January 1937, which concluded

---

[1] F.O. Memorandum of 1 March 1937 in FO 371 21368.
[2] F.O. Memorandum of 1 March 1937 in FO 371 21368.

The Royal Navy and the siege of Bilbao

We observe with regret that for a very long time no French man-of-war, worthy of the name, has anchored in the Bay, or taken some small part in the evacuation of refugees, above all Europeans, who are now stranded in Spain. In contrast to the magnificent English ships, the absence of our flag is the object of severe and entirely justified criticism.[1]

The pressures on 'the magnificent English ships' were various and compelling. On 16 March Angus Malcolm, Third Secretary at the Embassy in Hendaye, sent his mother a graphic account of the problem at his end.

Our efforts to rescue people multiply apace so that I can hardly keep up with them. People pour in all the time and I get almost distracted. In particular I feel so ashamed telling them, even in the most impossible cases, that I'm sure the Consul will do his best and that I feel confident that, given time, all will come right, when I know perfectly well that usually there isn't an earthly chance of success. The word seems to have gone round (as I knew it would in the end) that we are the only people who can do anything in either camp . . . At the moment I am carrying on single-handed a scheme, supported by cajolements and threats, to get handed over to us the 100 odd Red women and children who were captured last week [from the steamer GALDAMES taken by the Nationalist cruiser CANARIAS on 5 March] . . . It will be a great triumph if we can take them safely back to Bilbao after all. We shall get plenty of people away from Bilbao in return.[2]

His views, incidentally, were echoed by Captain McGrigor, who argued that the Royal Navy should continue to bear its humanitarian burden because only the Royal Navy was trusted by both sides. The Admiralty found his views 'very interesting' but contrary to Admiralty policy.[3]

Honest broker of human lives and liberty was thus an established rôle for British diplomacy and the British Navy, but a new task was already appearing on the horizon. Perhaps the first hint of it came in a resolution sent to the Foreign Office on 3 March by the Manchester branch of the Women's International League, calling for an international effort to evacuate

[1] ADM 116 3512.   [2] Malcolm.   [3] ADM 116 3512.

38

civilians from bombarded areas in Spain.[1] Bombardment was still only intermittent in the north, but the concept of rescuing people, not from persecution but from the effects of war, had other applications. Although the northern front had been stable, indeed almost quiescent, for nearly six months, the shortage of food in the Republican area, particularly in Bilbao with its large additional population of refugees, had long been acute. The Nationalists maintained a loose naval blockade (they had told Chilton at the beginning of the year that it would be dangerous to enter Government territorial waters after 8 January) and had succeeded in snapping up some of the Basque ships that had ventured out of Bilbao, while discouraging others from even trying. That same letter of the 16th from Angus Malcolm had continued 'I am also up to the eyes in a scheme for evacuating 1,600 orphaned, abandoned or necessitous children from Bilbao (where food is short) to refugee colonies in France where they can be fed, cared for and educated until happier days return.'

On the 21st he was able to report a first instalment of success 'This afternoon two destroyers brought in 450 children with about 25 nurses etc. from Bilbao. . . . All fervent little Reds, of course, they gave Captain McGrigor the "clenched fist" salute as they disembarked.'

Busy the Embassy and the British destroyers in northern Spanish waters certainly were, but their activities had hitherto been less dangerous, delicate or controversial than elsewhere and Commander Caslon of H.M.S. BLANCHE was pleased when he was ordered to take his division of the Fourth Destroyer Flotilla to that coast. It would be quieter there than in the Mediterranean, where the Spanish Nationalist Navy had been active and the fighting on land had extended to the coast. The contrasting calm of the Cantabrian Sea was such that the presence of a Post-Captain no longer seemed essential and, when Captain McGrigor returned to home waters, Caslon succeeded him as Senior Naval Officer North Spain and could look forward to a spell of independent responsibility. He took

[1] FO 371 21368.

39

up his appointment on 24 March 1937, called on the Ambassador and the British Consul from Bilbao (Stevenson was then on a visit to Hendaye) and, the very next day, sailed for Bermeo (the nearest mine-free port, in the Admiralty's view, to Bilbao) with Stevenson to embark 111 refugees and take them to Saint-Jean-de-Luz in France.[1] Once they had been landed, the ship had to be thoroughly cleaned and decorated for a cocktail party on board – on the 28th – at which the Chiltons were the guests of honour. Then another refugee trip – in the opposite direction this time – was due. Routine – as nine months of civil war had established it off the northern coast of Spain – was continuing its accustomed course.

This routine was one which made considerable demands of the man on the spot. Senior Naval Officer North Spain was a resounding title for a Commander, but it brought Caslon no additional resources for his new tasks. McGrigor, as Captain (D) commanding a flotilla, had enjoyed the services of staff officers and extra signallers. Caslon had to manage as best he could with the normal complement of his destroyer. For intelligence of the situation afloat he had to rely on what he and his officers could see for themselves, for news and guidance concerning political and military developments on his intermittent contacts with the Embassy, on out-of-date copies of English newspapers, on the sparse bulletins of the B.B.C. Nobody on board, for instance, was even capable of reading the Spanish press.[2] The Admiralty's confidence in Caslon's unsupported judgment was impressive and, as events would show, not unjustified, but it suggested a certain complacence in London, a reluctance to envisage problems before these had actually arisen, a confidence that, whatever happened ashore, the waves would still rise and fall in the rhythms of peace.

Beneath these calm waters there lay an unsuspected reef. If four British destroyers sufficed to provide Commander Caslon with the title of Senior Naval Officer North Spain – in its quiet way as arrogant a territorial claim as the contemporary British appointment of a Rear-Admiral Yangtse – this was largely

[1] ADM 116 3512.   [2] Caslon.

because the main battles of the Civil War were being fought elsewhere. Ever since their initial success in establishing control of a broad belt of northern Spain, the Biscayan enclave always excepted, the Nationalists had been battering their way towards Madrid, already menaced from the north. An offensive from this direction being repulsed, the Nationalists advanced from Seville, established command of south-western Spain and launched an assault on the western suburbs of Madrid. By the end of 1936 the capital was closely invested on the west and in the south, more distantly threatened from the north. The Republican Government had left for Valencia on 6 November. They were not alone in regarding the fall of Madrid as imminent. The President had fled to Barcelona even earlier. Yet the Republican defenders not merely survived a succession of fierce battles but, on 18 March 1937, won a significant tactical victory at Guadalajara, north of Madrid. In eight months of war the Republicans had lost more than half of Spain, but they still kept Madrid, most of the Mediterranean coast and its hinterland, and their Biscayan enclave. Their prospects were reckoned as poor, but not as hopeless.

Meanwhile the political character of the war had been further polarised. First the Communists, then the Anarchists, had joined the Republican Government. Political commissars were appointed in its army and, as the struggle became increasingly desperate, so control at every level passed more and more to the extremists of the Left, those most inclined to commit themselves to unlimited resistance. The Nationalists, for their part, appointed General Franco as Head of State, gave him the title of Caudillo and, but for their professed devotion to the Catholic Church, became more avowedly Fascist, the number of proclaimed members of the Falange, as their party was known, rising from 75,000 in July 1936 to nearly a million by the end of the year.[1]

What was even more alarming to British opinion was the accompanying growth in foreign support for the two sides in

[1] Hugh Thomas, *The Spanish Civil War* (Eyre and Spottiswoode, 1961), p. 355.

Spain. Russian arms, including tanks and aircraft, reached the Republicans in substantial quantities during the latter months of 1936. So did Russian and other Communist political and military advisers. So, too, did many thousands of foreign volunteers, including British subjects, who were organised into International Brigades and took a prominent part in the defence of Madrid. They were more than matched by the Condor Legion, drawn from the German Air Force, and organised formations of Italian Blackshirts under Italian officers. Non-Intervention, still officially accepted by all the governments concerned, had demonstrably failed to prevent the Spanish Civil War from becoming a trial of strength between the Soviet Union, half-heartedly and surreptitiously supported by France, on the one hand, and Germany and Italy on the other. At best the doctrine of Non-Intervention had limited and disguised the reality of intervention, preventing this from assuming the character of a dangerously open confrontation. At worst – and this view was increasingly argued in Britain, one of the few countries which effectively banned the export of arms and at least discouraged the flow of volunteers – it had unilaterally handicapped the Republicans and advanced the cause of Fascism, of Germany and of Italy.

British attitudes towards the Spanish Civil War were now more sharply divided and conflicting views more deeply felt. More Britons had been personally involved – as volunteer fighters, as relief workers, as political agitators at home. The refuge from commitment offered by Non-Intervention – still the dogma of the Government and the panacea of the apprehensive majority – seemed daily less convincing and more casuistical. Yet the dangers of support for Republican Spain – the form of commitment most often and most vociferously urged upon the British Government – had visibly increased. Not only was Germany's own strength growing: she was extending her links with Britain's other potential enemies. The proclamation of the Berlin–Rome Axis in November 1936 was promptly followed by Germany's Anti-Comintern Pact with Japan. The nightmare of the British Government and, above all, of the British

Admiralty – an alliance among Britain's three main naval rivals – could no longer be dismissed as an imaginary danger. It might well be hastened if British attitudes towards Spain angered Germany and Italy. On the other hand, it might conceivably be averted by a conciliatory policy aimed at detaching one partner from this formidable combination. On 2 January 1937 a 'Gentleman's Agreement' to preserve the *status quo* in the Mediterranean was signed with Italy.

The British Government accordingly persevered in Non-Intervention, even contriving to invest this doctrine with fresh verisimilitude by securing general agreement, on 8 March 1937, to a system of observers, by land and sea, to prevent the introduction of additional arms and volunteers into Spain. It was this agreement which had compelled a reluctant Admiralty, always conscious of the strain imposed on the Navy by these Spanish deployments, to contemplate the probable need to provide more destroyers for the Biscayan coast, one of the sectors for which British warships would have to furnish the International Naval Patrol. It would complicate the Admiralty's administrative arrangements, but promised, by investing the British naval presence on that coast with an added legitimacy, to ease those of the Foreign Office.

What nobody realised at the time, what they could hardly be expected to know, was that General Franco would react to the repulse of his troops at Guadalajara by deciding on a new offensive in the North. As long as the landward front of the Biscayan enclave had been quiescent, British destroyers could scurry to and fro on their independent errands, with no more to worry them than the occasional air-raid or the mines laid by Nationalist warships, whose loose blockade of the Biscayan coast seldom interfered with British shipping.[1] It was an uneasy situation, but not acutely dangerous, and one that was generally expected to be resolved by developments elsewhere in Spain, a side-show.

[1] CAB 23 88. There had been a couple of minor incidents off Bilbao in November 1936, which had resulted in representations to the Nationalist authorities. ADM 116 3677.

CHAPTER 4

Opening movement

I remember how we suddenly leapt
into speed that day.

Steer[1]

Two days before Commander Caslon took up his new appointment, General Franco reached his decision.[2] The attack on Madrid would be suspended and the Nationalist Army of the North would be reinforced for an offensive against the Basques. Heavily supported by aircraft, including the German Condor Legion, the Nationalists would advance westwards through the hills that ran inland from Ondarroa, on the Biscayan coast. The starting date was to be 31 March 1937 and a quick victory was expected to offset the depressing effects of the repulse before Madrid.

The imminence of this new phase of the war was not suspected in London, at Hendaye or aboard H.M. ships off the northern coast. As late as 16 March Malcolm wrote 'the outcome of the war must be plain to both sides. The fall of Madrid may produce a general collapse . . .'. Even when Madrid did not fall, British eyes remained on that city and the extent of the new offensive was not apparent before the attacks were in full swing. Least of all was it realised that Basque resistance would have to be broken by an intensified blockade as well as by bombing.

On 19 March, for instance, in answer to a letter from Mr Grenfell, a Labour Member of Parliament, the Parliamentary

---

[1] G. L. Steer, *The Tree of Gernika* (Hodder and Stoughton, 1938), p. 189.
[2] Thomas says the decision was taken on the 22nd, Lojendio on the 21st. (Hugh Thomas, *The Spanish Civil War* (Eyre and Spottiswoode, 1961), p. 399. Luis Maria de Lojendio, *Operaciones Militares de la Guerra de España 1936–1938* (Montaner y Simon S.A., Barcelona, 1940). Everyone agrees that the offensive began on 31 March.

Under-Secretary for Foreign Affairs wrote 'the Non-Intervention Agreement does not prohibit the carrying of food to Spain by ships of the participating countries. II.M.G. would in fact protest against any interference on the high seas with British ships carrying food or other commodities, and the Navy would prevent such interference whenever they could'.

The text of Lord Cranborne's letter had been cleared with the Foreign Office Legal Adviser, but there is no indication in the file that the Admiralty were consulted.[1] Perhaps they would have been if the Embassy had by then had time to report a protest received the same day from General Franco's administration about British vessels engaging in commerce with 'the Reds'.[2] This communication did not prevent the Ambassador from having Major Troncoso to lunch. 'The lunch was for men only: we got the Argentine Ambassador and the two captains from the new flotilla and it was a rousing success.'[3]

A more serious view was taken in London, where the Foreign Secretary told the Cabinet on 24 March that he proposed, perhaps a little belatedly, 'to confer with the Admiralty on the subject and he informed his colleagues that it might be necessary to issue a new warning to the Insurgent Government'.[4] On the 30th, indeed, when *The Times* reported a broadcast from General Franco's H.Q. at Salamanca warning British steamers 'to respond quickly to any signals by Insurgent warships off the coast of Spain', the diplomatic correspondent was able to add the obviously inspired comment that 'the British Government are not prepared to tolerate the stopping of British steamers on the high seas'.

In retrospect it seems obvious that the elements of a potential confrontation were in the making but, at the time, the significance of the broadcast of 30 March was not appreciated. Even the aerial obliteration of Durango[5] that opened the offensive on the 31st and the shots fired by a Nationalist warship at the

---

[1] FO 371 21368. [2] FO 371 21351.
[3] Malcolm. [4] CAB 23 88.
[5] Steer, *Tree of Gernika*. In his despatch of 3 April Stevenson described the attach on Durango as 'frightfulness', an expression dating from the First World War. FO 371 21290.

French ship CAP FALCON[1] off Santander on 1 April were seen as unconnected incidents. They were not mentioned when Commander Caslon reported regretfully, on 30 March, that the Nationalist authorities at San Sebastián had gone back on their previous undertaking to release a number of Republican prisoners for him to take to Bilbao. He was not impressed by the excuse that these could not be allowed to reveal the secrets of the coming offensive and commented that an indignant reaction from the Basques (who had released their own prisoners against a promise of reciprocity) was inevitable and would probably prevent the further evacuation of Nationalists from Bilbao. Stevenson, who had accompanied him, was most depressed and even Captain Caveda (who had himself been hoping to get his two sisters out of Bilbao) was full of regrets at the communication he had to make. Nevertheless, when BRILLIANT took Stevenson back to his post that same day, she also carried two English ladies who wanted to investigate the condition of the local children[2] and, when the National Joint Committee for Spanish Relief in London proposed, on 1 April, to send £200 worth of medical stores to Bilbao, the Foreign Office readily agreed that the next British destroyer visiting Bermeo should carry this consignment.[3] Events were following the accustomed pattern, which naturally included the occasional *contretemps*. Nobody seems to have realised that Bilbao was now the main objective of Nationalist military endeavour; that the victuallers of Bilbao were twelve technically British ships chartered or otherwise engaged by the Basque Government;[4] and that, in the altered military situation, Nationalist warships were unlikely to regard the voyages of these food-ships in quite the same light as the Foreign Office Legal Adviser.

Until April 6th, the day on which BEAGLE took me back to Bilbao, Franco's navy on the North Coast of Spain had always given the right of way to British cargoes. But I remember how we suddenly

---

[1] *The Times*. The ship was allowed to proceed after an exchange of protests.
[2] FO 371 21290.   [3] FO 371 21368.
[4] Steer, *Tree of Gernika*, p. 89; *The Times* 29 April 1937; Thomas, *Spanish Civil War*, p. 407.

leapt into speed that day, and how the crew stopped spitting and polishing the little bronze beagles that decorated the destroyer and the decks were clearing for action and the torpedoes put their warheads on as we entered Bermeo bay. The radio had spoken.[1]

What had happened was that the day before Commander Taylor of H.M.S. BRAZEN had decided that reports of a concentration of Nationalist warships off Bilbao, for which port various British merchant ships were known to be heading, made that stretch of coast a suitable area for him to patrol. While thus engaged, late in the evening of the 5th, he encountered the British freighter THORPEHALL, who signalled that she was bound for Bilbao and expected to enter that port at first light on the 6th. Commander Taylor decided to continue his patrol. Perhaps the CAP FALCON incident of the 1st – and the following day's announcement that French warships had orders to protect French merchantmen on the high seas –[2] had made THORPEHALL communicative and BRAZEN solicitous. But there was no general sense of emergency. BRILLIANT was oiling from the Royal Fleet Auxiliary tanker PRESTOL at the Spanish Nationalist port of Corunna, BEAGLE was due for a routine refugee run to Bermeo, giving the representative of *The Times* a lift when she did, and Commander Caslon himself in BLANCHE had been paying a round of visits at the western end of his area: dropping Stevenson at Republican Gijón, oiling at Corunna and calling on the Nationalist Vice-Admiral at El Ferrol. It was probably then that the Admiral told him there was no such word as neutral in the Spanish language: he who was not for us was against us. The Commander had stoutly replied that many thousands of Spaniards on both sides owed their lives to the contrary belief of the Royal Navy in an impartial humanitarianism,[3] a retort which evoked, with an inconsequence no Latin would have recognised as such, an emotional expression of the Admiral's sincere gratitude for the rescue of his niece and her children by BLANCHE from Red Cartagena in February.[4]

BLANCHE was rounding the north-western tip of Spain, on

---

[1] Steer, *Tree of Gernika*, p. 189. [2] *The Times*.
[3] Caslon. [4] ADM 116 3512.

her way back to Gijón, when Commander Taylor's signal was received at 2039 (G.M.T.) on 5 April reporting the Nationalist warships gathered off Bilbao and BRAZEN's own patrol in that area. It made no great impression: British merchant ships had not previously been molested on that coast. Indeed, when a Nationalist complaint had been received on 15 March that the freighter HAMSTERLEY had 'forced the blockade' of Bilbao under the protection of ENCOUNTER, investigation revealed that the destroyer had actually been in port at the time and that her 'protection' had been no more than an exchange of wireless signals (presumably intercepted by the Spaniards) with HAMSTERLEY. So, as Caslon later recorded, even another signal from BRAZEN, at the chilly hour of 0559 on the morning of 6 April, to say that she was investigating a complaint from THORPEHALL of being fired on, caused no particular concern. It was doubtless some mistake which Commander Taylor would sort out. BLANCHE herself hove to off Gijón and re-embarked Stevenson, who had come out 3 miles to meet the destroyer in a launch, having now concluded his visit to this outpost of his Consular district. At 0615 BLANCHE continued eastwards at the economical speed of 17 knots.

BRAZEN, too, had not initially been much perturbed when she sighted two ships stopped, when she identified them as THORPE-HALL and the Nationalist armed trawler GALERNA or when THORPEHALL signalled, at 0556, that she had been fired on. This was 10 miles off the coast and BRAZEN flashed a message to GALERNA to cease her interference and herself sent a boat to THORPEHALL to discover the exact position. It was the subsequent arrival of a more formidable challenger that transformed the situation and decided Commander Taylor to go to Action Stations, a process obvious to any observer, because it entailed men running over the open deck to their guns and torpedo tubes, to say nothing of the removal of the guard rails along the ship's sides. Then, in the words of the subsequent Report of Proceedings, 'I took BRAZEN between the British ship and the cruiser ALMIRANTE CERVERA which was then approaching from the direction of Bilbao. The trawler went away to the other side of the cruiser. I informed ALMIRANTE CERVERA that the British Government did not permit of any action being taken against the merchant ship.'[1]

ALMIRANTE CERVERA was a serious opponent for a destroyer. Much larger and with a crew three times the size of BRAZEN's, her designed speed was only 2 knots less, she had eight 6 inch guns to BRAZEN's four 4.7 inch and twelve torpedo tubes to BRAZEN's eight. If BRAZEN was to get her way only bluff would do it – or persuasion.

There followed an exchange of signals. BRAZEN pointed out that THORPEHALL was only carrying food; ALMIRANTE CERVERA replied that she could nevertheless not permit that ship to enter Bilbao, as victuals were as important as war materials at this time. At 0722 ALMIRANTE CERVERA emphasised her intentions by a simple manoeuvre: she and GALERNA placed themselves between THORPEHALL and the coast. This was an awkward impasse for an officer with no very precise instructions to cover a contingency which no one had envisaged in quite this form. Hoping that his senior officer was fast approaching in BLANCHE, Commander Taylor prudently decided to stall: 'I therefore advised THORPEHALL not to try [to enter Bilbao] and remained in company to see that she was not interfered with again.'

Commander Taylor could only hope, because wireless communications were giving trouble. When BLANCHE increased to 26 knots at 0800 this was because nothing further had been received since BRAZEN's first message. Wireless was still rather primitive in 1937, when many British merchant ships did not carry it and even the Royal Navy sometimes found it unreliable. Indeed, when continued lack of news began to worry Commander Caslon and he ordered BEAGLE to land her refugees and join BRAZEN, the signal he sent at 0844 did not get through till 1006. In vain did BLANCHE's operator minutely adjust his dials: there was only the crackle of static, the waxing and waning wail of interference, the gibberish of unwanted or undecipherable morse. At 0925 Commander Caslon could bear it no longer.

---

[1] ADM 116 3512.

Anything might be happening ahead of him and he wanted no hostages in a Nationalist harbour if action was in progress or imminent. He ordered BRILLIANT to raise steam and escort the tanker PRESTOL out of Corunna, then herself to join BLANCHE. Then, at 0937, a signal was at last received from BRAZEN: it reported the action taken two hours earlier by ALMIRANTE CERVERA to bar THORPEHALL's passage to Bilbao. Commander Caslon increased to 32 knots and cleared for action.

Fortunately the Spanish commanders had been in no hurry to force the issue. It was 1015 before ALMIRANTE CERVERA and GALERNA, some decision having evidently emerged after much pondering on their instructions and the proper interpretation of international law, again began to approach THORPEHALL. BRAZEN followed their example. At this moment, just as a real confrontation seemed imminent, there was a new and most unexpected arrival on the scene: a German pocket battleship, or *Panzerschiff* as the Germans themselves called these vessels. There were, admittedly, known to be two of them in the Bay – ADMIRAL GRAF SPEE had visited Saint-Jean-de-Luz on 27 March and BLANCHE had sighted one early on the morning of 6 April – but for one of them to turn up just as this encounter was becoming a trifle tense can scarcely have been very welcome to Commander Taylor. If ADMIRAL GRAF SPEE or ADMIRAL SCHEER – none of the British officers reporting the incident was certain which of these two ships they were confronted with – chose to make her influence felt, then six 11 inch guns and eight 5.9 inch would provide her with rather compelling arguments. Indeed, in the face of such preponderant metal, the arrival of BLANCHE, hot-foot from the west, at 1042, scarcely affected the balance of disadvantage. To Commander Taylor, however, conscious that the responsibility for coping with an increasingly tricky situation had now passed from him to the Senior Naval Officer North Spain, it must have been a considerable relief to watch the urgent foam of BLANCHE's bow wave subside as she too joined the growing group of ships rocking in the Biscayan swell.

Curiously enough, the German ship's arrival seemed to be

having the opposite effect to that which might have been expected. Indeed, Commander Caslon formed the impression –
presumably an exchange of signals had been noted – that the
newcomer had actually advised ALMIRANTE CERVERA against
proceeding to extremes and might even have prompted the
unexpected withdrawal, at 1100, of the two Spanish vessels.
Acting on his guess, Commander Caslon then signalled to the
German, who was flying a Rear-Admiral's flag, that BLANCHE
would follow the Spanish ships in order to explain that THORPE-
HALL, which had come from Valencia, then one of the principal
Mediterranean ports of Republican Spain, had been inspected
off Gibraltar by Spanish Nationalist as well as British authorities and given permission to proceed to Bilbao. The German
ship signalled back 'thanks for kind information' and added that
she was resuming her own patrol.

It had been a revealing little incident. Obviously the stopping
of THORPEHALL indicated a change in Nationalist policy since
she had been cleared at Gibraltar and, if Commander Caslon
was right in his deductions about German advice, a change
which even a sympathetic foreign naval officer could not regard
as consonant with a prudent interpretation of international
law and custom. But Caslon was sensibly intent on resolving
the dispute amicably if he possibly could and, having ensured
that the *Panzerschiff* was aware of his pacific intentions, set out
in pursuit of GALERNA (ALMIRANTE CERVERA was already out of
sight), first telling THORPEHALL to continue her voyage to
BILBAO and BRAZEN to accompany her as far as the 3 mile limit.

GALERNA was easily overhauled at 1150, but did not respond
to lamp signals, even when the message these conveyed had
been translated into Spanish by Stevenson. So BLANCHE closed
to hailing distance and the Consul bawled the information
through a megaphone, having first been disguised – why is not
obvious from the Report of Proceedings, but perhaps for the
linguistic honour of the Navy – in a naval cap and greatcoat.
There was no particular reaction, but BLANCHE had done all she
could and turned back to join BRAZEN, arriving from the west
at almost the same moment as BEAGLE from the east, the latter

having on board Steer, who afterwards remembered that 'everybody was somewhat excited in our destroyer, and there were happy whispers forward of "dirty work" '.[1]

It was just as well for, soon afterwards, at 1352, ALMIRANTE CERVERA again appeared, heading towards THORPEHALL at some speed and with at least the appearance of mischievous intent. This time, however, the odds were rather less unequal and Caslon promptly ordered his three destroyers to form line ahead, choosing a course and speed that not only placed them between the cruiser and THORPEHALL, but also gave them the position which any naval officer would recognise as that most favourable for a torpedo attack – parallel to ALMIRANTE CERVERA's course, but ahead of her. The delicate hint – at no stage did Caslon commit the impropriety of pointing a gun or a tube – evidently sufficed and at 1415, when THORPEHALL was off the harbour mouth, Caslon was able to order his destroyers to turn in succession and to lead them back, past ALMIRANTE CERVERA (with whom no signals were exchanged this time) and on an opposite course. The Spanish cruiser had made no attempt to renew her interception even after THORPEHALL had crossed the 3 mile limit, thus sparing Caslon the potentially awkward choice between attempting protection inside territorial waters (which might have been illegal) and allowing a British ship to be arrested under his very eyes (which could have been embarrassing). It must have been with some relief that, at 1555, he transferred Stevenson to BEAGLE (so that, together with Steer, he might continue his interrupted journey to Bermeo) and himself set off for Saint-Jean-de-Luz to tell the Ambassador (who kept him to dinner) and to compose his own report to the Commander-in-Chief.

He had a good deal to say and his report was destined to be quite as important as the 'judgment and initiative', 'good sense and readiness to take responsibility' he and Commander Taylor of BRAZEN had displayed (and on which they were rightly congratulated by the Commander-in-Chief and Admiralty) in

---

[1] Steer, *Tree of Gernika*, p. 189.

this prolonged confrontation with forces that were, at moments, greatly superior. His most telling point was that incidents of this kind could easily recur and, if they did, might not pass off so smoothly on other occasions. This time, for instance, the only shot fired had been the one from GALERNA – across THORPEHALL's bows – which opened the ball in the early dawn. If trouble was to be avoided in future, he had two recommendations: the reinforcement of British warships on the northern coast of Spain and measures to discourage British ships from attempting to enter Bilbao. Given his understanding of British policy – that the over-riding principle was Non-Intervention – these were reasonable recommendations. But he added a sentence, intended as no more than a straightforward summary of his argument, of which the explosive echoes still rumble controversially through history books written quarter of a century later.[1] He said the blockade of Bilbao was effective.[2]

This statement, of which the significance and the repercussions will be explored in later chapters, was supported, as were Commander Caslon's recommendations, by both Admiral Sir Roger Backhouse, the Commander-in-Chief Home Fleet, and Sir Henry Chilton. The Ambassador, indeed, rather revelled in naval detail, listing Nationalist strength on the north coast as one battleship, one cruiser, one light cruiser, one destroyer and one armed trawler; too much, he argued, for Commander Caslon's four destroyers. He accordingly recommended that British merchant ships should be informed that henceforth no protection could be provided on voyages to Bilbao.[3] All these recommendations, from Caslon, from the Commander-in-Chief, from the Ambassador, were to be hotly disputed, even denounced. But British policy had hitherto been dominated by what the Foreign Office called 'our determination not to waste our substance on a dispute which does not concern us'[4] and anyone accepting that principle was almost bound to reach

[1] Thomas, *Spanish Civil War*, p. 408.
[2] ADM 116 3514.   [3] FO 371 21352.
[4] Memorandum on the Spanish Civil War prepared by the Foreign Office for the Imperial Conference of 1937. FO 371 21296.

Chilton's conclusion from his reasonable premise that 'yesterday's affair ended successfully, but this type of emergency is likely to recur at any moment and to become increasingly dangerous'.[1]

Indeed, if British politicians, diplomats and naval officers had hitherto been a little slow to appreciate just what was brewing off the northern coast of Spain, they now responded more smartly to its new possibilities than did *The Times*. That newspaper, Steer's presence on the scene notwithstanding, gave the incident of THORPEHALL's rescue just six lines on 7 April: it was the first item on the agenda of the Cabinet when they assembled at eleven that morning.[2]

[1] FO 371 21352.   [2] CAB 23 88.

CHAPTER 5

The battle in London

Supplicamos al Primer Ministro o
al que mas manda en Inglaterra.
The children's letter[1]

'Whoever most rules in England' was a prudent reservation, because the question was to be somewhat disputed that spring of 1937. As early as 24 March the Foreign Secretary had had occasion to complain to the Cabinet 'that the difficulties of the present situation were being very much increased by the attitude of the Press and Parliament. For example, that afternoon no less than twenty-five Questions had been addressed to him and some of them were calculated to irritate Signor Mussolini.'[2] Many influential Britons were unwilling to regard the Spanish Civil War as 'a dispute which does not concern us' and their partisanship was inflamed with each fresh indication – and these came thick and fast – that Non-Intervention had a different meaning for the French, German, Italian and Russian governments. 'All that spring Spain had been an incessant topic for question-time and for debates on foreign affairs.'[3]

So when, at their regular meeting on 7 April, the Cabinet considered the reports that had come in about the interception of THORPEHALL, they did so in full realisation that they were discussing a situation as potentially controversial at home as it was delicate, and even dangerous, abroad. At this early stage, however, discussion was somewhat confused and inconclusive. The First Lord of the Admiralty, Sir Samuel Hoare, made the

---

[1] 'We entreat the Prime Minister or whoever most rules in England.' Letter of 19 June 1937 from the Basque children at North Stoneham Camp, Hampshire, to Mr Neville Chamberlain. FO 317 21372.
[2] CAB 23 88.
[3] Hugh Thomas, *The Spanish Civil War* (Eyre and Spottiswoode, 1961), p. 409.

point that a new situation had arisen: this was the first time that General Franco's forces had interfered with a British ship carrying food, one of those ships which, unlike vessels carrying munitions, it had hitherto been British policy to protect on the high seas. What was more the Commander-in-Chief Mediterranean (he meant Home, but the First Lord was inclined to be a little uncertain on these points of detail) thought that General Franco now had the power to do so: his blockade was effective. Perhaps the situation ought to be reconsidered. There were, after all, supposed to be another eight or nine of these food ships on the way.

The discussion that followed rambled a little. For a Conservative Cabinet presumably dedicated to the principle of free enterprise, there was surprisingly little sympathy for the owners of British ships trading to northern Spain. They were described as 'blockade-runners' and 'adventurers' and even the President of the Board of Trade, usually a staunch upholder of the rights of British shipping, emphasised that this rush to Spain was by no means characteristic of the shipping industry as a whole. The owners of these ships were after war profits and some of the ships concerned had only just been transferred to British registry. These were somewhat irrelevant issues, though more was to be heard of them during the following weeks. Eden got rather closer to the heart of the matter when he quoted Ogilvie Forbes, who had just completed his tour of duty as Chargé d'Affaires in Madrid, for the view that, in the Civil War, time was on the side of the Republicans. This was promptly countered by Hoare, who said that the Commander-in-Chief Home Fleet, who had recently visited some Spanish ports in his flagship, thought otherwise. This was an appropriate confrontation, for Eden and Hoare were to become the spokesmen of opposing factions during the next few weeks.

Lacking strong guidance from the Prime Minister – Baldwin, still exhausted by his exertions during the Abdication Crisis, was about to retire and is not recorded as having said anything on this occasion – the Cabinet decided to set up a special committee to consider the question of protecting shipping in its legal, political and practical aspects. But it was already apparent that, to Ministers, the problems were less clear-cut and straightforward than they appeared on the coast of Spain.[1]

Nevertheless the sense of urgency was there. The Cabinet Committee on the Protection of British Shipping (Spain) held its first meeting that very afternoon.[2] The interval had clearly allowed Ministers to obtain fuller information and advice from their officials, but had hardly been long enough for them to get at the roots of the problem that confronted them. The First Lord, for instance, opened with a solemn warning against a course of action nobody had proposed: 'in the view of the Naval Staff we should be undertaking a very grave obligation, and incurring very grave risks, if we now undertook to protect British ships within Spanish territorial waters'. The President of the Board of Trade, who, as he complained at the morning's Cabinet, 'had not been warned that this question was going to arise', had profited by the luncheon hour to increase his knowledge and to modify his attitude. There were no more derogatory references to 'adventurers'. Instead he emphasised the importance of maintaining the Government's position in regard to legitimate shipping activities in Spain and of ensuring that there was no interference with British ships bound for Bilbao and likely on their return journey, to carry cargoes of ore – 'having regard to the present grave shortage of iron ore in the U.K.'. This was a point of more than commercial importance at a moment when Britain was belatedly beginning the process of rearmament.

But neither contribution went to the heart of the matter: food was now a weapon in the struggle for Bilbao and Ministers had to decide whose hands should wield it. There was no chance, in the light of all that had been said and done before – Mr Grenfell, for instance, would not have forgotten Lord Cranborne's letter of 19 March – of avoiding this act of choice, of remaining passive, neutral, inert. The Basque Government had chosen British ships to bring their food – had spent good money to

---

[1] CAB 23 88.   [2] CAB 27 639.

ensure the ships should be British – precisely because they had believed British statements that such ships could count on the protection of the British Navy. If that protection were now denied, this would imply a change in British policy and the outcry from the numerous British supporters of Basques or Republicans or both would be considerable. There was equally little chance of the Nationalists merely acquiescing in the continuation of previous British policy. The British ships earlier protected had not been of the first importance to either side, objections to their passage had not been serious or sustained and the intervention of British warships scarcely resented. It was different now. To protect food-ships to Bilbao would be to do what the Republicans could not: break the Nationalist blockade.

Whatever Ministers decided, therefore, they were going to inflict real injury on one side or the other. In Bilbao, a fortnight's ration, admittedly supplemented by a little fish, seagulls and – a rare delicacy – the occasional fat cat from a British ship, was 'a pound of soup paste, two pounds of rice, half a pound of sugar, a pound of dried peas and a little less than half a pound of cabbage'.[1] Either way there was going to be a major row. It was a dilemma which might perhaps have been resolved by a careful analysis of likely terminal situations: which course of action would produce the least disagreeable result? There was no time for such methods that afternoon, when most of the Ministers were also due at a meeting of the United Kingdom Delegation to the Imperial Conference. Without much further discussion Ministers decided, to use the sometimes expressive jargon of Whitehall, to 'fluff' the issue. They would not change the existing naval instructions, whereby protection was given outside, but not inside, territorial waters. But they would warn British shipowners that the Basque coast, 'particularly off Bilbao', was 'specially dangerous at present for shipping'. And they would send Mr Pack, the Commercial Secretary at Hendaye, to tell the Nationalist authorities that H.M.G. did not recognise either side in Spain as having belligerent rights and to

---

[1] G. L. Steer, *The Tree of Gernika* (Hodder and Stoughton, 1938), p. 198.

persuade the Nationalists not to interfere with British ships unless these were carrying munitions.[1]

These were not, at first sight, decisions likely to have any very immediate impact on the coast of Spain or to solve any of the problems which the Commander-in-Chief and the Ambassador, to say nothing of Commander Caslon, had considered so urgent. However highly Mr Pack's powers of persuasion might be regarded, he was, after all, being given rather a difficult task. It was inherently unlikely that ALMIRANTE CERVERA had been cruising the Cantabrian Sea in complete ignorance of the views of His Majesty's Government on belligerent rights. And, if the British shipowners concerned had no idea that the vicinity of Bilbao was particularly dangerous to shipping, they must have been exceptionally sharp businessmen to secure those 'war profits' which had so shocked the Cabinet.

British policy, however, is seldom simply and explicitly decided: it evolves, or it crystallises, by processes that are biological or chemical, rather than logical. In this instance the true determination of Ministers had been implicit: they wished to avoid the disagreeable choice that confronted them and they thought they had discerned the germ of an idea that might enable them to do so. It was an ingenious idea. Indeed, as events were to prove, it was over-ingenious. On the 7th it was still vague, but on the 11th it would actually be put into words in the course of the Cabinet's discussions: 'One suggestion was that British Merchant Ships might be warned against proceeding to Bilbao owing to the dangers from submarine mines and air bombing, against which no protection could be offered by the Navy. From a Parliamentary point of view this course offered attractions, because it would avoid any appearance of yielding to General Franco's demands.'[2] In the light of this later clarification, as of the action taken by Departments on the Committee's decisions, we may reasonably assume that, as early as the 7th, Ministers dimly envisaged an ideal compromise:

[1] CAB 27 639.   [2] CAB 23 88.

discreet warnings of dangers quite unconnected with the Nationalist blockade would sharply reduce the numbers of British ships going to Bilbao; this would give General Franco the substance of his desires and he would accordingly refrain from interference with any British ships disregarding this warning. The arrival of a minority only of the ships they had expected might not silence Basque complaints, but it would enable H.M.G. to disclaim responsibility: their policy had not changed, but British shipowners had reached their own decisions on grounds of commercial prudence. And there would be no more potentially dangerous incidents.

Amid the passions and intransigence of the Spanish Civil War, this was probably an unattainable ideal: only the British Government regarded the avoidance of trouble as important and were accustomed to reaching discreet compromise through a nod, a wink and a murmur. But what little hope of success may ever have existed depended on complete comprehension by all the British executants of the precise intentions and aspirations of their masters. Either Ministers broke up too soon for that or their Secretary, Sir Rupert Howarth, lacked Lord Hankey's courage in making explicit what Ministers had felt but failed to express. Whatever the cause, the results are plain: the telegrams despatched by Admiralty and Foreign Office were clearly animated by diverse understandings of what Ministers had decided and, at the other end, created even more divergent impressions.

The long telegram sent by the Foreign Office to Chilton on the following day, for instance, gave a possibly exaggerated impression of Ministerial resolution. It was all about urging General Franco to leave British ships alone and the news that 'the Board of Trade are sending a private warning to ship-owners' against letting their ships go to Bilbao suggested that this would, indeed, be a very discreet communication.[1]

The impression the Admiralty gave to Commander Caslon was rather different. Admittedly he was told that his action

[1] FO 425 414.

had been approved though 'destroyers should bear in mind that they are not expected to engage forces in greatly superior strength', and that his recommendation of reinforcements was to be met by asking the Commander-in-Chief Mediterranean to send an 8 inch gun cruiser. But the emphasis in the Foreign Office telegram on the 'private' character of the Board of Trade's warning to shipowners was absent from the Admiralty instructions.[1]

It would, in any case, have come too late. As early as the evening of 6 April Caslon had begun broadcasting on the wavelength used by most of the tramps likely to be concerned: 'Any British Merchant Ship approaching Bilbao and within 100 miles is to communicate with H.M.S. BLANCHE.' He meant to make sure there would be no further incident while the Admiralty were making up their minds. When the freighter MARIE LLEWELLYN came into Saint-Jean-de-Luz on her own initiative on the 7th to seek advice – she had no wireless, but had heard the news of THORPEHALL's encounter on the Captain's portable radio – Caslon urged the Master not to try for Santander, his destination.[2] On the 8th, when the Admiralty belatedly told him that warnings to shipping should not be broadcast,[3] BRILLIANT intercepted OLAVUS at sea and BLANCHE's signal brought SARASTONE, HAMSTERLEY and LEADGATE into Saint-Jean-de-Luz.

Once again Commander Caslon had displayed initiative and readiness to take responsibility and again his actions were approved by the Admiralty, who told him on the 10th to do what he had begun already on the 8th: divert British ships to Saint-Jean-de-Luz, and detain them there. Admittedly Ministers were later to grumble that they had not actually meant him to *order* British merchant ships – something the Government had no power to do anyway – only to advise them. They should have made the nuances of their intentions clearer to this loyal, straightforward and energetic officer. In any case, there was not all that much difference between Caslon's forthright letter on

---

[1] FO 371 21352.   [2] Caslon.   [3] ADM 116 3514.

61

the 9th, 'you are not to leave Saint-Jean-de-Luz for any port in the hands of the Spanish Government on the North of Spain until further orders', and the officially approved instructions sent on the following day by the Board of Trade to H.M. Consul at Bordeaux: '. . . inform British ships now in Saint-Jean-de-Luz that British Government desire them not to enter Basque ports for the time being on account of the dangerous situation there and to wait at Saint-Jean for further communications'.[1]

And these fine distinctions were futile. Regardless of the precise intentions of Ministers, whatever shades of meaning anyone's words might bear, the actions taken on and after 6 April by Commander Caslon were already calling forth some unforeseen reactions, and had launched on an erratic course a minor political avalanche. Just when the first irreversible slide took place in the deep-piled drifts is uncertain, but the alarm rang on the evening of the 9th, when the Ambassador asked Caslon to pass an urgent message to London – the Embassy had no proper ciphers. Troncoso had called that evening with a distinctly menacing communication from General Franco, who knew there were four British merchant ships at Saint-Jean-de-Luz waiting to proceed to Bilbao: the entry of British merchant ships to Bilbao 'would be resisted by insurgent warships by all possible means, even at the risk of a serious incident'.[2]

This message had been born in as much misunderstanding as it durably engendered. General Franco's administration had read Captain Moreu's reports on the affair of 6 April, they had intercepted BLANCHE's broadcasts of that evening, their agents had observed the growing concentration of British merchant ships in Saint-Jean-de-Luz. The conclusion was obvious: the perfidious British navy, having broken the Nationalist blockade on the 6th with a single ship, was now planning a more ambitious operation. An entire convoy was being assembled in Saint-Jean-de-Luz, so that it might be forced through to Bilbao under

---

[1] Hansard, vol. 327, debate of 14 April 1937. [2] CAB 23 88.

the protection of British warships.[1] Clearly the British did not realise that the blockade of Bilbao was a serious part of General Franco's purposes: this must be made plain to them.

This was a sad mistake. ALMIRANTE CERVERA's manoeuvres on the 6th had conveyed a message that was clear without seeming excessively blunt. British Ministers had already drawn what General Franco would have considered the appropriate conclusions. In their slow, uneasy, self-conscious fashion they were gradually putting these into effect, being careful meanwhile not to let the left hand know what the right was up to. Now the tactless Troncoso had brushed these Whitehall cobwebs away, had brutally confronted Ministers with the character of their own conduct.

Afterwards, when Troncoso's message became public knowledge, the British opposition and the press and, of course, Mr Steer, made great play with it as the threat before which the Cabinet had cowered. This was scarcely true. The eagerness to avoid another incident, the disposition to connive at the blockade of Bilbao had emerged beforehand. Ministers, the Admiralty, even Commander Caslon, had been of one mind and actively working together on the 8th and 9th. On the 10th when the report of Troncoso's message reached London and an *ad hoc* meeting of Ministers – it was a Saturday – assembled to consider it, the trio of Foreign Secretary, First Lord of the Admiralty and President of the Board of Trade took only one new decision: to send to the northern coast of Spain what was then reckoned as the world's most powerful single warship, H.M.S. HOOD.

The three ministers also considered – and Mr Baldwin reluctantly agreed – that the full Cabinet should meet on the following evening to discuss the new and explicitly ominous situation that now confronted the British Government. There had not been a Sunday Cabinet since the Abdication Crisis – though one of those, on 22 November 1936, had also had a

---

[1] Captain Caveda told Commander Caslon on 10 April that this had indeed been the assumption on which Major Troncoso's warning had been based. ADM 116 3512.

Spanish item on the agenda. This Sunday there was only the one subject to discuss, but it took the whole of their time. There is no need to follow Ministers as they thrashed around in their efforts to escape from the freshly sharpened horns of their dilemma. We have already noted the fallaciously attractive issue on which they fastened. But two features of their discussion deserve remark, because these were to recur. One was the determined pacifism of the First Lord of the Admiralty – even the naval superiority which the arrival of HOOD would confer seemed to him an argument for discretion rather than valour: 'there was no doubt that we should possess overwhelming strength, so that whatever decision the Cabinet might reach, it would be based on strength and not on weakness'. The other was the disingenuous character of the arguments with which Sir Samuel Hoare had been furnished by his professional advisers: the Insurgents 'now had one new battleship armed with 12 inch guns' to help maintain their 'effective blockade' of Bilbao.[1] Now ESPAÑA was rated as a battleship and she had been commissioned as late as 1921 – five years after ROYAL OAK and one year after HOOD. But her construction – which had been delayed by the First World War – had begun in England in 1912 and had been inspired by a deeply conservative distrust of Fisher's new-fangled DREADNOUGHT and all this nonsense about oil fuel. To call this coal-burning eccentricity with her enormous funnel, her staggered turrets, her Victorian secondary armament of twenty 4 inch guns on separate broadsides a 'new battleship', as if she had been another ADMIRAL SCHEER, was an imposition on an ignorant Cabinet. A hundred feet shorter than ALMIRANTE CERVERA, she was at least as much less efficient, even if Steer were right in supposing her mutinous gun-layers to have been replaced by Germans. Acorazado was her official designation and, in ESPAÑA's case, the dictionary's rendering of 'iron-clad' is the least misleading translation. The Spanish sailors themselves called her 'El Abuelo' – the grandfather.[2]

---

[1] CAB 23 88.
[2] Almirante Francisco Moreno, *La Guerra en el Mar*, ed. Moreno de Reyna (Editorial AHR, Barcelona, 1959), p. 42.

Nevertheless the conclusions reached by the Cabinet strove to maintain the increasingly fragile compromise after which Ministers still hankered. Mr Pack's mission was cancelled but Chilton was to tell General Franco that His Majesty's Government could not tolerate any interference with British shipping *at sea* – this deliberately ambiguous phrase was the result of Hoare's argument, or of 'that affable familiar ghost which nightly gulls him with intelligence', that the Royal Navy would be profoundly embarrassed if ships they had protected on the high seas were to be arrested within their sight in territorial waters. But – and this was the important, the saving clause – the Government were themselves advising ships not to go to Bilbao. There followed some suggestions – based on a conversation Caslon had had with the obliging Caveda – that British ships might nevertheless still proceed to Santander and, in ballast and only for the purpose of loading iron-ore, even to Bilbao.[1]

This was the Cabinet's compromise, but they reached one conclusion, which may not unfairly be attributed to the intimidating effect of Troncoso's message and which certainly represented the high-water mark of Hoare's influence on their deliberations: the Admiralty were instructed to inform H.M. ships that naval protection was to be withdrawn from any British ships which might choose to disregard official advice and press on regardless for Bilbao. Even this, however, was something less than Hoare's tentative suggestion that the carriage of food to Bilbao might be prohibited by Order in Council.

It had been a busy Sunday evening in London and the day had not been inactive even at Hendaye, where the Embassy, most of whom had attended the dance given the night before in Saint-Jean-de-Luz for the crews of BLANCHE, BEAGLE and BRILLIANT, received three telephone calls from the Foreign Office, one of them from the Secretary of State in person.[2] He was eager to explore the possibility of British food ships

---

[1] CAB 23 88.   [2] Malcolm.

unloading their cargoes at Santander and continuing their voyage
to Bilbao in ballast – so as to be able to load iron ore at the latter
port.[1] In a sense, however, it had been a quiet day, the last
opportunity that politicians and Admirals, officials and Ambassadors, would have to handle this delicate and distressing
problem on their own.

The news broke next morning. It was inevitable – a Sunday
Cabinet, those battered tramps tossing at anchor in Saint-Jean-
de-Luz beneath the hotel windows of so many journalists, the
contempt of both sides in Spain for the discretion so beloved of
British Ministers, the departure from Gibraltar of the cruiser
SHROPSHIRE, the cancellation of shore leave for the crew of
HOOD. It was a meaty budget for the place of honour in the
middle page of *The Times* – the front page, in those more
decorous days, being reserved for Births, Deaths, Marriages,
the Agony Column sacred to Sherlock Holmes, and advertise-
ments for the tasteful restoration of cathedrals. Bilbao had
made the headlines and Major Attlee, the Leader of His
Majesty's Opposition, sent in a Private Notice Question to the
Prime Minister.

Mr. Baldwin did his best. He told the House of Commons:

His Majesty's Government can not tolerate any interference with
British shipping at sea. They are, however, warning British shipping
that, in view of conditions at present prevailing in the neighbourhood
of Bilbao, they should not, for practical reasons and in view of the
risks against which it is at present impossible to protect them, go
into that area so long as those conditions prevail. The Vice Admiral
Commanding the Battle Cruiser Squadron has been sent to the
North coast of Spain.[2]

The first and last sentences had a fine resonance and the
Prime Minister displayed all the skill of long practice in evading
the flurry of indignant supplementary questions. But the
Opposition gave notice of a motion of censure and the following
day the *Manchester Guardian* published a long and censorious
leader: 'it looks very much as though the Government were
using the threat of mines and bombs to extricate itself from the

[1] CAB 23 88.   [2] FO 371 21352.

embarrassing position of having to deal with the attentions of Franco's warships ... it is unfortunate that the British Government, with its rigorous 'non-intervention' so often intervenes in fact against the Spanish Government. It is doing so again now.'

This was a conclusion widely drawn and not only among the hot partisans of the Republican cause. Eden had some difficulty that same day in convincing the French Ambassador that Bilbao was mined and unsafe for ships to enter, that 'ships were indeed more liable to be attacked, so we were informed, within the 3 mile limit than outside it'.[1] In France itself, the left-wing press was terse: 'Londres favorise Franco dans les blocus maritimes que ce dernier semble vouloir adopter'.[2] In a couple of days Chilton was to learn that General Franco 'was very satisfied with our attitude'[3] and in Bilbao itself Mr Consul Stevenson was moved to compose a nine page despatch on the 13th. This was something of an event. As a deeply conscientious official, Stevenson did not lightly question the policy of his Government. Nor did he wield a fluent pen. Yet his tortured sentences reveal the intensity of his emotions:

The Basques, it cannot be gainsaid, are displaying amazing fortitude ... their last source of food supplies, built upon carefully planned British charter parties and paid for in advance, would now appear to be cut off by Franco's diplomacy, or by a change in policy, hardly credible, of His Majesty's Government, however well camouflaged and to the contrary statements in regard thereto may have been uttered at Westminster.[4]

The respectful protests of Consuls are, however, easily ignored and, although Steer may be guilty of some chronological exaggeration in his claim – 'I take to myself the credit that I, before anyone else, exposed the fake in the blockade and recovered the truth',[5] it must be admitted that his urgent advice to the Basque leaders and his own telegrams to members of the Opposition in London were more efficacious. Before the censure debate began on the afternoon of the 14th a good deal of

---

[1] FO 425 414.   [2] *L'Oeuvre*, 13 April 1937.
[3] FO 371 21352.   [4] FO 371 21291.
[5] Steer, *Tree of Gernika*, p. 193.

information had reached London without passing through the Admiralty filter. Even the Cabinet, at their meeting that morning, had a long telegram before them from the President of the Basque Republic explaining just why Franco's blockade of Bilbao could not be regarded as effective.

This was not, of course, the only subject on the Cabinet's agenda that day. They began by discussing the King's desire that certain of their papers should be communicated to His Royal Highness the Duke of Gloucester and they had also to consider the problems of Belgium and the Treaty of Locarno, Air Raid Precautions, the pasteurisation of milk, marriage, Sunday trading and the law of inheritance. But Bilbao, with a motion of censure pending, was undoubtedly their main concern and President Aguirre's message worried some Ministers. Were they really on firm ground in maintaining that mines alone constituted an insuperable obstacle to British ships bound for Bilbao? Even Hoare confessed to some doubts on this point, but the Cabinet were reassured by the Home Secretary, Sir John Simon. Having been entrusted with the duty of answering the motion of censure on behalf of the Government he had, so he explained, taken the precaution, with the consent of the First Lord of the Admiralty, of discussing this problem with 'two officers from that Department'. 'The Naval Officers he had consulted had insisted that the British Fleet could, of course, force a way into Bilbao, or any other Spanish port, but only if minesweepers were used.'[1]

One wishes that Simon had mentioned their names, for they at least must have known one of the Admiralty's more closely guarded secrets. On 20 March 1937 Captain MacGrigor, whose ship was at Bermeo collecting refugees, reported '[I] took the opportunity of calling on the authorities at Bilbao unofficially, accompanied by Mr Stevenson our Consul, as I was anxious to appreciate for myself the extent of the mine menace in the approaches to this port'. After lengthy discussions with Eguia, who showed him charts of the sweeping operations and provided

---

[1] CAB 23 88.

particulars of all the mines recovered, MacGrigor (who had heard the Nationalist story and seen their charts two days earlier), reported: 'I have no doubt that the entrance to Bilbao is absolutely safe and that our ships and oiler could use it under the conditions proposed without risk.' He had been concerned, as had his superiors, with the lack of suitable harbours where British destroyers could refuel and rest their crews and wished to use Bilbao for this purpose. He accompanied his report with a detailed appendix on the results of minesweeping at Bilbao.

His recommendations were not endorsed by the Commander-in-Chief Home Fleet – it is the privilege, indeed the duty, of Admirals to be more cautious than their Captains – so the Admiralty cannot be blamed for not accepting them. But the pencil annotation they placed in the margin of Captain MacGrigor's Report of Proceedings – 'Omit to B. of T. and F.O.' – is less susceptible of innocent explanation. Why did they not want these two departments to know that one of their best Captains – he ultimately became First Sea Lord – considered Bilbao 'absolutely safe' not merely for merchant ships but for his own destroyers?[1] And why was the Prime Minister advised to tell the House of Commons, on 12 April, that Bilbao was indeed dangerously mined – by both sides?[2] Admittedly, Steer exaggerated when he said 'in the period March 15th, when the Basques found the last (empty) mine of the January brood, to May 1st, during which all the talking was done in Parliament, the entry to Bilbao was completely clear'.[3] MacGrigor himself saw a floating mine on 24 March,[4] BRAZEN sank one on 5 April and, on 6 April, BLANCHE saw another, but, being at full speed to the aid of THORPEHALL, had no time to do anything about it.[5] Nevertheless, Hoare – a seasoned if not always a fortunate politician – was right when he told the Cabinet on the 14th: 'there would be difficulties if we based ourselves too much on the danger from mines'.

The trouble was that the Cabinet still refused to recognise

[1] ADM 116 3512.
[2] CAB 23 88.
[3] Steer, *Tree of Gernika*, p. 206.
[4] ADM 116 3512.
[5] FO 371 21290.

the inevitability of coming down on one side or the other. They even instructed the Admiralty to reverse their orders about withdrawing protection to British ships – because these were inconsistent with the Prime Minister's statement to the House on the 12th – and the Vice-Admiral Battle Cruiser Squadron, who had by now reached the Bay of Biscay and assumed charge of British naval forces on the northern coast of Spain, was told late that night: 'if a British ship proceeding to Bilbao in spite of Government advice calls on you for protection in a particular case you should render protection on the High Seas'. Vice-Admiral Blake, another vigorous and forthright sailor, found the wording of this new order somewhat lacking in clarity,[1] and a personal signal from the First Sea Lord (to Flag Officers only) recognised the delicate situation they had been placed in.

Ministers, however, were not alone in entering the House of Commons that afternoon with an armoury of disingenuous argument. Labour members accustomed to vote against the Service estimates and to proclaim their preference for scholar-ships rather than battleships were flushed with a new-found enthusiasm for the traditions of British naval supremacy. H.M.S. HOOD, whose arrival off Saint-Jean-de-Luz on the evening of the 12th had been evocatively described by *The Times* – 'a great crowd watched her as she entered the outer bay and dropped anchor some four miles from the shore' – aroused them to particular heights of patriotic, even jingoistic, fervour. Duncan Sandys had every right to poke fun at the Palmerstonian attitude adopted by Attlee in deploring 'the failure of H.M.G. to give protection to British merchant ships on their lawful occasions', but the Government, obliged to argue that the Nationalist blockade was effective, not on the high seas, where H.M.G. 'can not tolerate any interference', but in territorial waters, had the stickier case to defend. And, if both sides had to pretend that the course of action they preferred would constitute Non-Intervention, the Government laboured under the disadvantage of having actually taken an initiative –

---

[1] ADM 116 3514.

the issue of instructions to British merchant ships – which, unlike Commander Caslon or the Admiralty, they were reluctant to press to its logical conclusion. The ambivalence of their attitude – for Eden had expressly undertaken that British ships would be protected up to the 3 mile limit if they persisted in going to Bilbao – was expressed in rhyme by one opposition member, Lt Commander Fletcher:

> Mother may I go out to swim?
> Yes, my little daughter,
> But mind, if you go out to swim,
> Don't go near the water.[1]

The Government's majority was solid – even such occasionally independent members as Winston Churchill and Harold Nicolson supported them – and *The Times*, Mr Steer's efforts notwithstanding, gave them continued backing in its leaders. But the debate had done its work. The compromise favoured by Ministers had been too delicate and contrived to withstand the rough blasts of public controversy. And these now began to blow from all quarters – with as much violence as the westerly gale that drove Franco's warships from their blockading stations, dragged BEAGLE from her anchorage in Saint-Jean-de-Luz, distracted midshipmen undergoing examination in BRAZEN and sent HOOD out to the open sea.[2] Indeed it was from HOOD herself that the first, and sharpest, blast struck the startled Admiralty. Ministers had no time to rejoice at the size of their majority before they were reading Vice-Admiral Blake's report of the 14th that he had seen no more than one Insurgent warship at a time, that the blockade was not effective and that British naval forces were adequate for the protection of British shipping.[3] This was awkward – the Admiralty hastily telegraphed back for more particulars, pointing out with some emphasis that the Government's whole policy had been based on contrary assumptions. Then the Spanish Embassy, who had earlier insisted that there were no mines and that the coastal batteries of Bilbao could keep Insurgent warships 15 miles

[1] Hansard, vol. 327, debate of 14 April 1937.
[2] *The Times*, 15 April 1937.   [3] FO 371 21352.

from the coast, published a list of the ships that had entered and left that port without incident between 7 and 13 April.[1] On the 15th THORPEHALL herself left Bilbao, was intercepted by ESPAÑA, but allowed to proceed on the intervention of BRAZEN, whom she informed that Bilbao Bay seemed to be clear of mines.[2]

It was becoming increasingly difficult for Ministers to 'avoid any appearance of yielding to Franco's demands' as long as they maintained their 'advice' to British shipping. Even the ship-owners were being unhelpful – a deputation had visited the President of the Board of Trade on the 14th to ask if they could not at least go to Santander[3] – and the iron and steel industry of South Wales was complaining of a serious shortage of ore.[4] Worst of all, perhaps, was the massive publicity being given by the British Press to the food ships pitching impatiently off Saint-Jean-de-Luz. Thanks to the journalistic flair of David Scott, the special correspondent despatched by *The Times* from Paris, this had become a dramatically human story. Malcolm had mentioned casually to him that the Navy, confronted by no less than three ships' masters all called Jones, had distinguished them by nick-names, and Scott, delighted, succeeded in making 'Potato Jones', 'Ham-and-Egg Jones' and 'Corn-Cob Jones', (all but the first being his own invention)[5] into characters of brief but world-wide notoriety. Potato Jones, in particular, was described as 'the picture of a bluff sea-captain, with an added dash of independence derived from half-ownership of his vessel. His opinion of the present dilemma is expressed more by elo-quent silences than by words. His potatoes are growing long shoots through their sacks and the smell from the holds suggests that they will soon be no use to any Spaniard, rebel or Repub-lican.'[6] Instead of the profiteers the Cabinet had deprecated there was built up a picture of bluff, British sea-dogs whom only government orders restrained from gallantly running an imaginary blockade with food for starving women and children. It was not altogether a fair or an accurate picture, but it added considerably to the embarrassment of Ministers.

[1] *The Times.*   [2] ADM 116 3512.   [3] CAB 27 639.
[4] *The Times.*   [5] Malcolm and Caslon.   [6] *The Times.*

On the 16th, they gave a little ground, Hoare still resisting as best he could. The Committee on British Shipping decided to alter the emphasis of their advice: 'other Basque ports as well as Bilbao are not free from risk. The degree of risk may vary from day to day. We cannot therefore advise proceeding, but in any case we shall, of course, give protection as already announced, if called upon on the high seas.' It was significant that, on this occasion, Eden and Runciman were unexpectedly supported by Simon. General Franco's administration had over-played their hand. Not only had they allowed some of their overt threats against British ships to reach the British press, but they ignored compromise proposals for ships at least to load iron ore at Bilbao or Santander. Ministers now had to face the possibility that continued acquiescence would lead to the exclusion of British ships from all Spanish ports not already under Franco's control.[1] Although this was the day that Chilton reported General Franco as 'very satisfied with our attitude', the slide was already on and General Franco's spokesman did his cause no good by repeating this comment to the *Times* correspondent in Salamanca on the 18th. The *New Statesman*, the *Manchester Guardian*, the parliamentary opposition – who put down many questions on the 19th – were all on the warpath. Even *The Times* commented that 'the Opposition displayed deep anger' and started putting 'blockade' in inverted commas.

Indeed, it was not so much the partisan campaign in press and parliament that was pushing Ministers away from their chosen policy as the steady erosion of those fallacious arguments on which they had originally elected to found their case. If they had been willing, openly and from the outset, to adopt the robust and defensible language of the Foreign Office memorandum and to proclaim 'our determination not to waste our substance on a dispute which does not concern us', they might well have got away with it. But they had allowed the sophistries of the Admiralty – no one can be more Machiavellian than the Admiral (there is one in every generation) who

[1] CAB 27 639.

73

develops a real taste for the in-fighting of Whitehall – to lead them into positions so indefensible that successive exposures were ultimately to drive them to the opposite extreme.

On the 20th, for instance, another debate on Bilbao tempted Hoare to a rash assertion of Franco's ability to maintain an effective blockade of Bilbao within territorial waters alone. When first the Cabinet and then the Committee on British Shipping met the following day, he was confronted by reports from Stevenson that no Nationalist warship had ventured within range of the Basque shore batteries since 5 March (when CANARIAS had been hit), that thirty-two ships had arrived and seven left since 1 April, and, in *The Times* that morning, that the British freighter SEVEN SEAS SPRAY had entered Bilbao to a triumphant welcome and under the escort of Republican destroyers and armed trawlers, on the 20th. Steer rather spread himself, that day and the next, about the cool courage of white-haired Captain Roberts and his daughter Fifi, who accompanied him, as did the wife of the Chief Engineer. He did not mention – probably did not know – that HOOD and FORESTER had been waiting off Bilbao – just in case. Vice-Admiral Blake could display just as much initiative and independent judgment as Commander Caslon, who had sailed for Portsmouth on the 19th, when he had been relieved by Captain Danckwerts and the Sixth Destroyer Flotilla.

Once again an embarrassed Admiralty had to signal for Vice-Admiral Blake's opinion on the effectiveness of the blockade. This controversy, to which we shall have to return, was as much due to sheer misunderstanding as to any deliberate deception. The position was clear enough on the Biscayan coast, where Malcolm had explained to his mother on the 18th: 'the blockade by sea has hitherto taken place mostly on the high seas' because the Basque batteries kept Insurgent warships out of territorial waters and 3 miles afforded insufficient space and time for the proper processes of visit, search and capture as opposed to the doubtfully legal expedient of shelling. A British ship escorted to the territorial limit was thus likely to accomplish the rest of the journey without interference, but there was a risk that a British vessel inside territorial waters might be shelled by a Nationalist warship outside. This had been pointed out by Vice-Admiral Blake as early as the 16th and some correspondence had been needed to establish the precise obligations of British warships in such circumstances.[1] But Hoare was still unwilling to concede the point that, once a British ship reached the 3 mile limit, her subsequent interception was unlikely except as a result of extreme measures. He argued on the 21st that the Insurgent warships had only been temporarily dispersed by the gale. But the Board of Trade's case for letting British merchant ships enter Bilbao was one calculated to appeal to Conservative Ministers: 'it would please the shipowners, the steel industry and South Wales'[2] (which had eighteen steamers engaged in carrying Welsh coal to the Basque ports and returning with Spanish iron-ore).[3]

And the next day, before the Vice-Admiral's reply had even arrived, Ministers, still daily battered by questions in the House, had to read in *The Times* of the growing feeling among the masters of merchant ships at Saint-Jean-de-Luz that the blockade was not in fact effective at all. These were underlined by Steer's report of the dinner (it went on till five o'clock the next morning) given to Captain Roberts of SEVEN SEAS SPRAY at Bilbao by the Basque Ministers of Finance, Commerce and Supplies. The gallant captain was presented with a cigarette case, and his daughter Fifi with a bracelet, both embossed with the Basque flag. Even without Steer's advice, or, on this occasion, a hint from Ojanguren, the British Pro-Consul, the Basques understood the uses of the right kind of publicity: as early as 30 January they had reciprocated Steer's sympathy for their cause by placing a trawler at his disposal, when the tragic death of his wife in child-birth made it necessary for him to leave Bilbao in a hurry. They had also paid his hotel bill.[4]

But it was the Vice-Admiral's reply that really tipped the trembling scale. He had probably been getting tired of the

[1] FO 371 21352.   [2] CAB 23 88.   [3] *The Times.*
[4] Information given to the author in 1970 by Mr Angel Ojanguren (henceforth Ojanguren).

repeated signals appealing for his views on the effectiveness of the Insurgent blockade. He had given little comfort in return and now his predictions were blunt. He did not believe that Insurgent warships would interfere with British merchant ships *outside* territorial waters as long as British naval strength was adequate, which he had earlier said it was. As for what those warships might do *inside* territorial waters, 'I cannot express an opinion.' But, he added, he knew that three of the British merchant ships waiting at Saint-Jean-de-Luz now intended to try and enter Bilbao and this should provide a conclusive test of the effectiveness of the blockade. He ended – he was no equivocating Admiral – 'H.M.S. HOOD will be there.'[1]

That left little room for argument. With the crew of SEVEN SEAS SPRAY being feasted in Bilbao, with more and more Ministers yielding to clamour in London, with the Jones of Saint-Jean-de-Luz itching to go, with their own commander on the spot determined to assist, the Admiralty had been left in too weak and isolated a position for them to issue the positive order that would have been needed to arrest the momentum of events. Their reply approved Vice-Admiral Blake's intentions, though it pointed out that such measures would scarcely be practicable or desirable on every occasion that a British merchant ship wished to enter Bilbao.[2]

At about eleven o'clock on the clear moonlit night of the 22nd, the British steamers MACGREGOR, HAMSTERLEY and STANBROOK, all carefully darkened, crept slowly out of the anchorage of Saint-Jean-de-Luz and made for the open sea. Between them they carried 8,500 tons of food, including 2,000 tons of wheat.[3] A little later the numerous watchers on shore, who naturally included various agents of General Franco's, were also able to observe the undimmed lights of HOOD dwindling towards the HORIZON.[4]

[1] FO 371 21353.   [2] ADM 116 3514.
[3] *The Times*.   [4] Steer, *Tree of Gernika*, p. 206.

CHAPTER 6

A curious person

those curious people, our consular
agents.

Attlee[1]

Meanwhile, in Bilbao itself, Mr Consul Stevenson had been looking further ahead. Food-ships were important, of course, as were the vexed controversies of mining and blockade, and he did his best to furnish the Ambassador and the Foreign Office with information and opinions on each of these issues as it arose. But the problem on which his attention was concentrated arose from aerial bombardment. Admittedly the daily raids on Bilbao had not, at least in the first week of April, attained the proportions of the opening attack on Durango, where two churches full of worshippers had been destroyed and 250 civilians killed in half an hour.[2] Stevenson thought most of the Bilbao raids were directed against military objectives[3] and even Steer estimated the casualties inflicted at only nine deaths per raiding day.[4]

But this was 1937. Those successive triumphs of an advancing technology – Coventry, Dresden, Hiroshima – still lay ahead. Steer's description of the attack on Durango as 'the most terrible bombardment of a civil population in the history of the world up to March 31st 1937' did not then seem as absurd as it does in the present state of civilisation. The rudimentary techniques of the thirties, moreover, were matched by a corresponding archaism in the received conception of war. The notion still persisted that civilians, and more particularly women and

---

[1] Major C. R. Attlee in the House of Commons, 14 April 1937. Hansard.
[2] G. L. Steer, *The Tree of Gernika* (Hodder and Stoughton, 1938), p. 167.
[3] FO 371 21369.
[4] Steer, *Tree of Gernika*, p. 178.

children, ought somehow to be exempted from slaughter, and this idea found intermittent expression in the practical efforts of third parties – governments, international organisations, charitable societies and even private individuals – actually to rescue the victims of war.

Even in the thirties, of course, this form of humanitarianism was neither universally accepted nor untainted by ideological prejudices. Most people preferred not to let their minds dwell over much on the sufferings of foreigners, and the enthusiasm of those who did was often quenched – or heightened – by their political sympathies. But the impartial relief of distress caused by foreign wars was sufficiently part of conventional public morality to make it difficult and embarrassing for the British Government, once this principle was invoked, to resist all the pressures applied to them by individual philanthropists. And these, however diverse and mixed their motives, were both numerous and energetic. Their concern, moreover, tended to find its expression in the advocacy of measures which, however inconvenient, were often manifestly feasible and constructive. Nor were they content with mere agitation. People who felt strongly about the Spanish Civil War raised private money, sent relief supplies, themselves went to Spain: to investigate on the spot, to help in person, even to fight. These people who accepted a personal obligation and believed themselves capable of discharging it as individuals were a minority: their efforts were not enough to change the course of history, but they did modify the policy of the British Government and significantly affect the fate of numerous Spaniards.

To this extent, therefore, Stevenson was acting in the spirit of his age and addressing himself to a vulnerable audience when he telegraphed, on 8 April 1937, to the Foreign Office:

Owing to dangers to Bilbao civilian population from repeated aerial bombardments, I have in collaboration with French Consul, who is telegraphing in identical terms, proposed to Basque Government large scale evacuation of women and children. Basque Government are eager to accept proposal and promise to issue necessary passports without political discrimination. I submit for consideration most urgently by H.M.G. in consultation with the French Government the following points that have suggested themselves here.[1]

Nevertheless this was a remarkable telegram. To propose large scale evacuation from a theatre of hostilities under British naval protection – for this was an essential feature of Stevenson's scheme – was not an unprecedented initiative. What made it unusual was that – on an issue as controversial at home as abroad – Stevenson had not hesitated to discuss in detail with the Basque Government and with his French colleague the important new commitment he was, for the first time, suggesting to his own Government. If his proposals were rejected, for instance, his personal position would be most invidious. His telegram, though emphasising the 'extreme urgency' of the situation, offered no explanation or excuse for the unusual procedure he had adopted and it is hard to avoid the suspicion, which must also have been aroused in Downing Street, that he wanted to make 'no' the most difficult answer. This is sometimes an effective, but always a dangerous, gambit to employ against the Foreign Office, who do not take kindly to having their hand forced by their representatives abroad.

Their first reaction was certainly not encouraging. When they invited Chilton's comments the following day, they remarked that there could be no question of using H.M. ships or, as Stevenson had suggested, of manning Spanish ships with British naval ratings, that General Franco's consent would have to be obtained and that any need for a naval escort could be avoided by letting the British and French Consuls travel on board the refugee ships, a measure which both sides ought to regard as a sufficient deterrent to interference or improper exploitation of these voyages.

This last suggestion was not vindictively intended and, though it elicited a sarcastic comment from Eden when it later came to his notice, was not then as absurd as it seems today. It merely reflected the remarkable prestige which was still enjoyed by the British Consular Service, stemming from a

[1] FO 371 21369.

long tradition of British readiness to employ force in support of their representatives abroad, nourished by a genuinely international climate of respect for the inviolability of diplomatic and consular agents and, inevitably, exaggerated by the Foreign Office in particular, and by British public opinion in general. Lord Strabolgi, for instance, later told the House of Lords that 'he hoped that the British Consul would not be withdrawn from Bilbao if the advance on that town continued. The presence of a British official always had a calming effect on bloodthirsty and victorious soldiery.'[1]

These high expectations then rested on slender material foundations. Stevenson's only full time assistant was his Basque Pro-Consul, Mr Angel Ojanguren; he had no official transport, cyphers or 'wireless receiving set', this last, as the Foreign Office pointed out with censorious finality when Eden suggested its provision, being 'an expensive installation'.[2] His meagre salary was not supplemented by a tithe of the allowances paid to his successors thirty years later and a suggestion from the Embassy that the vicissitudes of war (Stevenson had to maintain a separate home for his family in England and was himself bombed out of two houses in Bilbao) warranted some financial compensation for Consuls serving in Spain drew a chilling minute from the Head of the Consular Department: 'The good civil servant should not think that routine ought to be altered or rules relaxed because he is in a position of discomfort or danger.'[3]

This austere vision of the dedicated official may have come more easily to one who was the grandson of a Duke and had himself never served abroad, but the attitude it reflected was deeply impressed upon the Service as a whole. Duty had to be done for its own sake, or for those rare and not very material rewards, the letters after one's name or the curt sentence in the Foreign Office telegram: 'I approve your action', 'I approve your language' or, supreme accolade, 'I entirely approve your

---

[1] *The Times*, 29 April 1937.   [2] FO 371 21290.
[3] FO 369 2475. Stevenson himself did, however, receive a small extra allowance.

language.' The money was minimal, promotion agonisingly slow (Stevenson had done better than most in getting his first step after only sixteen years) and most of the work – signing off the crews of merchant vessels, bailing out drunken tourists, reporting on the commercial reputation of local business-men – excessively tedious. But the Service appealed – the entrance examination was stiff and highly competitive – to that section of the educated bourgeoisie more concerned with status (Consuls held the King's Commission and were indubitably gentlemen in an age when that mattered), a degree of authority and responsibility, and the sense of serving one's country, than with affluence or material comfort. This significant sub-class, which also supplied the Indian Civil Service, the Colonial Service, most of the officers of the Army and Navy and a diminishing proportion of the Civil Service, tended to lack the wealth and aristocratic connections that led their possessors to the Household Brigade or the Diplomatic Service. But there was usually a background of Public School and Oxford or Cambridge, often a small private income, almost always a strong sense of superiority to those, however rich they might become, whose income was derived from 'trade'. They thought, though they seldom said, that, if one had to work for someone else, it might as well be the Crown.

Crudely stated, these are not entirely attractive characteristics and, when aggravated by the rigid bureaucratic discipline imposed by the Foreign Office, it is not altogether surprising that Consuls, even excluding the rather small minority driven to drink, eccentricity or outright lunacy, tended to strike the casual observer as stuffy, narrow-minded and out of touch with the aspirations either of *l'homme moyen sensuel* or of the political idealist. Theirs was a mandarin class and the rigidity of its code, the incentive to its members and the reason for its existence had a single source: the difficult and honourable task of maintaining for Britain a degree of international authority disproportionate to her resources. It will be a curious problem for future historians to determine which crumbled first, the class or its mission.

The Royal Navy and the siege of Bilbao

At the period with which we are concerned, the first symptoms of decay were evident in both, but had not touched Stevenson. Perhaps he had reacted against his slightly unorthodox background – partly German schooling and the London School of Economics rather than Oxford or Cambridge[1] – towards an extra degree of conformity with the mandarin ideal. Courteous and pleasant, but not sociable, containing his strong feelings, persistent in the application of his principles, this reserved and reticent official was easily underestimated by some of his British visitors, particularly by those crusaders – flamboyant, eloquent, thrusting – whom the Civil War attracted to Spain. This was a mistake seldom made by his colleagues, by naval officers or even by the Basques. Weeks before Stevenson was impelled into the centre of the stage, Captain MacGrigor had summed him up (the Navy usually reported on the Consuls they encountered and whole volumes are occupied by their complaints about the staff at Marseilles): 'Mr Stevenson, our Consul, obviously carries great weight with [the Basque Ministers] and I can well understand his great success in securing the reprieve and release of prisoners and hostages. He is a most admirable representative of our Country.'[2]

His influence, and not on the Basques alone, was to be severely tested. Few shared his belief that saving lives should take priority over considerations of political advantage and those who did sometimes lacked his grasp of practical possibilities.

His humanitarian course had three main reefs to surmount: the principle of evacuation without political discrimination, the principle of non-intervention and the practical necessity of a naval escort. It was typical of Stevenson to have taken the initiative in insisting, as he did throughout, on the first and last of these, for one was unwelcome in Bilbao and the other in London. Bombs might fall impartially on the just and unjust alike,

---

[1] Stevenson was actually successful in the Consular Service examination (he came fourth out of sixty-one candidates) without having had the benefit of any university training at all: he took the examination as soon as he was discharged from the Army and went to the L.S.E. afterwards. Information given to the author in 1970 by Miss J. Stevenson (henceforth Miss Stevenson).   [2] ADM 116 3512.

but it seemed illogical to the Basque leaders, and still more so to their politically harsher Spanish supporters, to consider those who sympathised with the motives of the bombers as equally entitled to rescue as those whose resistance the raids were intended to break. Besides, if General Mola's advance continued, then the wives and children of his supporters would make useful hostages and ought not prematurely to be removed from Bilbao. This was an argument which Stevenson always refused to entertain and he was supported in his obduracy from London. Only an impartially humanitarian evacuation could deserve British assistance.

It was not that Stevenson was unsympathetic towards the cause of Basque autonomy. On the contrary, his long despatch of the 13th, which has already been quoted, contained a rhetorical question which even Steer might have admitted as an adequate presentation of their case: 'is he [the Basque] not superior in every way except numbers to his Spanish oppressor?'.[1] And he had personally suffered what Steer so eloquently described, also from experience: 'the *sirena*, the grind of engines in the air, the dash for the shelter, the explosions, and the *sirena* again'.[2] He knew the tautening of the nerves and the bitterness these raids produced in a half-starved population. He was aware that the secrets of their defences, such as they were, had just been betrayed by a Basque sympathiser of General Franco's. But he still insisted that all the women and children of Bilbao must be eligible for British assistance.

The Foreign Office agreed, but they also strove, with Chilton's support, to eliminate from this assistance any naval contribution. They repeated their views on the 12th. These were only partly prompted by the Admiralty's reluctance to risk H.M. ships in the dangerous waters off Bilbao: there was also the principle of non-intervention. As Chilton explained, when commenting on a proposal by the Save the Children International Union that merchant vessels escorted by warships should take food to Bilbao and bring away the children of

---

[1] FO 371 21291.   [2] Steer, *Tree of Gernika*, p. 180.

Nationalist sympathisers, General Franco could not be expected to acquiesce in a removal of 'useless mouths' that must prolong the resistance of beleaguered Bilbao. To enforce such measures with a British naval escort would be flagrant intervention.

There was much support in London, in Foreign Office and Admiralty alike, for these views, but there was also an unexpected and important dissenter. When Chilton's report of 13 April reached the Foreign Secretary on the 17th, Eden minuted: 'I an not happy about this. Surely they should be protected to territorial waters anyway.'

This was not the first time he had differed from his officials on this issue. Already on the 15th, when he read Stevenson's telegram insisting that the Basques would not risk either their ships or their families on the high seas without a British naval escort, Eden had written: 'I should like us to help the Basques on this, if we can; more particularly if our ships are not allowed to go tomorrow.'

It was an odd suggestion – that refugee ships should be escorted because food-ships were not – but this bringing together of two problems hitherto handled separately had important and paradoxical consequences. It ought to have helped the objectors by emphasising the complications which any use of the Navy would entail, but it was actually exploited by Eden to expose some of the flaws in the arguments elaborated to support the official case. On the 16th, for instance, when the Foreign Office again urged on Stevenson their view that his presence on board a refugee ship should obviate all need for a naval escort, Eden intervened rather sharply when he saw the outward telegram in his distribution. Why, he wanted to know, were the Department prepared thus to risk the Consul's life, when the waters of Bilbao were supposed to be too dangerous for British ships even to enter?[1]

It was an awkward question and the officials to whom it was addressed inevitably appear in a less sympathetic light than either Stevenson, with his consistent humanitarianism, or

---

[1] FO 371 21369.

Eden, with his intermittently generous impulses. But there was a stronger case behind their reluctance than their arguments always revealed. What they feared was that, the dam of non-intervention once breached, there would be no end to the demands for the Navy to rescue Spaniards from the consequences of civil war, that each operation would create a precedent for others more extensive and more provocative to General Franco, that, at the very least, Britain would irretrievably alienate the probable victors, that there might be actual clashes and that, at the worst, these might lead to counter-interventions by General Franco's allies. As Eden had throughout insisted, and as he repeated in a public speech on 12 April, 'ever since the outbreak of the Spanish conflict' the Government had tried 'to prevent that conflict from spreading beyond the borders of Spain'.[1] This fear of a widening war has often been criticised by historians, as it was at the time, as exaggerated, even insincere, but, twenty-five years later, American intervention in another civil war was to grow from just as small beginnings and just as great an initial reluctance. As long as the proclaimed policy of the British Government was one of appeasement, the Foreign Office can scarcely be censured for seeking consistency in its application.

Unfortunately Sir George Mounsey,[2] the official principally concerned, was not content with the rigour of this defensible, but necessarily abstract and long-term, line of reasoning. He had yielded to the seduction of his friends in the Admiralty and adopted their arguments. It was so much easier and more convincing to maintain that mines, bombing and General Franco's warships simply made it too dangerous for ships to enter or leave Bilbao. The reply he put up to the Secretary of State therefore explained that the Consul would run no risks because he would only go if the evacuation had received General

---

[1] FO 425 414.

[2] Then fifty-seven, this conscientious and hard-working official had been promoted Assistant Under Secretary in 1929, a rank he retained until his retirement in 1940, and, in 1937, supervised the Department responsible for Spain (League of Nations and Western Department) and himself played the major part in the formulation of recommendations on policy.

Franco's consent. On this essential assumption the Basques would be able, unmolested, to sweep a passage through the mines, bombers would not attack the ships and ALMIRANTE CERVERA would not drive them into the minefields.

The advantage of supporting long-term objectives by short-term arguments is that the relevance of the latter is immediate. So, unfortunately, is their liability, should they be unsound, to refutation.

In this case Eden, evidently a little wearied with well-doing, appended a resigned minute: 'Very well.' But he did so on the day when the fallacy of Admiralty arguments was exposed, the day that was to change British policy, 23 April 1937.[1]

[1] FO 371 21369.

CHAPTER 7

Saint George's Day

When the 'mighty Hood' appeared
on the scene, the other side's
chances were felt to be as good as
over.

Grenfell[1]

Until she blew up in her first battle in 1941, H.M.S. HOOD
'had been generally reckoned, in respect of the combination
of fighting power, speed and protection, to be the most powerful ship in the world'. The fatal weakness in her design was
known to the Admiralty, who were always meaning to do something about it[2], but had been sedulously concealed from out-
siders, who were deeply impressed by the 42,000 tons, the
eight 15 inch guns, the massive armour and the 31 knots of
this handsome and famous battle-cruiser. As she breasted the
Biscayan waves, waiting, with the destroyers FIREDRAKE and
FORTUNE, for the dawn to break off Bilbao on 23 April 1937,
Vice-Admiral Blake can have had few doubts concerning the
result of any encounter that might emerge from those early
morning mists.

But this was peace-time and bluff and determination would
be more critically tested than gunnery or armour-plating. The
mere sight of HOOD, for instance, did not deter the Spanish
warships, who were also expecting the arrival from Saint-
Jean-de-Luz of the three British merchant ships MACGREGOR,
HAMSTERLEY and STANBROOK. As soon as MACGREGOR came within
hailing distance of GALERNA, at 0635, she was ordered to stop
and, when FIREDRAKE intervened, ALMIRANTE CERVERA cleared
for action and steered to the support of her auxiliary, signalling

---

[1] Captain Russell Grenfell, *The Bismarck Episode* (Faber, 1948), p. 58.
[2] Grenfell, *Bismarck Episode*, pp. 58–60.

to FIREDRAKE: 'please tell steamers not to enter Bilbao'. The Spaniards were in no conciliatory mood.

With a brusqueness unwonted in the Royal Navy (perhaps because the International Flag Code was employed) and resented by Captain Moreu[1] the Vice-Admiral himself retorted 'stop interfering'. ALMIRANTE CERVERA's reply was flashed in more elaborate Spanish: it claimed jurisdiction within territorial waters extending 6 miles from the coast. FIREDRAKE, anticipating the flagship, ignored the claim and answered only 'please do not interfere outside territorial waters'. This drew an extended protest from the cruiser but, at 0717, the rough retort, from GALERNA, of a shot across the bows of the leading merchant ship, by now some 5 miles from the coast.

Things were warming up and FIREDRAKE's riposte was blunt: she turned her guns on GALERNA, a threat not previously employed by one warship against another in these encounters.[2] It was a tense moment. As one of FIREDRAKE's officers later recalled, ALMIRANTE CERVERA 'steamed slowly past us, giving us a good view of the very ragtag and bobtail guns' crews and I caught myself wondering whether his eight 6 inch guns could sink us before HOOD's 15 inch guns could stop him'.[3]

It did not come to that. Instead ALMIRANTE CERVERA flashed across to HOOD (whose signallers were having some difficulty with this stream of Spanish) her justification and her protest:

Tengo derecha para impedir entrada de Esos buques en Bilbao. . . .[4]

The subsequent exchange of signals, in which Captain Moreau again claimed 6 miles as the extent of territorial waters and the Vice-Admiral insisted that the British Government recognised only 3, allowed a useful twenty minutes for tempers to cool and sober reflection to prevail.

All this time the plodding tramps and the circling warships

---

[1] Almirante Juan Cervera Valderrama, *Memorias de Guerra* (Editora Nacional, Madrid, 1968), p. 146.   [2] ADM 116 3514.

[3] 'The Battle of Bilbao', *Naval Review*, 1937.

[4] 'I have the right to prevent entry of these ships to Bilbao . . .' the rest of the signal was mutilated, but clearly meant 'and I request you not to interfere in the exercise of my right'.

were moving slowly along the coast, still outside the 3 mile limit. By 0756 they were within range of the Basque battery at Galea Point[1] – five batteries of three guns each, according to Steer,[2] two 6 inch Vickers guns as reported after a later visit by the Assistant British Military Attaché at Paris.[3] Whatever they were, the guns opened fire on GALERNA, missing with every shot, but causing her to sheer off north-westwards. By 0827 the scattered cluster of disparate ships was off the entrance to Bilbao and ALMIRANTE CERVERA made a final effort: she trained her guns on the merchant ships. Commander Black of FORTUNE 'reported the fact to HOOD, who then trained her turrets on the Spanish cruiser, an action which resulted in the immediate training fore and aft of the guns in the latter ship'.[4] Actually, as the Vice-Admiral afterwards reported,[5] he had ordered HOOD's guns to be trained 20° off ALMIRANTE CERVERA, a subtle blending of menace and restraint which might, or might not, have been appreciated aboard the cruiser, but was certainly too sophisticated for HOOD's Gunnery Officer, who simply swung his great turrets straight at ALMIRANTE CERVERA, much to Blake's annoyance.[6]

The hint was taken and the cruiser watched passively as the three merchant ships crossed the 3 mile limit, where they were met by a Basque pilot boat, whose entire crew lined the rail and saluted FIREDRAKE as the latter steamed past on her turn away towards the high seas. This was a courtesy considerably more welcome than the shots fired by one of Eguia's armed trawlers, which had also come out to meet the convoy. Her shells were doubtless intended for GALERNA, but they fell significantly nearer FIREDRAKE, who peremptorily ordered her to cease fire.[7]

As H.M. ships made for the open sea and the Spaniards watched in impotent anger, 'two Basque armed trawlers, the

[1] ADM 116 3514.
[2] G. L. Steer, *The Tree of Gernika* (Hodder and Stoughton, 1938), pp. 192–3.
[3] FO 371 21295.   [4] ADM 116 3516.   [5] ADM 116 3514.
[6] Information given to the author in 1970 by Rear-Admiral W. J. Munn, at one time Vice-Admiral Blake's Flag-Lieutenant.
[7] 'The Battle of Bilbao', *Naval Review*, 1937.

The Royal Navy and the siege of Bilbao

BIZKAYA and IPAREKO-IZARRA, accompanied MACGREGOR, HAM-
STERLEY and STANBROOK into harbour'. This was a long 8
miles up the Nervión, but

enormous crowds cheered as the procession of three red dusters
passed slowly up river[1] . . . between two lines of hills running north
and south . . . the narrow river valley, an industrial ribbon packed
with tall, black chimneys, gasometers, foundries like giant dark pill-
boxes, clattering trains, crumble-faced slums. Iron-ore tilts at the
end of trailing steel aerial lines hung empty in the air, backed by
steep brown peaks of mine-waste which climbed the hill-side behind
them. Dozens of cranes stood at their full idle height, paraded at
ease along the solid granite grays of the Nervion.[2]

Through this valley of industrial desolation, watched by those
hungry and workless crowds, 8,500 tons of food came to
beleaguered Bilbao.

It was not, however, as Steer has beguiled even historians
into believing, the end of the Insurgent blockade of Bilbao.[3]
Nor did anyone in the Royal Navy then think it would be.
The first reaction of the Commander-in-Chief Home Fleet
to the Vice-Admiral's initial report on the day's events was to
order: 'In view of incident a heavy ship or cruiser should
always be in easy reach of destroyers patrolling off the Basque
coast'.[4]

From any other commander one can imagine the ripe naval
oath that might have rumbled across the Vice-Admiral's
cabin. He had said as much a week earlier and it was he, and
no one else, who had stationed HOOD off Bilbao both on the
20th and the 23rd. But Blake was a mellow man, blessed with
wealth, a vigorous physique and an alert and enquiring mind.
Meticulous, a stickler for detail, devoting fascinated attention
to the social responsibilities of his command, he had two
qualities that are everywhere unusual, but particularly unexpected in one of his temperament and background. He was a
gentle, considerate man, patient almost to excess with his

[1] Steer, *Tree of Gernika*, p. 207.   [2] Steer, *Tree of Gernika*, p. 124.
[3] Hugh Thomas, *The Spanish Civil War* (Eyre and Spottiswoode, 1961),
p. 411: 'No further attempt was made to prevent British shipping arriving
at Bilbao.'   [4] ADM 116 3514.

subordinates. And he surveyed the field of international politics with a wider knowledge and less bias than most naval officers of his day.[1]

This touch of intellectual sophistication doubtless heightened the contrast between Blake's robust confidence and the anxieties of Backhouse and Chatfield. But the facts seemed clear enough on the spot and that evening's signal must have tried his patience: yet another personal message from Chatfield – was the Insurgent blockade still effective, could the shore defences really deal with Insurgent warships inside the 3 mile limit, had the latter actually ventured into territorial waters? Posterity, however, may be grateful for these irritating signals (which promptly drew the blunt rejoinder that 'effective blockade was a misnomer which should never have been employed)',[2] for they were probably responsible for the extended analysis in Blake's final report of the 27th – he was relieved as Senior Naval Officer North Spain by Rear-Admiral Ramsey on the 26th. When this report – and the reactions it evoked – are contrasted with the paper 'Situation on the North Coast of Spain' which Chatfield prepared for the Cabinet meeting of the 26th, the true nature of the controversy surrounding this vexed question of 'effective blockade' is clearly revealed.[3]

This was not, as those historians seduced by the charm of Steer's compelling prose have too easily assumed, a dispute about the facts of the situation. Thomas, for instance, says 'it would certainly seem that the Navy gave incorrect information to the Government' and argues that their reports were based on Nationalist sources rather than 'a careful examination of the facts'.[4] But Caslon, who was the first to use the phrase 'effective blockade', based his report on his own experience: THORPEHALL's interception by ALMIRANTE CERVERA and the risky defiance of that cruiser by BRAZEN. He was recalling the lectures he had heard at the Naval Staff College,[5] which must have quoted the Declarations of Paris, in 1856, and of London, in 1909, as requiring an effective blockade to be supported by

---

[1] See note 6, p. 89. [2] CAB 27 639. [3] CAB 24 269.
[4] Thomas, *Spanish Civil War*, p. 411. [5] Caslon.

'une force suffisante pour interdire réellement' any access to the coast in question.[1] This was interpreted by a contemporary international lawyer as meaning 'supported by a force adequate to render all ingress and egress hazardous'.[2] Chatfield had no difficulty in demonstrating this to be the case: since the 23rd eight British ships had entered Bilbao and Santander, five of them being intercepted by the Insurgents but, when protected by British warships, allowed to proceed. On the 25th, for instance, 'ESPAÑA trained a turret on the British ship OAKGROVE and H.M.S. SHROPSHIRE, already at action stations, got ready for anything.' In spite of an angry signal from the Spanish battleship to OAKGROVE – 'if you do not avoid entrance I finish you for this time' – that incident ended with ESPAÑA turning away and OAKGROVE sailing into Santander.[3]

But Caslon – and Chilton – had been justified. Insurgent warships did intercept a high proportion of British merchant ships attempting entry to Basque ports – enough to render ingress 'hazardous' – and when H.M. ships intervened, the circumstances of their intervention did become 'increasingly dangerous'. Insurgent warships behaved with greater belligerence on 23 and 25 April than they had on the 6th. Factually, both Caslon's report and his prediction were accurate and were not invalidated by the safe arrival of SEVEN SEAS SPRAY and other vessels. An 'effective blockade' does not have to be 100% effective.

The true issue was legal and political and the controversy turned less on the facts than on their interpretation. If international law and British policy allowed British ships to be intercepted only after they had crossed the 3 mile limit, then, as Malcolm had explained to his mother on the 18th and as Chatfield repeated in his paper, such ships could only be stopped by firing into them, an expedient the Admiralty had pronounced to be intolerable to a watching British warship. British protection for merchant shipping up to the 3 mile limit accordingly

[1] Georg Schwarzenberger (ed.), *The Law of Armed Conflict* (Stevens, 1968).
[2] Norman J. Padelford, *International Law and Diplomacy in the Spanish Civil Strife* (Macmillan, New York, 1939).   [3] CAB 24 269.

implied, for practical purposes and in most cases, depriving the Insurgents of any possibility of maintaining a blockade even within territorial waters. Therefore, in Chatfield's view, because 'H.M. Ships have virtually taken steps to force six British merchant ships through as far as the limit of territorial waters', they had broken a blockade which, without their intervention, would have been effective. This was intervention on the Republican side.[1]

Blake, however, drew different conclusions from similar premises. His only divergence on the facts lay in his insistence that, on the 23rd as on the 25th, determined action by Insurgent warships would still have resulted in the capture of British merchant ships inside territorial waters. He thus regarded the Insurgent policy of interception outside the 3 mile limit as being, from their point of view, desirable rather than indispensable. But his objection to that policy was that it was illegal: they had not been granted belligerent rights. Therefore, when H.M. ships intervened to protect British merchant vessels outside the 3 mile limit, this 'does not deprive the Insurgent Naval Forces of any legitimate right. On the other hand, if we do not maintain *our* rights and allow ships to be turned back on the High Seas, we are granting a powerful concession to the Insurgents, to which they are not entitled. Such a policy in fact is intervention on the side of the Insurgents. Effective protection of British shipping is, therefore, strictly in accordance with the policy of non-intervention.'[2]

Whatever the British Government decided, there would be a senior British naval officer to support Spanish charges that this constituted intervention. And so it would. In the circumstances of 1937 it was idle to suppose that the British Government could altogether avoid taking sides. Britain was not merely a Great Power, but the leading naval power: the possessor of the world's largest merchant fleet; traditionally predominant

[1] CAB 24 269.
[2] ADM 116 3679. The Chief of General Franco's Naval Staff, however, subsequently admitted that he lacked the ships to maintain an effective blockade of all the enemy ports. Cervera, *Memorias de Guerra*, p. 136.

in trade with Northern Spain. Non-intervention might have some meaning for distant Japan or impotent Luxembourg: for Britain it was the merest hypocrisy. There was no relevant action – or inaction – the British Government could take which would not help – or hurt – one side in Spain more than the other. At the time, however, this obvious truth could not be admitted in official reports and recommendations, which had to cloak their partisan views in a pretence that these constituted the pure essence of that sacred myth: non-intervention.

Moreover, all the naval officers concerned tended to worry Caslon's red herring of 'effective blockade' as if they had been hounds worrying a fox. Blake was particularly emphatic: 'There is, however, one very clear line which should be followed and that is to get away at all costs from the term 'effective blockade'. It does not exist, it has never really existed, and the acceptance of it immediately introduces the consideration of belligerent rights in a particular area which must be strongly denied.'

His key sentence might almost have come from the pen of Steer: 'The bluff of Franco's so-called blockade and his claim to the extension of territorial waters has been met.'

He might have added – perhaps he thought it unnecessary and immodest – that it had been met by HOOD. The attitude of the British Navy was the factor missing both from his equation and that of his immediate superior, Admiral Sir Roger Backhouse, Commander-in-Chief Home Fleet, who expressed his disagreement when forwarding Blake's report: 'in actual fact, it [the blockade] would certainly have been effective for part of the time had none of H.M. Ships been there to interrupt it . . . we should regard a blockade as being fully effective had we a battleship and a heavy cruiser on the spot to enforce it.'[1]

This was an odd comment. Battleships and heavy cruisers (the latter as misleading a description of ALMIRANTE CERVERA as Hoare's earlier 'new battleship' for ESPAÑA) are unnecessary

---

[1] ADM 116 3679.

and inappropriate vessels to enforce a blockade against *merchant ships*, victims more easily intercepted by small, fast and, above all, *numerous* warships. A ship of force was only needed if armed opposition was likely and, on the high seas, such opposition could only come from the Royal Navy, which was more than capable of disposing of 'a battleship and a heavy cruiser'. Within territorial waters, admittedly, larger ships might have the advantage of offering greater resistance to the fire of shore batteries, but this, as Blake had pointed out, was a hazard which Spanish warships had hitherto preferred to avoid. For practical purposes the effectiveness of the Insurgent blockade depended entirely on the answer to one thoroughly awkward question: would the Royal Navy allow this blockade to be enforced on the high seas?

It is scarcely surprising that, once again, the Admiralty decided *not* to copy this correspondence to the Foreign Office.

But Blake's central recommendation had not merely been acted on, but anticipated: 'to avoid "incidents", i.e. the Spanish warship opening fire on a British merchant ship or warship, the British warship present must be unquestionably more powerful than the largest Insurgent ship. Two capital ships are therefore required, one preventing interference and one resting.'[1]

On 26 April, when Vice-Admiral Blake sailed in HOOD for Portsmouth, he was relieved by the Rear-Admiral commanding the Second Battle Squadron, flying his flag in the battleship ROYAL OAK and followed by her sister-ship RESOLUTION.[2]

Nevertheless, in spite of Vice-Admiral Blake's accurate predictions, his successful accomplishment of a delicate and hazardous mission and the adoption of his major recommendation, there must have been some pregnant silences when he accompanied Admiral of the Fleet Sir A. Ernle Chatfield, First Sea Lord and Chief of the Naval Staff, to meet the Cabinet Committee on the Protection of British Shipping (Spain) on 28 April. The Committee, to whom the full Cabinet meeting

---

[1] ADM 116 3679.   [2] ADM 116 3514.

that morning had remitted the problem, had clearly been more impressed by the encounter of Saint George's Day than by Spanish reactions.[1] On the 26th, for instance, Major Troncoso had called on Sir Henry Chilton to convey General Franco's indignant protest against Blake's actions. In the course of 'a heated interview'[2] Chilton (who was rather deaf) had listened in silence and concluded the conversation by turning his other ear towards Troncoso and emitting an interrogative, but diplomatically non-committal grunt;[3] 'Senor Troncoso even went so far as to say that if we wanted war we could have it . . . he added that commanding officer of "ADMIRAL CERVERA" [sic] had attempted to commit suicide from mortification.'[4]

This moment of drama, however, had been followed, as Ministers knew, by a later telegram from Chilton reporting the receipt of friendly overtures from a Nationalist official.[5] Either Troncoso had exceeded his instructions or his superiors had had second thoughts. The Committee decided that General Franco should be informed that 'while unable to advise British shipping to enter Bilbao, they are determined, in the event of British ships ignoring the warning, to give them full protection on the high seas if called upon to do so'.

Chilton was also to remind General Franco that the British Government had taken a similar attitude towards the Republican blockade of Insurgent ports in August 1936. These instructions to the Ambassador were accompanied by others to naval commanders restricting the protection to be afforded to British ships *inside* territorial waters to the prevention of excessive force, i.e. continued firing after submission. A British ship which had submitted *inside* territorial waters and afterwards escaped to the high seas was 'not to be afforded further protection', an order in which Runciman acquiesced only 'with reluctance and misgiving' in this serious departure from the policy of unqualified protection to British vessels on the high seas.[6]

It was thus in vain that Chatfield had reminded Ministers

[1] CAB 27 639. [2] FO 371 21353. [3] Malcolm.
[4] FO 371 21353. [5] CAB 23 88. [6] CAB 27 639.

of the progressive watering down of the Government's original warning to Bilbao-bound shipping and of the simultaneous increases in the degree of protection they were prepared to afford. Far from retracting their steps, Ministers had now gone even further than he had feared. And, ironically enough, it is hard to resist the conclusion that, as much as political pressures at home and Blake's success in the Bay, Chatfield's own arguments were responsible for the rejection of his views. If he had not insisted so much at the start – doubtless prompted by his consistent desire to avoid all risk of 'incidents' until the progress of rearmament had restored the strength of the Navy – on dangers which subsequently proved to have been exaggerated, Ministers might have been less ready to disregard his advice.

Another paradoxical stiffener of Ministerial resolution may have been the broadcast, which was reported by *The Times*, of 26 April from the Insurgent transmitters at Ferrol and Ceuta that:

all ships, whatever their nationality, navigating in the territorial waters of Northern Spain between the meridians of Cape Bidio and Cape Machichaco less than 3 miles from the coast, which do not stop at the request of the ships of the National Fleet will be bombarded or fired at by those ships or by aircraft.

In those days British reactions to overt and public menace still tended more towards defiance than submission, particularly when there was clear and recent evidence that the threats might contain rather a large element of bluff.

At home, of course, the shift in the Government's attitude was welcome. Already on the 24th the *Manchester Guardian* had devoted a leader to HOOD's action of the preceding day and had congratulated the Government on their 'second thoughts'. On the coast of Spain, the reactions of naval officers had initially been characterised by some bewilderment and a degree of contemptuous mockery for the ambiguities beloved of British politicians. On the 23rd, for instance, Commander Black of FORTUNE, having suggested as an expedient for consideration in future incidents laying a smokescreen between a British merchantman and a Spanish warship trying to intercept her,

97

added the sarcastic comment: 'But should the smoke subsequently be blown inside territorial waters, the question as to whether this was a grave act of intervention or purely an Act of God would, it seems, probably arise!'

These destroyer captains, the cream of the Navy, were often as distinguished for their wit as for their dash and seamanship. FURY's captain, for instance, reporting a request for advice about entering Bilbao from the British ship JENNY, demurely recorded: 'She was told that the Government's advice is that the situation varies from day to day inside territorial waters and cannot be assessed. As the Master did not understand English, this advice did not confuse him.'[1]

For British ships, as we shall subsequently discover, were sometimes more British in the names they bore and the flag they flew than in the nationality of owners, officers or crew.

But, and this is the essential point, by 26 April, the unfolding of events had clearly demonstrated that the blockade of Bilbao existed, or did not, at the pleasure of His Majesty's Government and according to the nature of the instructions they issued to H.M. ships. The excuses had been exposed, the alibis exploded: the choice – whether food should go into Bilbao or refugees should come out of it – lay clearly and inescapably in Downing Street. And something else had happened, on that very day of 26 April, to sharpen the emotional edge of the dilemma that now, and inescapably, confronted Ministers.

[1] ADM 116 3516.

CHAPTER 8

Guernica

Popular feeling forced the Government of Great Britain to take two
decisions: to admit 4,000 Basque
children refugees to the United
Kingdom, and to agree to protect
all shipping, whether British,
foreign or even Spanish, which was
taking children, women and men
past military age away from the
horrors of Bilbao.

Steer[1]

Thirty years after the event books were still being written to
support the proposition that Guernica, a market-town of some
10,000 inhabitants, the ancient capital of the Basques and the
symbol of their traditional rights and liberties, was not destroyed in three hours of concentrated bombing by German
aircraft in the afternoon of 26 April 1937, but was deliberately
dynamited and set on fire by Communists in order to create an
artificial story of atrocity.[2]

This was not a view widely accepted by British public
opinion at the time. Steer's report – he had visited Guernica
and interrogated some of its surviving inhabitants a few hours
after the raids ended – received two full columns on the leader
page of *The Times* of the 28th and carried general conviction.
He was supported in other papers by the correspondents, who
had also been there that night, of Reuter, *The Star*, the *Daily
Express* and *Ce Soir*. Stevenson, who had the advantage of

[1] G. L. Steer, *The Tree of Gernika* (Hodder and Stoughton, 1938), p. 259.
[2] See, for instance, Luis Bolín, *Spain: The Vital Years* (Cassell, 1967), who
is supported by James Cleugh, *Spanish Fury* (Harrap, 1962) and, more
hesitantly, by Brian Crozier, *Franco* (Eyre and Spottiswoode, 1967).

fluent Spanish to aid his enquiries in Guernica on the 27th, added his confirmation on the 28th. In response to a subsequent request from the Foreign Office for further particulars, he reported on 2 May that he was sending them two German incendiary bombs he had picked up in the ruins.[1] These were taken by destroyer to the Embassy in Hendaye, where they caused some embarrassment, the Foreign Office regulations concerning Diplomatic Bags making no provision for the despatch of such genuinely inflammatory material.[2]

The reactions were predictable: a joint protest by the Labour Party and the Trades Union Congress against this 'outrage upon humanity', a meeting of M.P.s to listen to the Basque Delegate in London, indignant leading articles – even *The Times*, in spite of the Editor's constant efforts 'to keep out of the paper anything that might have hurt [German] susceptibilities' – had to join in. Guernica, as Watkins says in his survey of the effect of the Spanish Civil War on British political opinion, 'probably did more to engender anti-Nationalist hatred internationally than any other incident of the war'.[3]

In Britain its most significant impact was probably not on the Left – though even there it was a powerful extra stimulus towards humanitarian action – but on moderate Conservatives. Influential men and women whose opinions and position in life had not previously inclined them towards the Republican cause were shocked by what they considered a deliberate atrocity. Harold Nicolson, for instance, who had supported the Government in the censure debate of 14 April, was among those attending the Basque Delegate's meeting on the 28th;[4] Winston Churchill, who had argued on the 14th that food was a legitimate object of blockade (as the British Navy had treated it during the First World War) later denounced 'such experimental horrors as the bombing of the defenceless little town of Guernica'.[5] Their reactions were partly, as we have seen, a reflection of the different moral standards of a more innocent

[1] FO 371 21291.   [2] Malcolm.
[3] K. W. Watkins, *Britain Divided* (Nelson, 1963).   [4] *The Times*
[5] Winston S. Churchill, *The Gathering Storm* (Cassell, 1948), p. 168.

era, but partly also a response to pressure on a nerve that was peculiarly sensitive in contemporary British public opinion. Steer's diagnosis is shrewd: 'Bombardments of cities have always meant more to the British, who have to defend the greatest and most vulnerable of them, than to any other people.'[1]

Moreover, this realisation that the precedent of Guernica, if unchallenged, might find future application against British towns, reflected a general fear of bombing not confined, as it sometimes seemed during the nuclear disarmament agitation of the fifties and early sixties, to a single political party. Baldwin, for instance, who was still Prime Minister on 28 April 1937, had almost an obsession with the horrors of bombing:

I think it is well also for the man in the street to realise that there is no power on earth that can protect him from being bombed. Whatever people may tell him, the bomber will always get through . . . When the next war comes and European civilisation is wiped out, as it will be . . . [1932]

I have been made almost physically sick to think that I and my friends . . . should be spending our time thinking how we can get the mangled bodies of children to the hospitals . . . [1935]

more may be destroyed in four years of bombing than Goths and Huns and Vandals could accomplish in a century. [1939][2]

When, therefore, an Englishman who was conservatively inclined, but not so partisan as to take the extreme course of rejecting the evidence, heard of the bombing of Guernica, the double shock to his sensibilities was such as to weaken his resistance to the avowedly humanitarian proposals already being urged upon him, from various motives, by the Left and their allies. On the 27th, for instance, the National Joint Committee for Spanish Relief (which had a Conservative M.P., the Duchess of Atholl, as one of its members and a Liberal M.P., Wilfred Roberts, as its Secretary, in addition to some very left-wing members and supporters) had formally proposed to the Foreign Office (who referred the matter to the

[1] Steer, *Tree of Gernika*, p. 258.
[2] Quotations from G. M. Young, *Stanley Baldwin* (Hart-Davis, 1952), pp. 174, 203, 249.

Home Office) that a refuge should be offered in England to Spanish children evacuated from northern Spain.[1] The idea first put forward by Stevenson on the 8th (and which the Foreign Office had unsuccessfully endeavoured to discourage him from pursuing) had since attracted other supporters. Leah Manning, one of the prime movers, but writing from memory over thirty years later, dates her arrival in Bilbao for the express purpose of investigating and organising such an evacuation on 24 April.[2] The bombing of Guernica did not generate the idea of evacuating children, even of evacuating them to England, but gave a powerful impulse to its supporters and did much to undermine its opponents.

The stubborn obstruction that had blocked the proposal submitted 'most urgently' by Stevenson on the 8th, that had dissuaded even a sympathetic Eden on the 23rd, was suddenly swept away by a whirlwind of activity raging through Whitehall and leaving Sir George Mounsey to gasp indignantly for breath. On the evening of the 28th the Spanish Ambassador (a Republican) in London called on Lord Cranborne with an official request for British assistance in the evacuation of Basque women and children and Cranborne (it is uncertain on whose authority) agreed in principle, provided there was no political discrimination in the selection of those to be evacuated. The next day the Home Office agreed, also in principle, that some children from Bilbao might come to England, Eden himself drafted a telegram warning Chilton to be prepared to approach General Franco on the subject[3] and, in the evening, a group of Ministers (who actually met as the United Kingdom Delegation to the Imperial Conference) approved the action already taken by the Foreign Secretary. 'Pending replies to these enquiries' (General Franco's concurrence was to be sought as soon as Basque assurances about non-discrimination had been received) Eden told his colleagues 'the question of British naval protection did not, at the moment, arise, but

FO 371 21369.
[2] Leah Manning, *A Life for Education* (Gollancz, 1970), ch. 10.
[3] FO 371 21369.

certain influential persons were proposing to write to the newspapers on the subject and Parliamentary Questions might be anticipated".[1] Indeed the matter had already been raised in the House of Lords, where Lord Strabolgi had strongly supported the idea of assistance from the Royal Navy.[2] Even the French Ambassador had assured Eden that his Government were prepared to co-operate in any steps His Majesty's Government might take for the evacuation of civilians from Bilbao, though the Ambassador's inability to answer Eden's immediate question – did this mean that the French Navy would help in escorting refugee ships? – rather diminished the impact of his offer. He had, it appeared, no instructions on that point and would have to consult his Government[3] (who had, of course, received Stevenson's original proposal from their own Consul at Bilbao three weeks before).

Curiously enough, when the Cabinet Committee on Foreign Policy met the next day, both Eden and Hoare agreed that it would be better not to seek assistance from the French Navy. Otherwise the Committee's proceedings, which began with a brief discussion of the bombing of Guernica, were dominated by an overwhelming sense of urgency. Eden said the Basque Government wanted to start the evacuation the next day, that Bilbao and the ships in the harbour 'were being bombed at that moment'. Although Basque assurances about non-discrimination had not yet been received, Ministers decided to act on the assumption that these would be forthcoming and that General Franco would raise no objection. Chilton was accordingly instructed, without more ado, to inform General Franco's representative that British warships had been ordered 'to afford all possible protection to any ships leaving Bilbao with these non-combatant refugees on board on reaching the high seas'. Meanwhile Stevenson was to expedite the necessary assurances from the Basques and, later that day, was actually able to report that these had been given by President Aguirre. The wheels of Whitehall were whizzing too fast to be checked

[1] FO 371 21370.   [2] *The Times.*   [3] FO 371 21370.

by the receipt, on 1 May, of General Franco's refusal to agree or by Sir George Mounsey's long minute of protest on the 2nd: Eden made the Cabinet's decision irrevocable on the 3rd by announcing to the House of Commons, when his words drew loud cheers,[1] that, in spite of General Franco's objections, the Government had decided: 'to instruct H.M. Ships to afford all possible protection on the high seas' to ships carrying refugees from Bilbao.[2]

In less than a week Ministers had been whirled from their anxious discussion, on 28 April, of the extent to which it would be appropriate to protect British shipping, to the startling decision, in open defiance of General Franco's strongly expressed objections, to convoy Spanish ships escaping from the blockade of Bilbao. Even though their resistance had been eroded by the exposure of earlier fallacies and by the conspicuous success of Vice-Admiral Blake, it is hard to resist Steer's conclusion that this abrupt reversal of policy, so deplored by both their naval and their diplomatic advisers, was prompted by the impact on British public opinion, particularly on important elements hitherto sympathetic to the Government's views, of 'the total furnace that was Gernika'.[3]

[1] *The Times.*   [2] FO 371 21369; FO 371 21370.
[3] Steer, *Tree of Gernika*, p. 241.

CHAPTER 9

Our Bilbao babies policy[1]

The generous surge of indignation and compassion that had operated upon the sentiments of Ministers in London was soon to find practical expression in the evolutions, described in Chapter 1, of H.M.S. ROYAL OAK. But her manoeuvres were only the first stage in a protracted series of encounters and arguments. Moreover, the considerations, whether moral or political, which had apparently converted Ministers, found imperfect reflection either abroad or in the entrenched reluctance of a grudging British bureaucracy. Before we resume the story, from that moment on 6 May when ALMIRANTE CERVERA sheered off and allowed the convoy to proceed undisturbed on its course for France, it will be as well to turn aside and consider the characters and motives of those now engaged in sometimes embittered debate over the future of the children of Bilbao.

This debate, so far as we are concerned, turned upon two distinct questions: whether the British Navy should take steps to ensure that children were able to escape from Bilbao and whether some of these children should come to England. To the children, to their parents, to General Franco and to foreigners generally, the first question was far more important than the second. At no stage was it ever envisaged that more than an insignificant fraction of the evacuated children should find a refuge in England. It was in its impact upon the policy of the British Government and on the conduct of British officials and ordinary British people that the second question assumed the importance it will receive in the next chapter.

[1] This derisive phrase was employed, to describe a policy he would be reluctant to defend, on 17 May 1937 by Mr D. E. Howard, Assistant in the League of Nations and Western Department of the Foreign Office, when explaining why he did not want to protest to the Italian Embassy against attacks on Stevenson in the Italian press. FO 371 21292.

But, at the moment we have reached – the aftermath of Guernica – it was the first question that still predominated and which, while the war continued in Spain, caused fresh difficulties to be discovered in Whitehall and the dangers of creating precedents to be rehearsed anew. In Bilbao matters wore a different aspect.

Stevenson himself, as might be expected, had been deeply stirred by his visit to the ruins of Guernica. Under its influence and the menace of the contracting front and the minor, but nerve-rackingly reiterated, raids on Bilbao, he took a new and even more surprising initiative. On 28 April he called on President Aguirre and urged him to spare his people useless slaughter by surrendering a city that was already doomed[1] – Stevenson expected the defences to collapse at any moment.[2]

This was a doubly remarkable move. First of all, it was made entirely on his own initiative and proved equally unacceptable to the President and to the Foreign Office in London. It thus deserves some consideration, together with Stevenson's other initiatives, by those historians whose repetitive tic compels them so constantly to inform us that the invention of the electric telegraph had long before made Ambassadors, to say nothing of junior Consuls, the merest puppets jerking at the end of a wire. Secondly, it provides a convincing refutation of the label so often fastened on Stevenson by the supporters of General Franco – *el consul rojo*. Even so moderately Leftish a partisan as Steer would never have regarded the saving of life as justifying a premature capitulation.

In fact Stevenson was as conservative in his political views as he was in his ideas on dress, morals, finance and general behaviour. Even his habitual humanitarianism was occasionally lacking in his comments on such problems of capitalism as unemployment, while his attitude towards strikes or even trade unions was distinctly old-fashioned. Nor did he much care for women who meddled in politics[3] and his reception of Mrs Leah Manning, a former Socialist M.P. and official of the National

---

[1] FO 371 21291.   [2] FO 371 21369.
[3] Miss Stevenson and Ojanguren.

Union of Teachers,when she arrived on his doorstep to announce her intention of organising the evacuation of Basque
children to England, was frankly unenthusiastic. He offered her
hospitality for the night, but urged her to go home the next
day. As Dame Leah Manning very fairly remarks in her
account of this incident, Stevenson had already had 'trouble
enough over the Romillys with Churchill demanding they be
got out'.[1]

And the irrepressible Jessica Mitford[2], whom Stevenson
and the Navy had tried to lure away from Bilbao with the bait
of luncheon on a destroyer, was by no means the only exasper-
ating English adventurer to descend upon his Consular district.
At a later stage, for instance, there was the romantically named
– and behaved – Rupert Belleville, a wealthy amateur pilot
fond of claiming official connections and secret missions which
did not actually exist. This enterprising gentleman first flew to
San Sebastián, with a young lady, and later, intending to celebrate the capture of that town by General Franco's forces, to
Santander – this time with a case of wine. Arriving one day too
soon he was taken prisoner by the Republicans and removed to
Gijón, from which grim citadel of the extreme Left he was
eventually rescued, after a good deal of trouble and without his
aircraft, by H.M.S. FORESIGHT.[3]

Mrs Manning, of course, was a far more serious person and
Stevenson was eventually to recognise the value of her crusad-
ing enthusiasm, her gift for publicity and her organising
ability. But even the most broad-minded of Consuls, which
Stevenson was not, might have been excused some annoyance
at the eruption of so vehement and loquacious a lady, flourishing her personal acquaintance with Republican leaders and
Basque representatives, fervent in her mission, convinced,
then and later, that the evacuation of children was her own
particular idea and responsibility.

Not only had this project given Stevenson much trouble and

---

[1] Leah Manning, *A Life for Education* (Gollancz, 1970), p. 124.
[2] Her account will be found in Jessica Mitford, *Hons and Rebels* (Gollancz,
1960).   [3] ADM 116 3679.

anxiety since he first conceived it, but he was now beginning to wonder whether, after all, the children should receive the first priority. On 26 April, for instance, he had succeeded in extracting authority from a reluctant Foreign Office 'to arrange such evacuation facilities as the navy may be able to provide' for 'prominent Basques including the Government'.[1] On the 28th he reported the French Consul as concurring in this recommendation[2] and on the 29th, when he said the collapse of the Bilbao defences was daily expected, he asked that two destroyers should stand by to evacuate the Basque Government and other leading personalities – about 500 people altogether.[3]

His reasoning was clear, though his expectation of military collapse was premature. He believed, rightly as it turned out, that the victorious Insurgents would be unlikely to molest children, particularly if Bilbao were surrendered before it fell, but that many prominent Basques would have to face the firing-squad. He thus wanted, in what he supposed to be the few days remaining, to save those most acutely threatened. When the Foreign Office, in response to the changed mood of Ministers, invited his comments on their plan for protecting the evacuation of children, Stevenson replied on the 30th that surrender was the best expedient for preserving the lives of the civilian population, but that British warships should evacuate the endangered Basque leaders. The Foreign Office had to telephone ordering him not to pursue this idea,[4] which was becoming almost an obsession and to which he nevertheless returned again on 2 May, when Sir George Mounsey again telephoned a refusal,[5] which he tried to soften by the somewhat fallacious argument 'that a Basque destroyer and other ships' were available for evacuating the government.[6] CISCAR's good-for-nothing crew of mutinous Spaniards would not, of course, have faced ALMIRANTE CERVERA on such an errand, but Mounsey had a better reason for retracting his earlier consent. On 30 April Rear-Admiral Ramsey had bluntly signalled his readiness to send FAULKNOR into Bilbao harbour to evacuate Stevenson,

---

[1] FO 371 21403.   [2] FO 371 21291.   [3] FO 371 21369.
[4] FO 371 21370.   [5] FO 371 21369.   [6] FO 371 21403.

Our Bilbao babies policy

British residents and their families, the two or three remaining foreign consuls and their families, 'a total of about 30 people and *no one else*'.[1]

It was a time of great tension and anxiety. In the hills to the east the front seemed to be crumbling and the Basque troops demoralised, while the Junkers and Heinkels came across Bilbao half a dozen times a day, sometimes bombing, sometimes just circling 'at leisure over the population for the moral effect produced'[2] on a hungry and frightened people, who had more than the example of Guernica to ponder. For it was reported on the 29th – though neither Chilton nor Steer could afterwards find evidence to confirm the story – that General Mola had threatened to raze Bilbao to the ground so that 'its bare and desolate site shall make the British people regret for ever the aid which they made to the Basque Bolshevists'.[3] Stevenson was not the only pessimist in those black days, but he caused anxiety to the Embassy and irritation to the Navy by his refusal to leave on the destroyer sent to fetch him on 1 May, when 'she was damned near bombed'.[4] As Chilton telegraphed a little plaintively to the Foreign Office (he thought Stevenson might take more notice of them): 'My impression of Mr Stevenson's character leads me to fear that if left to himself he would minimise the danger.'[5]

Stevenson, on the one hand, and the Embassy, the Navy and the Foreign Office, on the other, had drawn different conclusions from the same premise that the fall of Bilbao was imminent. He saw this as demanding immediate measures to save life and his own continued presence to organise the work; they regarded the fall of Bilbao – and the prior evacuation of Stevenson and of the British community – as the only means

[1] A signal preserved in an interesting scrapbook in the National Maritime Museum at Greenwich, the Executive Officer's Log of the 1936–1938 Commission of H.M.S. ROYAL OAK (henceforth RO Scrapbook).
[2] *The Times*, 30 April 1937.
[3] The story appeared in the French Press and in the English *Daily Herald*, but Chilton could not find it in any Spanish paper. FO 371 21290 and G. L. Steer, *The Tree of Gernika* (Hodder and Stoughton, 1938), p. 260.
[4] Malcolm. [5] FO 371 21290.

of escape from an increasingly intolerable dilemma. The Admiralty and the Commander-in-Chief Home Fleet were worried that more and more of their ships would be sucked into ever-expanding commitments of increasing delicacy and danger; the Embassy and the Foreign Office that the policy of non-intervention was being undermined and Britain ever more alienated from the winning side in Spain.

There was some substance in both complaints. A second battleship (H.M.S. RESOLUTION) had sailed from Portland on 29 April[1] to join ROYAL OAK in the Bay of Biscay and, as Rear-Admiral Ramsey later pointed out, the use of Spanish merchant ships (which were legitimate victims for the Insurgent navy even on the high seas) for evacuation greatly increased his burdens, because these vessels had to be protected both on their outward and their return journeys.

But the administrative problems, which tend to arouse some impatience in the civilian reader when Ramsey goes on to grumble that such duties were diverting ships from the Coronation Naval Review at Spithead,[2] were secondary to the fundamental objection: the Navy was being employed in a manner calculated to make new enemies for Britain at a time when she was not yet prepared to meet the ever more imminent menace of Germany. The attitude of the Admiralty throughout this affair, their often misleading advice, their seeming tendency to exaggerate dangers and difficulties that were cheerfully surmounted in the Cantabrian Sea, can only be understood in terms of their central preoccupation. As Admiral of the Fleet Sir Ernle A. Chatfield, First Sea Lord and Chief of the Naval Staff, later summarised his policy in a letter of 11 November 1937, to the Commander-in-Chief on the China Station:

I am using every effort I can and such influence as I possess to reduce our enemies and to avoid our rushing into dangerous situations which we are not prepared to follow to the end. It is essential that we should make friends and not enemies while . . . our defence

[1] *The Times.*   [2] FO 371 21370.

position is still weak . . . I shall be glad when the next two years are safely past. . . .[1]

Whether Britain or Germany had more to gain by thus deferring a conflict for which neither was then ready still remains an issue too extensively controversial for resolution within the narrow scope of the present work. All that need be said is that Chatfield's view, indeed the entire policy of appeasement, represented a possible, a consistent, an intellectually defensible line of conduct. Unfortunately it was sometimes pursued by rather devious paths. On 2 May, for instance, Sir George Mounsey composed a long minute of protest against the proposal that British warships should protect an evacuation carried out in defiance of General Franco's objections. This would constitute a flagrant intervention in the Spanish Civil War, it would expose the refugees to danger from mines or attack in territorial waters and it would be less efficacious than an acceptance of Franco's offer to designate a safe zone for the refugees in Spanish territory. Although his views were strongly supported by Vansittart, then Permanent Under-Secretary, and seen by the Secretary of State,[2] they did not influence the decisions of the British Government and they did not deserve to. For the arguments employed, whatever the possible merits of Mounsey's underlying motives, were fallacious. Even though ESPAÑA had hit a floating mine off Santander on the 30th and, to the huge delight and encouragement of the Basques, had sunk,[3] the mine menace off Bilbao

---

[1] From the Chatfield Papers by kind permission of Lady Chatfield and thanks to the courtesy of Professor A. Temple Patterson, who provided this revealing quotation.   [2] FO 371 21370.

[3] Her sinking was first claimed by Republican aircraft – a story that brought the British Air and Naval Attachés hot-foot from Paris to investigate a possibility so acutely controversial between the Royal Air Force and the Royal Navy as the successful bombing of a battleship – but was finally established as due to one of the mines earlier laid by the Insurgent ship JUPITER. Though both sides in Spain at one time attributed, whether in glee or fury, her loss to the intervention of the Royal Navy, there was no truth in this either. The best account of the sinking is that composed by Mr Consul Bates on 12 May 1937 (FO 371 21291), while Basque reactions are described in Steer, *Tree of Gernika*, and the Attachés' journey from Paris by Malcolm.

had by now been thoroughly exposed as mythical by the mere passage to and fro of so many British ships. And Chilton's telephonic summary, on the preceding day, of the protest received from Troncoso contained a sentence which should finally have demolished the notion of effective blockade: 'the blockading forces are unable to use force on ships in territorial waters except at a distance owing to the coastal batteries'. This was General Franco's own representative explaining why British naval protection on the high seas would constitute 'blockade breaking'.

Troncoso's communication, indeed, can scarcely have been of much assistance to Mounsey. The suggestion that evacuation represented a ruse 'by the Russian leaders in Bilbao' to enable them to blow up that city as they had blown up Guernica was not well attuned to British public opinion. Nor was the statement that the safety of Consulates in the harbour area could not be guaranteed, a veiled threat publicised on the 3rd[1] and, according to Mr Ojanguren, acted on when the house occupied by Stevenson was destroyed by raiding aircraft.[2] Even the offer to designate a secure zone in Spanish territory, either Republican or Nationalist, to which women and children might be evacuated, was not one which, at this stage of the Civil War, the Basques could be expected to trust or accept.[3] As the International Red Cross were later informed, there were no villages between Bilbao and Santander capable of housing such large numbers, while the Embassy at Hendaye subsequently learned that General Franco's proposal (of which the British Government unsuccessfully sought further particulars), had only been made in the hope of discouraging British assistance.[4] The only valid argument was that rescuing women and children constituted intervention, but this was a threadbare dogma with which to oppose the emotional pressures of humanitarianism.

---

[1] *The Times.*

[2] The house was indeed destroyed, but Stevenson did not take the threat seriously and it would have implied a capacity for precision bombing seldom attained by any Air Force.

[3] FO 371 21369.   [4] FO 371 21371.

Our Bilbao babies policy

These were still gathering force, both in Bilbao, where Leah Manning had somewhat prematurely told President Aguirre on 30 April that 4,000 Basque children would be offered a refuge in England[1] and in London where *The Times* published an appeal for funds to assist in the evacuation on 1 May.[2] In Bilbao, too, the masters of the nine British merchant ships then in that port met at the British Consulate to discuss how they could best assist, while the Basques set up an evacuation committee which decided to commission the liner HABANA to carry the first shipment of refugees to France, where the Confédération Générale du Travail had promised to provide hospitality for 2,300 children.[3] And Mrs Manning had started her 'blistering broadcasts' to England from Bilbao Radio.[4]

These, of course, in common with most of the public agitation, were concerned with the still vexed question of evacuation to England. The principle of British naval protection for Spanish refugee ships had been publicly announced on the 3rd and, on the 4th, Rear-Admiral Ramsey issued his preparatory orders concerning the first convoy to France.[5] All that remained was for Stevenson to certify that the children to sail on HABANA and GOIZEKO-IZARRA had been selected without political discrimination, a condition on which the Cabinet were most insistent. He, and the Basques, did their best. The opportunity of evacuation was publicly proclaimed, by press and radio, as open to all and the registered political parties were all invited to propose names from among their members. Stevenson and his Pro-Consul, Ojanguren, who had been working in the Consulate since 1919 and knew everyone in Bilbao, were given every facility to observe the processes of registration and selection.

[1] *The Times.*
[2] The signatories were Katharine Atholl, Noel-Buxton, Arthur Salter, Ellen Wilkinson, Eleanor Rathbone, Irene Ward, Megan Lloyd George, John Withers, Harold Nicolson, Thelma Cazalet, Philip Noel-Baker, Anthony Crossley, Lytton, Patrick Hannon, David Grenfell – representing all parties and very diverse opinions, but including none of the major politicians.   [3] *The Times.*
[4] Manning, *A Life for Education*, p. 127.   [5] ADM 116 3516.

They would probably have detected, and they would certainly have denounced, any gross abuses. In a sense, however, the idea of non-discrimination was an impossibly quixotic, a typically English ideal. Although the children of Franco's supporters were equally vulnerable to bombing and to starvation, they had less to fear from the fall of Bilbao. Their parents thus had less incentive to seek their evacuation. On the other hand, these parents were necessarily lying low. To present themselves at the offices of the Asistencia Social and to request the evacuation of their children was to expose themselves to enquiry and, whether or not the children were accepted, to possible persecution. It was thus almost inevitable that the children of Franco's supporters would be under-represented.

It was equally predictable that any official in a position to choose could and would argue that, the more committed were the parents to opposition to Franco, the greater the need of their children for evacuation. And, all altruistic and abstract arguments apart, there was the traditional, and very defensible, Latin tendency to emphasise the moral primacy of the obligation to support and assist one's own family, one's own friends, one's own associates and supporters. It would have been a miracle if the children selected for evacuation had not, in the overwhelming majority, come from families opposed to General Franco.

There is little evidence that any miracles occurred in Bilbao during the month of May 1937. On 8 May, for instance, Chilton telegraphed to Stevenson: 'Vice-Consul Innes[1] informs me that refugees in HABANA [this was the evacuation of 6 May 1937 protected by ROYAL OAK] were almost entirely children who landed saluting with clenched fists singing Internationale and that GOIZEKO-IZARRA contained mostly families of Basque Government.'[2]

It is hard to understand how an experienced British diplomat could have expected anything else, but Chilton went on:

---

[1] A British businessman who had been Honorary Pro-Consul in Bilbao and had been evacuated to Hendaye (he and his family sympathised with Franco), where he worked in the Embassy.   [2] ADM 116 3516.

'You should remind latter of their promise of impartiality and insist on its execution, which is an essential condition of British naval protection.'

Stevenson, always conscientious, replied regretfully: 'although I was satisfied at the time of embarkation that impartiality had been observed, I learned subsequently that preference was given to families of Government employees and of other influential persons who embarked in yacht.'[1]

He was given fresh assurances, but on 16 May he was so disturbed at the methods of selection employed that he refused his certificate to another shipload of refugees on HABANA. It made no difference: there was no time to alter the naval dispositions and a British destroyer escorted the liner to the Gironde.[2]

The problem created by the Spanish moral code – which is neither better nor worse than the British, merely different – was compounded by the children themselves. Brought up amid fierce political passions, hardened by a year of civil war, it never occurred to them that they could be helped, protected, sheltered by anyone but a political sympathiser. A clenched fist salute on landing was as much a gesture of courtesy and gratitude, a concession to the supposed convictions of their rescuers, as it was a profession of faith. It was certainly not the symbol of defiance it seemed to some British observers.

Nothing, indeed, was more productive of misunderstanding in this affair than the concept of an impartial humanitarianism. To most Spaniards, on either side, it was the merest hypocritical mask for the cynical purposes – which did occasionally exist – of perfidious Albion. Troncoso's protest of 1 May had begun by saying that 'British humanitarianism and impartiality are appreciated',[3] but this was Spanish politeness.[4] It was not

---

[1] FO 371 21370.   [2] ADM 116 3516.   [3] FO 371 21369.
[4] It could have been something more as far as Troncoso was concerned. Before Santander fell in August, he went to considerable trouble, and incurred some personal risk, to facilitate the evacuation by the Royal Navy of a mixed party of Basque leaders and Nationalist hostages. Perhaps prolonged exposure to contact with the British Embassy at Hendaye had tarnished his Latin logic.

only the Spanish – and the German and Italian – press which denounced Britain for her shameless, political exploitation of the children of Bilbao: on 11 May General Franco himself told the German Ambassador, for whose sake no pose was necessary, that British support for the evacuation of women and children from Bilbao was only a ruse to enable them to extricate some ships belonging to a Spanish company with British share capital.[1] Foreigners are apt to exaggerate both the subtlety and the stupidity of the British.

On the other hand, although the main weight behind British sympathy for these children, the support that finally influenced the Government, was unquestionably humanitarian, there were elements open to Spanish criticism. Katharine, Duchess of Atholl might have the purest motives for her efforts to help Basque children. She was, after all, an extreme Conservative, who had temporarily renounced the Whip in protest against the excessive liberality of her party towards India. In the thirties she was one of the first to expose the use of forced labour in the Soviet Union and, after the Second World War, she championed the cause of the oppressed peoples of eastern Europe. That she should be called the 'Red Duchess', that her humanitarianism and her attachment to the principles of a liberal democracy should ultimately entail the loss of her seat in Parliament: these were the absurd results of a political fanaticism that was then invading Britain itself.[2] But some of her associates were less impartial in their sympathy for the suffering and oppressed. Leah Manning, whose judgment was hardly distorted by right-wing prejudice, is explicit about the part played by British Communists and fellow travellers, while Watkins analyses in detail the connection between aid to Republican Spain and the power struggle inside the British Labour Party. British sympathy for the children of Bilbao and British assistance in their evacuation were factors which could be exploited to promote a more leftward orientation of British foreign policy.

[1] *Documents on German Foreign Policy*, series D, vol. 3 (H.M.S.O., 1951) (henceforth German Documents).
[2] Katharine, Duchess of Atholl, *Working Partnership* (Barker, 1958).

The possibility, indeed the existence, of such exploitation was constantly emphasised at the time to receptive listeners in the Foreign Office. Most of these warnings came from sources of equal and opposite bias, but there was one cautionary counsellor with greater apparent claims to credence. On 4 May 1937, Mr Golden, Secretary of the Save the Children Fund, told the Foreign Office that his Society were

absolutely opposed in principle to the removal of young children from their native country . . . he would sooner see them die in their own land than rot slowly in exile where they deteriorate physically, morally and mentally. From his own knowledge of the workings of the Joint Committee he had been forced reluctantly to the view that the desire to get the children sent to this country was actuated largely by political motives and he had been quite unable to understand why the Committee should not consider the very reasonable plan to remove the children to another part of Spain.

He went on to tell the Foreign Office of his fear that some of the Committee's more ardent members might attempt a *fait accompli* by bringing children to the United Kingdom before the Home Office had been able to approve a detailed scheme.[1]

These were somewhat extreme views, the merits of which may be reserved for later examination, but they came from a source that was *ex officio* humanitarian and the Foreign Office can scarcely be blamed for taking them seriously. They tended to undermine and to call in question all that warmth of emotional response that had swept aside Chilton's logical but chilling analysis: 'I find some difficulty in disposing of the contention that H.M.G., by using force, or the threat of it, to remove useless mouths from Bilbao, have used force, or the threat of it, to prolong the city's resistance.'[2]

That was a retrospective comment on 21 May, but it reflected one of the ideas dominant throughout the discussion raging in Whitehall and mirrored amid the anxieties of Bilbao. It was a discussion that continued in spite of the Ministerial decision announced to Parliament on 3 May because, contrary to expectation, Bilbao did not fall. Instead of a brief, once-for-

[1] FO 371 21370.   [2] FO 371 21292.

all operation of protecting a last-minute evacuation from a doomed city, the Royal Navy found themselves committed to the continuing task of convoying refugee ships, full or empty, and of protecting the freighters bringing food to the Basques and taking away their ore. Many of the latter, moreover, had only recently acquired their right to fly the Red Ensign – forty-seven vessels had been transferred to the United Kingdom register since 1 January.[1]

On 4 May, for instance, RESOLUTION had to rescue PORTELET and BLACKHILL;[2] the first evacuation followed on the 6th; THORPEHALL and BACKWORTH required the intervention of RESOLUTION on the 7th[3] when Captain 'Corn-Cob' Jones of MACGREGOR was also alarmed by ALMIRANTE CERVERA though no interception took place and FIREDRAKE's assistance was not needed.[4] On the 8th FEARLESS and FOXHOUND were despatched from Portland to reinforce the Sixth Destroyer Flotilla on the Basque coast[5] and on the 10th FOXHOUND, together with FURY, prevented the Insurgent destroyer VELASCO from interfering with the British ship MARVIA and the 242 refugees she carried.[6]

The Royal Navy, who were also kept busy ferrying Stevenson to and fro between Bilbao and Saint-Jean-de-Luz, were not alone in their activity. The three French ships sent to Bilbao on the 8th to collect 2,000 refugees had the imposing escort, in both directions, of the battleships BRETAGNE and LORRAINE, the cruiser EMILE BERTIN, the destroyer LE TERRIBLE and the despatch vessel SOMME.[7] ALMIRANTE CERVERA herself was continuously on patrol, to the subsequent admiration of Rear-Admiral Ramsey, from 30 April to 16 May and – an item of news calculated to increase the forebodings of the First Sea Lord – on the 10th DEUTSCHLAND, ADMIRAL SCHEER and the Second Destroyer Flotilla sailed from Wilhelmshaven for Spanish waters.[8]

Chilton and the Foreign Office were equally busy. Troncoso 'waxed very angry indeed' on the 1st;[9] General Franco's

[1] *The Times.* [2] FO 371 21292. [3] FO 371 21292.
[4] ADM 116 3518. [5] *The Times.* [6] FO 371 21292.
[7] ADM 116 3516. [8] *The Times.* [9] Malcolm.

Our Bilbao babies policy

Minister for Foreign Affairs denounced on the 6th the British 'attack upon the prestige of its navy and upon the sovereignty of Spain';[1] on the 7th Chilton complained of the 'frightful time' he had experienced in ascertaining from the French where HABANA and GOIZEKO-IZARRA were to land their passengers: 'it was not until midnight on the 5th/6th that we could get any information and even then the destination of HABANA was altered the next day'[2] – she went to La Pallice and GOIZEKO-IZARRA to Bordeaux.

Against the sombre and tragic background of the Civil War, measured by the suffering of the parents and the anxieties of the children – who, on arrival, were sent in batches to various places, including Hendaye, Saint-Jean-de-Luz, Bayonne, Cette, Dax, Audienne and Perpignan – these seem the petty woes of soulless bureaucrats. Perhaps they deserve no more sympathy than the Admiralty's grievances over the Coronation Naval Review or the reluctance of the Ministry of Marine 'to keep units of the French fleet in Spanish waters' at a time when manoeuvres were impending.[3] But the terrible truth of La Rochefoucauld's 'nous avons tous assez de force pour supporter les maux d'autrui'[4] also enshrines its sordid converse: ordinary men – and officials are nothing else – are easily convinced of the insupportable inconvenience of any interruption to their own routine.

ROYAL OAK had done her job. The first of many thousand children had reached safety in France. But the administrative task of giving effect to decisions taken in principle, not least, so far as we are concerned, that of the Home Office on 29 April, was only just beginning. The obstacles still to be surmounted before any children reached an English port will not be understood, or the need for the next chapter obvious, unless a lamentable fact is borne in mind – these children were not only 'useless mouths', a diplomatic embarrassment, a menace to established policies – they were also a nuisance.

---

[1] FO 425 414.   [2] FO 371 21369.   [3] FO 371 21370.
[4] Francois VI, Duc de la Rochefoucauld, *Maximes* (Cambridge University Press, 1945), no. 19.

CHAPTER 10

An English welcome

―――――

Suddenly the whole ship listed to
one side as four thousand children
crowded the rails and deck and
rigging to wave frantically to a blue
strip on the horizon. 'Inglaterra!
Inglaterra!'

Ellis[1]

Thirty-three years afterwards Dame Leah Manning wrote 'I
do not think the full story of the evacuations from Bilbao has
ever been told . . . there are many stupid errors . . . I should
like to put the record straight.'[2]

The full story still awaits a more determined and protracted
effort at research, particularly in the files of the Home Office,
if these still exist, and will not be attempted here. But it was not
quite so simple as it appears in Dame Leah's recollection, with
advantages, of her single-handed struggle against Stevenson's
obduracy and the obstruction of Whitehall. She remembers, for
instance, being asked by President Aguirre on 24 April to take
4,000 children to England and *The Times* of 3 May reports her
as calling on the President on 30 April to offer hospitality for
this number. But the first written proposal that any children
should come to England was made to the Foreign Office only
on the 27th and the agreement 'in principle' – always a sinister
phrase – by the Home Office was given on the 29th and was
subject to the National Joint Committee submitting a detailed
scheme for approval[3] The subject was not mentioned by the
Representative in London of the Basque Government, when he

―――――

[1] Article describing the children's arrival in *New Statesman and Nation* of
29 May 1937 by Dr Richard Ellis.
[2] Leah Manning, *A Life for Education* (Gollancz, 1970), pp. 127–31.
[3] FO 371 21369.

called on Vansittart on 3 May to convey his Government's thanks for the assurance of British naval protection and, incidentally, to explain that the Basques constituted something of a third party to the Civil War.[1] On 5 May, while the Cabinet were discussing the question of naval protection, the rumour was mentioned that a plan existed to bring children to England, but was dismissed as unfounded.[2] The Foreign Office, being rather better informed, (Eden had told the house of Commons on 3 May that 'no final arrangements have been made for the admission of the Basque children') telegraphed on the same day to Stevenson instructing him to make it quite clear to the Basques that no children were to be sent to England before the Home Office had given their approval.[3]

Clearly there was some misunderstanding. Mrs Manning says she told Stevenson flatly on 24 April 'I'm here at the request of the Basque Government, through their Delegation in London, and I propose to evacuate Basque children to England for dispersal throughout my country until Franco is defeated.' Mrs Manning seems to have been a little ahead of the National Joint Committee in London. One of the troubles, of course, was finance. The response to the appeal of 1 May had been inadequate and, on 6 May, both Wilfrid Roberts and the Duchess of Atholl wrote to Mr Baldwin, the Prime Minister, appealing for government funds. They emphasised that the committee included representatives of the Catholic Archbishop of Westminster, the Society of Friends and the Save The Children Fund as well as of the Trades Union Congress and Members of Parliament. The Foreign Office, when asked for their observations, urged the Prime Minister to insist that the evacuation should be financed entirely by voluntary contributions, both to preserve the principle of non-intervention and to prevent His Majesty's Government being exposed to similar demands in other cases.[4]

Only on 10 May did Wilfrid Roberts send two letters to the Home Office, one setting out the detailed scheme requested on

[1] FO 371 21291.   [2] CAB 23 88.
[3] FO 371 21370.   [4] FO 371 21371.

29 April for receiving Basque children in England and looking after them there, the other explaining that the Committee had now collected enough offers from other organisations to feel justified in doubling their initial proposal to bring 2,000 children to England.[1] Therefore, although Dame Leah's account suggests that 4,000 had been the figure envisaged since 24 April, this was only *proposed* by the National Joint Committee a fortnight later. And even then, when Baldwin replied on the 11th to the two letters he had received on the 6th, he not only refused any contribution from public funds but tried to discourage the whole idea of bringing children to England at all.[2] He did not, however, give a flat rejection, so that Wilfrid Roberts was able to reply on the 13th that the National Joint Committee intended to go ahead with their plan to bring 2,000 children to England.[3] Even this had still not been finally accepted by the Government, so that, when Stevenson sent a telegram on the 14th saying that it appeared that Mrs Manning had given the Basque Government to understand that preparations for reception in the U.K. of the children were sufficiently advanced for them to sail early during the following week, he added that he had again told them this would not be possible before he received instructions from London.[4] Only on the 15th did the Foreign Office telegraph to Stevenson that, as a result of that day's meeting between the Home Office and the National Joint Committee, which on this occasion also included representatives of the Salvation Army, approval had been given for the admission to the United Kingdom of *two thousand* children aged between six and twelve (900 boys and 1,100 girls) together with 100 women and 15 priests.[5]

This long delay in reaching a decision is open to criticism. The immediate causes were probably threefold: the National Joint Committee had conceived and announced the idea before they had either prepared a scheme or mustered the funds to pay for it; the Government would not put up the money themselves; and, although this is only a guess, Ministers and officials

---

[1] FO 371 21370; FO 371 21371.   [2] FO 371 21371.
[3] FO 371 21371.   [4] F.O. 371 21370.   [5] FO 371 21370.

no longer felt the same sense of urgency that had gripped at
least the former at the end of April. The emotional impact of
Guernica was wearing off and all the prudential considerations
discussed in the previous chapter were reasserting themselves.
Perhaps this procrastination was censurable, but it does not
fully justify Dame Leah's charge: 'no country was more guilty
of these cruel changes [in policy] than our own'.[1] There were
no changes in policy before 15 May, because that was the first
day that policy was decided, while subsequent changes were all
in conformity with Mrs Manning's wishes.

But Dame Leah brings a more serious charge, and this time
against Stevenson personally.

After the evacuations of May 16th [to France], I began to feel
anxious. It seemed as if we were never going to get away . . . I began
to send out imploring telegrams – to the Archbishop of Canterbury,
to the Catholic Archbishop, to Lloyd George, to Citrine. The
answers came back, helpful and encouraging. 'all right' said the
authorities, 'we'll leave it to the Consul to decide'. But Mr Stevenson
was adamant. He could not advise His Majesty's Government to
accept 4,000 children of all ages. I played my last card . . . I trailed
along to see Philip Jordan . . . [who] evolved a complete plan for out-
manoeuvring London . . . 'this evening', began the conspirator
[Jordan] 'we are going with Stevenson, by submarine, to St Jean, to
celebrate the Coronation. With the Consul out of the way, your
buddy the pro-consul is in charge. Get to work on him. Con him
into sending a telegram in the name of the Consul agreeing to your
arrangements.' I had no hesitation in doing all I could to persuade
Senor Oganguerren [sic] to send that telegram. It went off that same
night and the reply in confirmation, came in the morning. Mr
Stevenson never knew what had hit him. . . .[2]

The story is a good one, but it receives no confirmation from
the official records. There is no mention of representations
from any of the exalted recipients of Mrs Manning's telegrams,
no suggestion of referring to Stevenson a decision that was
peculiarly a matter for the Home Office, no hint of hostile
advice from Bilbao. Merely negative evidence would not, of

[1] Manning, *A Life for Education*, p. 127.
[2] Manning, *A Life for Education*, p. 130.

course, discredit the tale: too much was destroyed by clerks heedless of future historians. Nor does it matter that there were no British submarines on the north coast of Spain – naval nomenclature has confused even the most eminent of diplomatic historians. But Coronation Day was on the 12th and Stevenson, together with two Spaniards, left for Saint-Jean-de-Luz aboard the destroyer FURY on the 11th.[1] If Philip Jordan was aboard, he escaped the notice of FURY's Commanding Officer. Stevenson was certainly back in Bilbao on the 14th and 15th (when he was so dissatisfied with the selection of evacuees for France) but was probably away on the 17th, when Mr Angel Ojanguren did send a telegram to the Foreign Office explaining that, if their wishes were to be met on age limits and on the ratio between girls and boys, this would mean revising all the arrangements so far made and a consequential delay of from seven to ten days. It was a perfectly proper telegram, which expressly stated that it was sent by Ojanguren in Stevenson's absence and at the request of Mrs Manning.[2] Even without this documentary evidence it is, of course, inherently unlikely that this honourable man, after eighteen years of loyal service in the British Consulate, would have acted otherwise or that he would have been so gullible as to be 'conned' into an attempt to deceive the Foreign Office.

Moreover, Mr Ojanguren's own recollection of this incident is rather different. What he remembers is hearing one of Mrs Manning's broadcasts over Bilbao Radio, in which she appealed to the British people for assistance in the evacuation of Basque children to England. Not having heard of this plan before, he accordingly telephoned to suggest she should call at the Consulate to discuss the problem and, on her second visit, himself suggested the famous telegram. Naturally after thirty-three years, his memory is as fallible as Mrs Manning's, but the telegram is there and can be seen by anyone who cares to go to the Public Record Office.

The only truth in this entertaining anecdote is that, on the

---

[1] FO 371 21292.   [2] FO 371 21370.

following day, 18 May, the Home Office did tell Mr Wilfrid Roberts[1] and the Foreign Office did telegraph to Bilbao,[2] that 4,000 children aged from five to fifteen, with a preference for girls in the higher age groups, would be admitted to England. Whether this was due to Ojanguren's telegram is uncertain: Eden himself had, on the same day, received a strongly worded telegram from the Duchess of Atholl explaining that the National Joint Committee 'specially desire 4,000 to include girls about 15 to save them from terrible fate if Moors enter'.[3]

It is, incidentally, a curious illustration of the difference in political fashions then and now, that this blatant colour prejudice – this assumption that young girls were more exposed to rape, and that their fate would be more terrible, at the hands of General Franco's Moorish troops than at those of his Spanish, Italian or German soldiers – was exploited by Left and Right alike. Both Ojanguren and Mrs Manning remember broadcasts threatening just this by General Queipo de Llano, one of Franco's propagandists. Mrs Manning, however, was equally concerned at the prospect that any restriction on evacuation from Bilbao might leave 'young girls to be raped by the tercio'[4] (the name given to a particularly notorious formation on the other side). It is also a sad pointer to the innocence of a vanished era that neither of these ladies expressed similar fears about the boys of Bilbao.

But the exoneration of Stevenson and Ojanguren does not detract from the importance of Dame Leah's own exertions at the time. Without her flaming zeal, her emotional outbursts, her real organising abilities, her broadcasts and her telegrams to all and sundry, the obstacles erected in London to the reception of Basque children might not have been overcome. For the earlier defence of the Home Office, unlike that of Stevenson and Ojanguren, was formal rather than effective. In addition to the official correspondence preserved in the files of the Foreign Office, there must have been many informal exchanges, telephone calls, meetings to hammer out the proposals

---

[1] FO 371 21371.   [2] FO 371 21370.
[3] FO 371 21370.   [4] Manning, *A Life for Education*, p. 130.

that the National Joint Council later embodied in formal letters. It may be that a full account of all these transactions would do more to bear out Mrs Manning's complaints.

But it would still be unlikely to inculpate Stevenson, who seems to have done no more than act on the orders which, from time to time, he received from London. At first sight and in view of the initiatives he had earlier taken – and would again – this passivity seems unusual. Admittedly he was extremely busy: supervising the selection of refugees for ships to France, co-ordinating with the Navy the arrangements for protection, nipping to and fro between Bilbao and Saint-Jean-de-Luz. He may also have felt that he had burned his fingers a trifle over his repeated and impetuous proposals for the surrender of the city and the evacuation of leading Basques. Nobody had accepted his views and these had not been justified by events: Bilbao did not fall and, although General Mola's troops were creeping nearer, the first half of May somewhat diminished the general sense of imminent disaster. But there is a third, though equally conjectural explanation, which may also help to clarify some of the cross purposes between London and Bilbao. Stevenson may well have thought it more important to remove the maximum number of children from Bilbao than to ensure that some of them went to England. They would be just as safe in France, where a more familiar climate, the presence of a substantial Basque population and the readiness of the Government to contribute to their upkeep even offered advantages not available in England. Moreover, HABANA could, and did, make the return journey to a French port in half the time needed to get to England and back. Even in the absence of obstruction from Whitehall, the despatch of children to England might thus actually reduce the total numbers evacuated from Bilbao.

One wonders, therefore, whether the insistence on sending children to England may not have had a political as well as an humanitarian motive. The very obstacles that loomed largest in Downing Street – the added irritant to General Franco, the further erosion of British non-intervention – were positive incentives to anyone who still hoped for a Republican victory.

If such ideas were present to the minds of the Basque leaders – and it would be surprising if they were not – this would explain why they preferred to seek assistance from Mrs Manning and her friends rather than approach the British Government officially (as they had with the request for naval protection). Mrs Manning, unlike the Foreign Office or Stevenson, could be relied on to ask no awkward questions.

This is speculation. When the Ministerial Committee on Foreign Policy, with Mr Baldwin in the chair, discussed the matter on 19 May, they recorded that, in spite of their efforts to discourage the bringing of Basque children to this country, the Ministers concerned had reluctantly been convinced by a delegation from the National Joint Committee that there was a good case for this measure. The fact that the French Government had undertaken to admit and maintain large numbers in France had made it particularly difficult to refuse admission to the United Kingdom.[1] Consent had at last been given, though grudgingly – a factor that was to prove important subsequently – and the operation could proceed. Rear-Admiral Ramsey, who was told by Stevenson the same day, reported that 'The arrangements in Bilbao for this undertaking appeared to be largely in the hands of a Mrs Leah Manning who, as representative of the National Joint Committee for Spanish Relief, had proceeded to Bilbao some days previously.'[2]

In fact, of course, Mrs Manning had been at work in Bilbao for weeks. So, according to the *Manchester Guardian*, had a certain Mrs Alonso, but nobody else mentions her. There had, however, also been two British doctors and two nurses, who had left England on 8 May to carry out a medical inspection of all the children and reassure the Ministry of Health that these would bring no contagious disease to England. In fact most of the children struck Dr Ellis as healthier and showing fewer symptoms of privation than many children of unemployed workers in Britain. While these examinations, which were frequently interrupted by air-raids, proceeded, Mrs Manning

[1] FO 371 21371.   [2] ADM 116 3516.

was organising, as demanded by the Home Office, the preparation of an identity disc (inscribed *Expedición a Inglaterra*) and a separate record of personal particulars for each of the 3,805 children. This task was completed, so Stevenson reported, on the 20th,[1] and the children, Mrs Manning, the doctors, 99 female teachers, 120 female attendants and 15 priests were ready to embark. These last had also signed declarations promising to abstain from political propaganda while in the United Kingdom. It is amusing, in view of the predominant rôle in this undertaking of Mrs Manning, the Duchess of Atholl and many other highly political British ladies, that this precaution was not considered necessary for Spanish members of the fair sex. Stevenson also reported that it was impossible, without the hardship of separating families, to adhere strictly to the ratio of 9 boys to 11 girls: 'I did not insist on the letter of your instructions.'[2]

ROYAL OAK was ready. Unlike BEAGLE, BLANCHE, HOOD and many other of H.M. ships encountered in these pages she was not at Spithead for the Coronation Naval Review on 20 May 1937. The photograph published in *The Times*, which purported to depict this battleship at anchor and awaiting the Sovereign's inspection, aroused considerable irritation among the ship's company.[3] But that paper's naval correspondent – or his informant at Portsmouth – was a trifle out of touch with the harsher realities of the Civil War. On the 16th he was still expecting, a little doubtfully, the arrival at Spithead of the Republican destroyer CISCAR and only gave up hope on the following day.[4] Coronation Day itself, however, was properly celebrated aboard H.M. ships in Spanish waters, even if the printed programme of the festivities in ROYAL OAK ends on a cautionary note: 'Franco permitting'.[5]

Ramsey was regarded by some as a more diplomatic Admiral than Blake (who received the K.C.B. in the Coronation Honours) but he agreed with his predecessor on essentials. On 10 May he commented in his report to the Commander-in-

[1] FO 371 21370.   [2] FO 371 21371.   [3] RO Scrapbook.
[4] *The Times*.   [5] RO Scrapbook.

Chief Home Fleet 'Recent cases of interference with British merchant ships on the high seas by Insurgent warships had made it necessary that a heavy ship should be in the neighbourhood to support the destroyers on patrol . . . the likelihood of an unpleasant incident would obviously be considerably lessened by the presence on the spot of a strong force.'[1]

On the 18th he felt more confident and predicted that, as long as British warships were present, ALMIRANTE CERVERA would abstain from interfering. But he himself, with ROYAL OAK, had remained within supporting distance for the convoy of the 16th.[2] And, for the expedition to England his 15 inch guns would again be in the offing.

That expedition really began on the evening of 20 May 1937, when darkness fell and the German bombers ceased their destructive circling above the battered streets and the apprehensive citizens of Bilbao. The Estación de Portugalete began to swallow up swarms of children, chattering or frozen in tearful silence, thrilled or terrified, all gripped by the emotions of an experience that, to them, was unique. As priests, teachers, parents, soldiers, helpers, policemen, and officials pushed their way through the eddying mass, shouting, gesticulating, gradually reducing chaos to order and organisation, the first of many trains was loaded and at last began to move.

The children were taken down to the ship [the HABANA once again] in trainloads of six hundred and filtered down to every inch of accommodation.[3]

The quay was a thick black mass of parents, defying bombs as the children, some happy and excited, some in tears, were taken aboard in orderly companies. Head to tail the señoritas laid out our precious cargo – on the bulkheads, in the swimming pool, in the state rooms and along the alley ways, for all the world like the little sardinas about which they were always singing.[4]

One wonders how long these children remained 'laid out' so

[1] ADM 116 3516.   [2] ADM 116 3516.
[3] Chapter contributed by Dr Richard Ellis to *The Basque Children in England* by Yvonne Cloud (Gollancz, 1937).
[4] Manning, *A Life for Education*, p. 131.

neatly or how soon sleep came to anyone aboard. But Mrs Manning found time for a triumphant telegram to Eden. 'We passed the breakwater early next morning, accompanied by a Spanish destroyer, a yacht carrying other refugees to France [this was GOIZEKO-IZARRA], and two cargo boats; shortly afterwards we were picked up by our British convoy, the ROYAL OAK and a destroyer.'[1]

There were actually two destroyers, of which FEARLESS escorted HABANA all the way to the Needles, while FOXHOUND convoyed GOIZEKO-IZARRA to the Gironde.[2] 'As bad luck would have it, we found a strong wind and sea in the Bay. The next fifteen hours are best forgotten. Four thousand wretchedly seasick children crowded into an old boat whose very latrines are apt to regurgitate in sympathy, are not a pretty sight.'[3]

Perhaps the state of the sea also discouraged any interference from the Insurgent Navy, who were otherwise still active and resentful. On the following day, when three more refugee ships left for France, VELASCO and CIUDAD DE VALENCIA 'displayed their feelings by manoeuvring unnecessarily close' and ALMIRANTE CERVERA, though she did not interfere, broadcast a protest: 'The English nation again breaks the law of neutrality protecting one of the belligerents against an effective blockade.'[4]

Fortunately even the Bay of Biscay does not last for ever and, at 6.30 p.m. on the 22nd[5] HABANA, flying the Spanish Republican flag, the pennant of the Non-Intervention Control Commission, the Saint George's Cross and the yellow Quarantine flag, dropped anchor off Fawley in Southampton Water. By special request no sirens greeted her from other ships – lest these should be mistaken by the children for air raid warnings – but a tug went out carrying Dr Williams, Medical Officer of Health for Southampton, Mr Brinton of the National Joint Committee, customs and immigration officials, a consignment of food and

[1] Dr Ellis in Cloud, *Basque Children in England*.   [2] ADM 116 3516.
[3] Dr Ellis in Cloud, *Basque Children in England*.   [4] ADM 116 3516.
[5] The following account is mainly based on contemporary accounts in *The Times*, *The Daily Telegraph*, *The Observer*, the *Daily Express*, the *Daily Mail*, the *Daily Herald*, the *Daily Worker* and – fullest and probably most reliable of them all – the *Southern Daily Echo*, the local evening paper.

sweets for the children and a reporter from *The Daily Telegraph*, who particularly noted that this time there were no clenched fist salutes from the children.

These had been crowding the rails ever since first light, staring in astonishment at the long rows of little English houses – as unfamiliar after the tall tenements of Bilbao as the square loaves of white bread the better sailors had relished during the voyage. Esperanza Ortiz, who was one of the few not to be sea-sick, also remembers with appreciation her first slice of Madeira cake. Even Bautista Lopez, who had to be taken to hospital on arrival, has preserved the memory of the gay bunting that decorated the streets of Southampton. Only afterwards did the children discover that this was not actually in honour of their arrival, but an aftermath of the Coronation.[1]

Disembarkation did not begin until 10 o'clock the next morning, for Dr Williams had another medical inspection to carry out first. Apart from the after-effects of sea-sickness he found very little wrong, though Felix Gonsalez had to be taken to hospital for an operation and 400 of the children proved to be verminous and went first to the Corporation Baths for disinfestation and – to the despairing tears of some of the girls – a close crop of their long tresses. Buses took them, and the other children, as each batch passed Dr Williams' inspection, to North Stoneham, on the outskirts of Southampton, where 500 bell tents (250 of them hired from the Army) had been erected for their reception.

Here considerable chaos prevailed. Volunteer workers, the Duchess of Atholl among them, had still been frantically erecting tents and preparing the camp the night before. The problems of receiving the children, allocating them to tents and answering a million questions were complicated by language difficulties – scarcely any of the children spoke English and a few knew only Basque – as well as by the arrival of distinguished visitors (the Spanish Ambassadress, the Home Secretary and Lady Simon among them) and a horde of curious motorists

[1] Information given to the author in 1971 by Mr and Mrs Bautista Lopez.

who had made North Stoneham the target of their excursion that fine Sunday. Breakfast took four hours to serve and produced a near-riot as the hungry and over-excited children swarmed· round the steaming cauldrons of hot milk crying 'leche, leche!' The motorists, too, were charitably disposed and the presents they had brought created fresh pandemonium, not least because many of the voluntary workers tried to discourage the children from begging for cigarettes; the number who smoked was a constant source of surprise.

These voluntary workers were variously described according to the political predilections of the newspaper concerned. The *Daily Worker* said they were members of the Communist Party, the Labour Party and the Peace Movement; the *Daily Herald* substituted Friends of the Soviet Union for Communists and added the Southampton Co-operative Society, the Liberal Party, the Salvation Army, the Rotary Club and Toc H; but *The Daily Telegraph*, though mentioning 'men and women of all political parties', specified no organisations except the Roman Catholic Church, the Church of England, the Salvation Army, the Boy Scouts and the Girl Guides. In fact there seems to have been widespread, though perhaps not very lasting, local sympathy and support. The Mayor of Southampton had presided at a meeting on the eve of HABANA's arrival, where £157 had been collected and many offers received of help in kind.

To begin with, indeed, assistance was more conspicuous than organisation and it was a mercy that Sunday evening's thunderstorm was an isolated break in the hottest spell 1937 had yet produced. For the children, tense with weeks of accumulated emotion, separated from their families, camped in a strange land, struggling to grasp and express their experiences, and often unable to make their simplest needs understood, seemed to their more stolid English hosts wild, temperamental and undisciplined to an extent even beyond that to be expected from their age and situation. They rushed aimlessly about, they congregated in vociferous groups, they broke out of camp, they showed little comprehension of the extemporised sanitary arrangements. The organisers and their amateur helpers did their best. Good will and compassion abounded: the Air Ministry asked pilots not to overfly the camp, because all aircraft were hostile bombers to these frightened infants; Movietone News did penance for alarming the children with the muzzles of their cameras by sending a copy of the film, specially subtitled in Spanish, to Bilbao; Sir John Simon tried his Spanish in friendly conversations; nurses toured the tents at night to comfort and reassure. But two different worlds were groping for contact through a handful of interpreters: the messages of order and peace and benevolent routine percolated slowly through the bewilderment of exile and separation, the charged memories of fear.

Nor was it only the children whose attitudes, customs and reactions demand, even today, an effort at understanding. On the 26th, the day the first children left the camp for less temporary accommodation, there was a third medical inspection. It was not that the British people were afflicted with the collective neurosis of hypochondria, though any Spanish doctor might have been excused such a diagnosis. The phenomenon was political rather than medical. When Lord Lloyd, for instance, warned the House of Lords, on the 25th, of the peril of trachoma which these children had posed for the British people, he seemed quite as concerned with the dangers of political contagion. That, at least, was the conclusion of the Marquess of Dufferin and Ava, who expressed 'the opinion of His Majesty's Government that, at any rate for the moment, these children are unlikely to influence the electoral results in the next five years.'[1]

Nevertheless these apprehensions, the tip of an iceberg to be sounded in a subsequent chapter, had to be treated seriously enough to bring an ophthalmologist to North Stoneham. Officials wanted to leave no flank exposed. Every precaution must be seen to be taken, to limit and contain the consequences of these potentially infectious infants.

---

[1] Hansard (Lords), vol. 105, col. 229.

These fundamental considerations were mercifully beyond the ken of the children and of their parents in Bilbao. All the Basques knew was that their sons and daughters had arrived, they were safe, they were cared for. President Aguirre had more than politeness, and that lively expectation of further favours to come which is gratitude, to prompt his thanks to the British people for 'the wonderfully generous welcome accorded to our children at Southampton'.

It was still spring.

CHAPTER 11

That summer's dying fall

> Ship after ship bucketing across
> the right-angle of the Bay to the
> serenity of France, their holds a
> vomiting, rolling mass of refugees.
>
> Steer[1]

Early on the hot, sunny morning of Sunday 13 June, Stevenson left, for the last time, the house where he had been living in Bilbao's northern suburb, Las Arenas, and set off for the harbour.[2] He had an appointment with Captain McGrigor, who was awaiting him 4 miles off Cape Lucero in the destroyer KEMPENFELT, the new leader of the Fourth Flotilla. Stevenson, in the stately language of his final report, 'proceeded thither in a motor yacht placed at my disposal for this and similar purposes by the Basque Government'. He was accompanied by Eguia, creator and commander of the Basque auxiliary fleet, who wanted 'to ask a few questions about destroyer management. He had only ten days earlier turned out of the two Government destroyers J. L. DIEZ and CISCAR most of the crews, a sorry lot of idlers, and made up the complements of these ships with Basque seamen and fishermen.'

We do not know what advice McGrigor gave him or how he reconciled compassion, hospitality and the doctrine of non-intervention. But Eguia had left his questions more than a little late. The final assault on Bilbao had begun on the 11th and the exhausted defenders, dazed and battered by bombs, shells and the demoralising machine-guns of the Heinkels that dived at

---

[1] G. L. Steer, *The Tree of Gernika* (Hodder and Stoughton, 1938), p. 261.
[2] Except as otherwise indicated, this account of the last days of Republican Bilbao is based on Stevenson's final report in FO 425 414 and on Steer, *Tree of Gernika*.

them unopposed, were everywhere falling back in disorder. The legendary iron ring, the *cinturón de hierro*, of Bilbao had been pierced and, though General Mola himself was dead, his troops were pressing forward. Even the imperturbable Steer, tired out after a day with the retreating troops, stirred in his sleep when the Nationalists began 'shelling the centre of Bilbao with twelve-inch armour piercing shells', an improbable detail (how could he know?) as characteristic of his reporting as Stevenson's cautious statement that 'fifteen large shells'[1] struck the city was of his very different style. Air-raids were incessant – Stevenson's house was destroyed while he was down at the harbour – and the anguished citizens of Bilbao huddled in the cellars while their leaders weighed the dwindling possibilities of resistance against the dread prospects of surrender. Some of them packed a furtive bag.

For the hopes of May, of which Steer wrote retrospectively 'I am of the opinion that the Basques, had they had bombing aircraft, would have finished off the Italian division Flechas Negras in the crucial days of May 1st to 3rd, and with that disaster the attack on Bilbao would have been over' had been deceived and, for the Basques, the cruellest month was June. After a succession of minor repulses, of unsuccessful counter-attacks, their weary and dispirited troops were subjected to the final assault of their enemies on 11 June. For a few days longer the defenders flaggingly maintained their rearguard actions, but the eastern defences of Bilbao were shattered and the city's encirclement, its divorce from the still intact and accessible western enclave centred on Santander and Gijón, could only be briefly delayed. Although Stevenson commented that the 4,500 refugees who boarded HABANA on the 12th did so without the least thought of impending defeat, it never occurred to him to share their pathetic hopes. The end he had so long predicted was all too obviously imminent.

Indeed, one can not help wondering what Eguia and Stevenson found to talk about as, the last salutes exchanged,

[1] FO 371 21295.

their launch carried them away from the brief tranquillity of
KEMPENFELT – the pink gins, the captain's attentive steward, the
tactful conversation – towards the smoke that rose, sometimes in
tall, black persistent columns, more often in the puff-balls of
explosions, above their invisible, their dubiously attainable,
destination. To men of sensitive perceptions, there is always an
extra strain, an added embarrassment, in being only partly
involved in the danger of others. The staff officer on a brief visit
to the front line, the journalist, the diplomat: each of these may
find himself talking to men who must stay when he has gone,
who must continue to run the risks which it is his privilege, even
his duty, to escape. Sometimes it is necessary to question those
who will remain, to discuss their perils, perhaps to speculate
about their possible fate. Even among friends it can be hard to
strike the right note, to avoid the jarring phrase, in such
conversations.

Stevenson, admittedly, was returning to Bilbao in spite of the
contrary arguments, even the remonstrances, of Captain
McGrigor, because he still saw duties to be done there. He had
nothing to be ashamed of. But he knew he would not be staying
for long, that he risked nothing worse than a few hours' exposure
to the flying fragments of an unlucky bomb or shell. He cannot
have found it easy to talk to Eguia, to be overheard by the crew
of the launch, to know, even when he parted from them at the
mole, that he still had some time to spend among people whose
lives, whose families, whose whole future were going to be in
deadly danger when he himself was safely recounting his
exploits to appreciative listeners in London. It must have been
an awkward, as well as a disturbing Sunday.

Perhaps it was something of a relief to be summoned, at eight
o'clock on the evening of that unlucky 13 June, by President
Aguirre, who enquired whether His Majesty's Government
would be prepared to lend their good offices in arranging the
surrender of Bilbao. With commendable caution Stevenson
asked for a definite proposal, preferably in writing, but the
President explained that his enquiry was only tentative: he was
not yet ready to declare himself formally. Stevenson withdrew,

though where he does not mention, perhaps to the offices of the Consulate, which had surprisingly remained intact. In the Carlton Hotel, where the President had moved from his official residence – itself the special target of the enemy artillery – the arguments continued through the night, as Ministers, military leaders and foreign advisers (there really was a Russian general, though he had less influence than was supposed) struggled for agreement. At 3.30 a.m. Stevenson was summoned again. The President had changed his mind: there would be no surrender, but could the evacuation of non-combatants be accelerated?

Regretfully, Stevenson replied that he had already been instructed to tell the President that, from the 15th, the French Navy would be taking over from the British the responsibility of protecting refugee ships. This was a change long sought by the Admiralty, who found it illogical, as well as vexatious, that vessels carrying refugees to France should continue to be escorted by British warships. Indeed, they had hoped that HABANA's voyage on 6 June would be the last occasion on which the services of the Royal Navy would be required.[1] They were disappointed then and they would be again.

President Aguirre, however, was distressed by this news. Would the British Government change their mind, he asked, if he agreed to include in each shipload of refugees some of the Nationalist hostages held in Bilbao? The idea attracted Stevenson, but not the ratio proposed by the President: 50 hostages for every 5,000 refugees escorted by the Royal Navy. In one of the strangest negotiations ever conducted by a Consul – and these two men haggling amid the stale smoke of a commandeered hotel sitting-room were, and would remain, personal friends – Stevenson drove this President of a doomed republic up the scale of human lives until a bargain was finally struck: 250 hostages for every 5,000 refugees and Stevenson would do his best with the British Government.

By the time he had sent his telegram, there was little chance

[1] ADM 116 3516.

for sleep before the morning light renewed the barrage of bombs and shells that was to disturb Bilbao throughout Monday 14 June. At one o'clock that afternoon Stevenson decided that the situation was becoming serious and set off for Arregunega beach, where the submarine cable to Falmouth emerged from the sea. It belonged to the Direct Spanish Telegraph Company, who had a British engineer in charge. To him Stevenson entrusted a telegram calling for a destroyer, the date and time of her arrival being left blank for later insertion, despatch to await Stevenson's final confirmation. Then he returned to his own office, where he found a telegram from the Foreign Office agreeing to continued British naval protection for refugee ships.

This should have been a satisfactory communication for Stevenson to make, but, once again, the President had changed his mind. His Council, Aguirre explained, would not agree to part with their hostages at the very moment of crisis when these might be exploited to best effect. It was a very understandable point of view, but it disgusted Stevenson, who had no use for logic when human lives were at stake. He left in some indignation. On his way out he met Steer and another British journalist – was this when Steer, who has got his dates a little muddled, found him 'well-dressed, peaceful and engagingly friendly'? – and tried vainly to persuade them to leave before the city fell. Then he telephoned – the line, cut twice that day by bombs, had now been repaired – to Mr Rawlings of the telegraph company to send the prepared message. His two Pro-Consuls, Ojanguren and Eguia, refused to accept his advice to accompany him as soon as the destroyer arrived. They were involved (differently: for Eguia, not to be confused with his naval name-sake, was not as politically committed as Ojanguren) in a way that Stevenson was not. Every foreign crisis throws up these distressing dilemmas, when the local employees of British diplomatic or consular missions are torn between conflicting loyalties and interests. In this case they had been offered the chance of escape; they had declined; Stevenson had done all he could; no blame could attach to him. But he is certain to have felt the grief, the guilt, perhaps even the resentment, that only the entirely insensitive avoid on such occasions. It was not a happy night.

Although darkness had long since fallen, the bombs and the shells still descended on Bilbao. Small arms fire could be heard close at hand and the streets were full of deserters and stragglers. They were also filling with the energetic, the logical, the rationally despairing citizens of Bilbao, loading themselves, their families and such of their possessions as they could contrive, onto lorries, onto trawlers, even onto the hitherto immobile destroyers CISCAR and J. L. DIEZ. Those with reason to fear and those without the courage of desperation were preparing to leave a city that was visibly doomed. By the light of the moon, and with their tracer bullets, the enemy's aircraft speeded on the flight.

But there were still resolute men in Bilbao. At one o'clock in the morning of the 15th and again at three, Stevenson telephoned to the President, but on each occasion Aguirre refused to release the hostages. His Council would not agree. Haggard, sleepless, but stubborn, Stevenson thereupon formally refused to ask for further naval protection and announced that he himself would be leaving at dawn. Bilbao might be falling, but there could be no compromise with the principle of humanitarianism. At this last hour, of course, it was a principle only: the Navy had decided to concentrate their resources on the evacuation of British subjects and those refugee ships which got away on the 15th did so unescorted, and would have, whatever Aguirre had answered.[1]

At first light Captain McGrigor picked up Stevenson, and the handful of British subjects who accompanied him, from an open rock-encumbered beach. Only the perfect weather, so he afterwards reported, had made this belated evacuation feasible.[2]

His relief, as the smoky silhouette that marked the mouth of the Nervion receded beneath the after horizon, must have been less alloyed than Stevenson's. McGrigor had done his job, accomplished all he was asked or had intended. Stevenson had

[1] ADM 116 3517.   [2] ADM 116 3517.

left more than a beleaguered city; he had also had to abandon a cause to which he had committed more feeling than was altogether compatible with the coolness of his professional code. To him there must have been little exhilaration in the urgent throb of the engines, a diminished warmth in the June sun, an ambiguous gaiety in the glitter from the Biscayan waves, a certain sadness in the long, white wake that stretched back and back towards the city he would never see again. He, too, had done his duty, but he had hoped to do more and he had left, as the cheerful naval officers about him had not, some of his friends and illusions behind.

Some, but not all. The sympathetic distress of the outsider, the alien participant, exists, but must not be exaggerated. It was in Bilbao, which was not finally occupied by Nationalist troops until the 19th, that the real agonies occurred. And the thousands who escaped across the Bay to Santander – only two of the many craft that made the crossing, according to Steer, were actually captured – had more solid cause for regret than any foreign consul. Only the hostages, for whom Stevenson had striven in vain, could really rejoice. At the last moment, in a sudden spasm of chivalry, the Basques had unconditionally released them. As so often happens when men argue earnestly in moments of crisis, the long debate between Aguirre and Stevenson had made no difference, had been 'full of sound and fury, signifying nothing'.

But the fall of Bilbao was real and at North Stoneham, among the Basque children encamped in the peace and safety of Hampshire, the news detonated an explosion of agony and despair. The children stampeded, had to be rounded up, could not be reassured, had somehow to be quietened and comforted. Their hopes were shattered, their precocious anguish was quickened.[1] It was then that some of them, doubtless encouraged by adults conscious that action can alleviate the pain of sorrow and fear, composed that letter to the Prime Minister or 'to whoever most rules in England' asking for 'some big boat,

[1] Yvonne Cloud, *The Basque Children in England* (Gollancz, 1937), Leah Manning, *A Life for Education* (Gollancz, 1970) and newspapers.

one of those we saw in the sea on our way here' to be sent 'para que defienda a nuestros madres y hermanos y abuelos y enfermos nuestros' (to defend our mothers and brothers and grandfathers and our invalids).[1]

It is not, of course, only children who are helplessly involved in events beyond their ability to control, who must accept a fate that no choice of theirs, no exertion of will or intelligence, could reasonably have been expected to avert. The world of June 1937 held – as the world of today still holds – millions of adult victims who had neither elected to share its convulsions nor been afforded the option of escaping the consequences. The children of North Stoneham were more vulnerable only because the years had hitherto spared some of their illusions, had not taught them that resignation, compromise and reluctant adaptation are part of the human condition. On the contrary, they had been given cause to hope, had seen that rescue was possible: they were in England. All they asked was that some of their families – they knew enough of war's cruel logic not to seek more – might share the deliverance they had themselves experienced.

In some measure their plea was answered. Already on 17 June Eden had told the French Ambassador that, because of the sudden crisis in Bilbao, H.M.G. were continuing to protect refugee ships in spite of the earlier agreement that this task should be taken over by the French Navy. All he now asked was that evacuation from Santander should be a French responsibility.[2] This was to prove as vain a hope as the Admiralty's suggestion, made on the same day, that RESOLUTION might be withdrawn as soon as Bilbao fell.[3]

It was not the children alone who were being sucked along by the tide of events. The earlier decisions of His Majesty's Government had involved them in a situation that was developing and open-ended, in which British intervention – theoretically supposed not to exist at all – constantly threatened to escape from those bounds of time, of place, of political implication,

[1] FO 371 21372.   [2] FO 425 414.   [3] FO 371 21295.

within which Ministers struggled to confine it. As long as there were Republican ports in northern Spain, British merchant vessels to visit them and Spanish warships to attempt interception, the precedent set by Blake on Saint George's Day would continue to produce its consequences. On 22 June, for instance, the Prime Minister – by then Neville Chamberlain – told the House of Commons 'H.M.G. will be prepared to continue protection by British warships to ships carrying Basque women and children to France, provided that the conditions are similar to those in which such protection was given at Bilbao . . .'

This was, of course, a carefully qualified undertaking. Chamberlain went on to point out '. . . the circumstances with regard to the evacuation from Santander are in one respect widely different from those obtaining at Bilbao . . . There is no British Consul to supervise the evacuation and the Santander authorities, who are independent of the Basque Government, have as yet, given no assurances as to impartiality.'

Nevertheless, such were the pressures upon the British Government and the force of the precedents they had piled up around themselves, that this not very impulsive or warm-hearted statesman had to end by saying that the naval authorities had been instructed to continue protecting 'refugee ships, British and other, proceeding to France'.[1]

What neither side in the original British argument had fully foreseen was that the Spanish Nationalist Navy would just go on doing what they had done before. They did not abandon their blockade or stop interfering with unprotected British merchantmen. But nor did they succeed – at least at Santander – in making their blockade fully effective within territorial waters. It was still usually on the high seas that Spanish warships challenged blockade-runners and confronted (in a manner not noticeably sharper or more subdued) the Royal Navy. The original dilemma neither disappeared, nor came to a head in crisis: it persisted, but Blake and Ramsey had made it inescapable by their repeated demonstrations that, beyond the 3 mile

---

[1] Hansard, vol. 325, cols. 1027–8.

limit, Britannia ruled the Biscayan waves. What happened on the high seas to British merchantmen or Spanish refugees would thus be what British Ministers chose should happen and, for the moment at least, they were not ready to be seen as significantly departing from the choices that had earlier been forced on them.

All that summer long, therefore – indeed, well into October – British warships continued to be active on the north coast of Spain, though the protection they afforded to refugees was increasingly concentrated on those carried in British ships. This does not appear to have resulted from any express governmental decision. Chamberlain had promised protection to 'other' ships on 22 June and, on 1 July, Eden specifically said this would apply to HABANA, if she were to take refugees from Santander to Bordeaux.[1] The voyage does not, however, appear to have taken place before 5 July, when H.M. Ambassador at Paris was instructed to ask that HABANA should henceforth be escorted by French warships.[2] On 19 July, nearly a month after Chamberlain's original statement, the House of Commons were told that, since the fall of Bilbao, only British ships had actually been protected by the Royal Navy. Nine of them had sailed from Santander, carrying between them 16,091 refugees.[3]

The protection of British ships, of course, imposed much less of a burden on the Royal Navy, because British ships were only exposed to capture or interception in the vicinity of the Spanish coast, whereas Spanish ships were fair game anywhere and Nationalist warships did actually make captures as far afield as the English Channel and the North Sea. Even in territorial waters, where no ship could expect protection, the consequences of capture would be far less serious for a British ship. It would thus have needed a deliberate effort, an organised plan of evacuation and a regular channel of communication to overcome the various obstacles to the employment of Spanish vessels, under British naval protection, for the transport of refugees. These were conditions scarcely attainable by the authorities in

---

[1] Hansard, vol. 325, col. 1939.   [2] ADM 116 4084.
[3] Hansard, vol. 326, col. 1761.

Santander and Gijón, who lacked the advantages enjoyed by the Basque régime in Bilbao: an efficient administration, the sympathy of British officials (even in the Western Department of the Foreign Office the Basque Government could be described as 'the most innocent of all the participants in the Spanish conflict')[1] and the intermediary influence of Stevenson. Ideology, too, was now more potent than humanitarianism. Many of those who set sail were escaping from both sides and their ability to do so often depended more on their disposable assets than on their age or sex or peril. The merchant vessels which carried them did so as a business venture and were protected because they flew the British flag.

Both these factors were a source of some grievance to British naval officers. All through August the Admiralty received reports of the handsome profits being made by shipowners. Commander James of FEARLESS heard that STANGROVE carried 600 refugees on every voyage and charged them £2 6s a head without food;[2] another officer put the tariff at £3 a head and said 'intercepted wireless messages reveal that large cheques are paid by the owners to the home address of the ship's master when he enters a Spanish port'.[3] An article in *The Observer* of 22 August 1937 remarked that 'with the high freights now obtaining for ordinary merchandise into Spanish ports, two or three voyages suffice to pay for the ship and to leave a substantial margin of profit'. Time charters were said to bring in £1,100 a month.[4] All these figures have to be weighed against Commander James' report that STANGROVE had been sold outright to her present owners for a mere £1,000.[5]

Naval officers whose own pay had been *reduced* by a grateful country some years earlier (a Commander in 1937 was entitled, if he had less than six years' seniority in that rank, to under £2 a day) would have had to be more than human to feel no resentment at their task of protecting such profiteers, most of whom were not even their own countrymen. As Admiral Ramsey pointed out on 3 August: 'Many of the ships have nothing

[1] FO 371 21403.   [2] ADM 116 3518.   [3] ADM 116 3678.
[4] ADM 116 4084.   [5] ADM 116 3518.

British about them except their flag and registration, the Master and entire crew in some cases being foreigners and unable even to speak English.'[1]

More than prejudice, however, was involved. In the face of an active Nationalist blockade, the task of protecting British ships on the high seas, but not in territorial waters, was onerous and demanded constant snap decisions about the distance between a tramp tossing in the anonymous waves and the dimly discernible coast of Spain. One of the most vexing problems, which seemed to require the mature deliberation of lawyers, even of theologians, rather than the necessarily instantaneous judgments of naval officers, concerned the frequent cases in which a British merchantman was challenged by a Spanish warship within territorial waters, but succeeded in escaping to the high seas. The geographical facts alone were sufficiently difficult to establish – navigation was a less precise science in 1937 than it is today – but the legal question – had a British ship supposedly inside territorial waters indicated an intention of surrendering before subsequently crossing the 3 mile limit? – was necessarily a matter for subjective interpretation. On 22 July, for instance, ALMIRANTE CERVERA fired a succession of warning shots across the bows of MACGREGOR, which nevertheless escaped to the high seas and was there protected by KEMPENFELT.[2] A little earlier, however, a similar decision by Captain Sturdee of RESOLUTION concerning the British ship GORDONIA had been judged incorrect by Admiral Ramsey, who had actually apologised to the captain of ALMIRANTE CERVERA, an incident which drew a revealing comment from Chatfield:

I have no doubt that Sturdee made a very doubtful and probably unwise decision about the GORDONIA, but it is very difficult to make a right decision in those circumstances and I hope that when you see him you will tell him that I fully realise the difficulties of his position in having to make an instant decision without being quite clear perhaps as to what had happened. We cannot blame those we put into those positions if they do occasionally make an error of judgment, and I think it is remarkable that (as far as I know) it

[1] ADM 116 3679.   [2] Hansard, vol. 326, col. 2644.

is the first mistake that has been made during the whole time of this Spanish trouble.

I did not really mean Ramsey to go so far as to apologise to the ALMIRANTE CERVERA.[1]

This was the charitable judgment of a professional on an incident which had elicited three differing views from British naval officers. Members of Parliament were less indulgent and the First Lord had to defend Captain McGrigor against opposition insinuations that his successful defence of MAC-GREGOR had been insufficiently forceful.[2] Naval officers had some justification for the cynical view that, whatever they did, someone would pronounce them wrong.

Such encounters between British and Spanish naval vessels were frequent and, even if the growth of an informal understanding about the rights each side was prepared to concede to the other prevented these from developing into serious incidents, there was a perpetual strain and uneasiness in this curious relationship. Admittedly there was a tendency on the British side to minimise the extent of these frictions and to emphasise only the mutual courtesy that obtained between British and Spanish naval officers. Chilton said on 18 August that the Royal Navy had 'succeeded in retaining the liking and respect of both sides' and enclosed a fulsome letter from Caveda to his 'dear friend and companion in arms', Captain McGrigor, to prove his point.[3] When RESOLUTION was finally withdrawn in October, Rear Admiral MacKinnon exchanged cordial messages with ALMIRANTE CERVERA and paid tribute to her captain's willingness to co-operate 'and to accept gracefully my decisions'.[4] Even Chatfield, looking back on those anxious days, remarked that 'Extreme courtesy existed between the Spanish and British sailors, almost as in the days of Nelson.'[5]

The courtesy undoubtedly existed, but it was superficial. The

---

[1] Letter of 12 July 1937 to the Commander-in-Chief Home Fleet quoted from the Chatfield Papers by kind permission of Lady Chatfield and thanks to the helpful courtesy of Professor Temple Patterson.
[2] Hansard, vol. 326, col. 2644.   [3] FO 425 414.
[4] ADM 116 3679.
[5] Lord Chatfield, *It Might Happen Again* (Heinemann, 1947) p. 93.

then Chief of Staff of the Spanish Navy heard from one of ALMIRANTE CERVERA's officers how often his encounters with the Royal Navy had made him wish to die of shame, how the captain used to say, with tears of rage in his eyes, that nothing must be done to worsen relations with England. And, years afterwards, when Admiral Cervera wrote his memoirs, he still remembered the 'bitterness' which, from the very beginning of the war, these 'relations with England' had caused him.[1] Tactically, and in the short term, Rear-Admiral Ramsey had been justified in his comment of 4 June, 'There is no doubt that the knowledge that we have a battleship in the area has a salutary influence on the activities of the Insurgents in regard to our Merchant Vessels';[2] but a price had to be paid for this salutary influence. As the officials of the Foreign Office, Vansittart among them, had pointed out in a series of minutes in mid-May, British actions were widely misrepresented abroad as indicating a desire for 'the triumph of Bolshevism in Spain'.[3] Absurd as such suspicions must seem against a government headed since the beginning of June by Mr Neville Chamberlain (he held his first Cabinet on the 2nd),[4] they were about to receive a seeming confirmation from one of the most curious incidents of this strange episode.

On 27 August, in response to a request from Maisky, the Soviet Ambassador in London, Eden agreed that, if the Soviet Government were to charter a British ship to evacuate Spanish children from Gijón, a particularly 'red' town, that ship would be protected on the high seas by the Royal Navy.[5] Today Maisky's request and Eden's ready agreement seem significant mainly for their reminder of the astonishing revolution that subsequent years have effected in the hierarchy of nations. In 1937, however, there was no cause for surprise that the Soviet Union should seek the shelter of the British flag: everyone, as the Foreign Office and Admiralty constantly complained, was doing that. What then caused astonishment and dismay was

---

[1] Almirante Juan Cervera Valderrama, *Memorias de Guerra* (Editora Nacional, Madrid, 1968), p. 318.   [2] ADM 116 3516.
[3] FO 371 21292.   [4] CAB 23 89.   [5] FO 425 414.

Eden's seeming indifference to the political implications of according this protection. When the Soviet Government did charter the S.S. BRAMDEN and the Admiralty not merely ordered British warships to prevent her interception, but instructed her sailing to be reported, so that the Soviet Embassy might be informed, there was a vigorous protest from the British Chargé d'Affaires at Hendaye. Thompson, who did not usually share Chilton's sympathy for Franco, expressed himself at length on 13 September:

I venture in all earnestness to suggest that we should ask ourselves where we are going. For months we have seen the Royal Navy used to earn handsome profits for shady shipowners who have exploited to the fullest extent the humanitarian feelings of a certain section of our people. Now we are called upon to witness the menacing spectacle of a foreign government known to be deeply interested in the result of the Spanish Civil War taking a hand under the shadow of the Red and White ensigns. I find it hard to believe that the Soviet [sic] who have been shooting political opponents without mercy for months are really deeply concerned about the children of Gijón.[1]

His indignation was endorsed by Rear-Admiral Mackinnon and other naval officers on the spot, but it was later to be matched by that of Mr Wedgwood Benn, who accused the British Government of condemning the Royal Navy to the rôle of callously indifferent spectators on the occasion of the final fall of Gijón. According to Mr Benn there were thousands of refugees frantic to escape; there were British merchantmen waiting outside the 3 mile limit to take them aboard; there were British warships ready to afford protection on the high seas. But inside territorial waters there were General Franco's warships – evidently, though Mr Benn did not say so, making their blockade effective at last – and the refugees could not reach their rescuers. Mr Benn and his colleagues on the opposition benches thought that the Royal Navy should have intervened and were not in the least satisfied by the First Lord's argument that a line had to be drawn somewhere and that this had been done at the 3 mile limit.[2]

[1] ADM 116 3678.   [2] Hansard, vol. 328, cols. 57–75.

Mr Duff Cooper had a good case, but Mr Benn had a harrowing tale of human suffering to relate. Both, perhaps, were on stronger ground than either the Chargé d'Affaires or the Admiral when, in September, they had predicted dire results once news of the arrangement with the Russians reached the ears of General Franco. Thompson and Mackinnon may have been a little oblivious of the extent to which earlier British actions had already been misinterpreted, but Sir George Mounsey, at least, must have regarded the incident as justifying the worst of the forebodings which from the very outset, he had consistently expressed. In fact there seem to have been no extraordinary repercussions and, after this remarkable climax, British naval activities off northern Spain gradually diminished until the capture of Gijón on 21 October finally relieved the Admiralty and Foreign Office of this particular form of embarrassment. A hundred thousand refugees had escaped to France (89,000 of them under the protection of the Royal Navy), but no more would now leave a coast held from end to end by Nationalist forces.[1]

Events, emotions and the unexpected impact of some rather dubious arguments had conspired to divert the British Government and the Royal Navy from their chosen path of Non-Intervention. It was now less than ever likely that the end of the Civil War would fulfil the surprising prediction once advanced to support that always illusory, because unrealisable, policy: 'this country may hope to regain her influence in Spain and to be remembered with gratitude for her impartiality and for the respect she has shown for Spanish independence'.[2]

But the Bay of Biscay, at least, would no longer trouble British relations with the winning side in Spain and it would not be long before optimism broke out afresh in Downing Street. On 10 December 1937, for instance, the Foreign Office informed the Cabinet that the successful completion of arrangements for the evacuation of Nationalist supporters who had taken refuge in diplomatic missions in Madrid and Valencia 'has gone a

[1] Hansard, vol. 328, cols. 57–75.
[2] Memorandum prepared for Imperial Conference. FO 371 21296.

long way towards removing the mistaken impression prevalent in insurgent territory, ever since the evacuations from Bilbao, that the humanitarian activities of H.M.G. were confined to the relief of supporters of the Spanish Government'.[1]

It was, indeed, a mistaken impression, as the preceding account of British activities has amply demonstrated, but the motives, and tactics, of British ministers, officials, diplomats and naval officers had always been sufficiently mixed to warrant the widest variety of misinterpretation. Stevenson alone had been consistent in the application of his peculiar principles, but there is no evidence to suggest that he had ever entertained any illusion that these would be understood or appreciated. He had done what he believed to be right: others, as the Basque children in England were soon to discover, were equally, and perhaps no less justifiably, exercised by what was expedient.

[1] CAB 24 273.

CHAPTER 12

Ebb tide

Have you your return-ticket?[1]

It had always been assumed, of course, that the children would soon be able to return to Bilbao. Even Leah Manning, when she spoke of keeping them in England 'until Franco is defeated',[2] probably thought she was setting an early, if still uncertain, date for their repatriation. But the Marquess of Dufferin and Ava was perhaps a little quick off the mark, a fraction more explicit than was entirely hospitable, in telling the House of Lords on 25 May – the very day *The Times* published President Aguirre's thanks for 'the wonderfully generous welcome accorded to our children' – that 'the presence of these children, as we hope, will be short and of temporary duration'.[3] He was undoubtedly expressing the views of the Government to which he belonged, but the retrospective reader can scarcely escape a twinge of regret, almost of embarrassment, at the chilling clarity of his words.

The Noble Lord was, after all, talking about children and he was only the first of many whose tone of voice, or turn of phrase, would sometimes seem lacking in the indulgence which convention accords to this particular category of victims. As the months passed there developed something of a gap between the attitudes of those involved in meeting the children's daily needs and those to whom they constituted a 'problem' or, worse still, an 'issue'. The latter were not confined to a single political party or trend. Those wishing to repatriate the children to demonstrate their confidence in General Franco were sometimes

---

[1] The words of welcome prescribed for use by British Immigration officials when greeting foreign visitors.
[2] Leah Manning, *A Life for Education* (Gollancz, 1970).
[3] Hansard (Lords), 1937, vol. 105, col. 230.

answered by others reluctant to lose such useful sticks for beating him. It is not difficult, as one turns the dusty pages of Hansard, to guess which ingenious questioner was concerned with political pawns and who actually cared about human beings.

Even on the surface of debate, however, those who argued that the children would be happier with their parents now seem to deserve more sympathy than Members – or Peers – agitated by the threat these children posed to the health or the safety of the British people. On 7 June, for instance, the House of Commons were told that five cases of typhoid, two of diphtheria and two of measles had been diagnosed among the children.[1] This produced a crop of anxious questions on the 10th and a well deserved rebuke from Mr Davidson: 'Would the Minister arrange for a supply of tabloids to the Members opposite who are afraid of infection?'[2]

An even more remarkable intervention was that of Sir T. Moore who, on 28 July, asked the Home Secretary to send the children back to Spain 'in view of the repeated attacks made on British citizens'. Mr Lloyd, who answered for the Government, was commendably dismissive of these exaggerated rumours,[3] but they had earlier engaged the attention of the Cabinet, whom the Home Secretary had informed on 14 July, when announcing his rejection of requests to receive more children, 'that reports on the Spanish refugees were not of a favourable character'.[4] There had, indeed, been various minor incidents, of a kind not altogether unexpected from children separated from their parents and congregated, in circumstances of extreme emotional tension, among strangers whose language and customs were unfamiliar. The indignant reactions of British politicians ought, however, to be weighed against the following anecdote, for which the author is indebted to one of the children.

Marcel Segurola, who was a little more than twelve when he embarked on HABANA, came from an inland village in the province of Guipúzcoa, so that, in May 1937, his family were

---

[1] Hansard, vol. 324, col. 1413.   [2] Hansard, vol. 324, cols. 1949–50.
[3] Hansard, vol. 326, cols. 3126–7.   [4] CAB 23 89.

already refugees in Bilbao itself. For this same reason, and unlike most of his fellow-passengers, he spoke Basque and had largely to learn Spanish after his arrival in England. He spent some three weeks in the camp at North Stoneham and was then transferred to a farm at Baydon in Wiltshire, where three huts had been erected for about a hundred children. In October he moved again, this time to the relative luxury of a recently bankrupt hotel at Bray, close to the Thames. It was here that a group of Basque children out for a walk encountered a party of English school-children who, from the obscure motives that prompt young boys, greeted them with shouts of 'Franco'. A fight ensued in which the Basques seem to have had the upper hand. That evening the police arrived at the hotel, accompanied by some injured English boys and their aggrieved parents. A parade was held, some of the Basque culprits were identified and arrests seemed inevitable, when one of the older boys, who spoke good English, stepped forward and made a speech. He explained why and how they had come to England, the circumstances in which they had left their parents and their reasons for reacting with emotional violence to the cries of 'Franco'.

The impact of his words might have surprised Sir T. Moore: the young English victims of assault burst into tears, their parents withdrew the charges and the police departed without their prisoners.[1]

These skirmishes were occasionally a little more serious. At Scarborough, where eighty boys were sent, a dispute took place about the food. In an impulsive reaction, which anyone starved at a British boarding school can only envy and admire, the Basques drew their knives and chased the cook out of the camp. Knives, however, are alien and alarming and some of the ring-leaders had to be transferred to Brechfa, in Wales. Even here the boys did not feel altogether at home: they started holding up motorists to demand money and cigarettes; cars and other property were damaged; finally, in response to local protests, there was a concerted raid on the village. Sterner measures were

---

[1] Information supplied to the author in 1970 by Marcel Segurola (henceforth Segurola).

required and fifteen particularly ill-behaved boys were actually deported.

Similar events took place among the Spanish children in France, where twenty-one children had to be deported after a riot in the camp at Saint-Cloud. But too much was made of relatively isolated incidents among the children scattered the length and breadth of England (only 500 were left in the original camp at North Stoneham by mid-August). The *Times* correspondent who carried out a survey of the problem summed it up neatly: 'the high-pitched whirr of axe-grinding which has been the accompaniment of the Basque children's career in this country has drowned the still, small voice of truth'.[1] And complaints of disorderly conduct only blurred the two issues of fundamental importance to the children, not that they were fully aware of them at the time: was it safe for them to go back to Spain and what were the obligations of the British Government? Arguments concerning both began early and continued long.

On 5 July 1937, for instance, the Foreign Office sought Chilton's views on the prospects for repatriation, but their enquiry crossed a telegram from the Ambassador reporting that a number of anxious and, in some cases, disgruntled citizens of Bilbao were already demanding the return of their children.[2] Were these requests genuine, representative and evidence that all the children could now return without fear of persecution or reprisal? On the 8th Chilton was still cautious: 'Bilbao will soon be sufficiently normal to permit of these young refugees returning.' Mrs Manning did not believe this,[3] but, in the House of Lords, no doubts assailed Lord Newton.[4]

In Bilbao itself, Mr Pears, the British business-man who had been Pro-Consul but, because of the sympathy of his wife's family for Franco, had preferred to leave for Hendaye, returned

---

[1] *The Times*, 11 August and 20 August 1937.
[2] FO 371 21372. But, two months later, the Secretary of the Basque Children's Committee (an offshoot of the National Joint Committee) wrote to *The Times* (6 September) to say that only thirty-nine requests had been received from parents for the return of their children.
[3] FO 371 21372.   [4] Hansard (Lords), vol. 106, cols. 223–34.

to the city on 29 June 1937. He reported the Consulate as intact, but for a few broken windows, and in the charge of his fellow Pro-Consul, Mr Eguia. Pears was given a cordial welcome by the local authorities and recommended the early appointment of a career consul[1] (it had already been decided in London that Stevenson's return would be unacceptable to the new régime). There was still some uncertainty at this period. A French journalist commented 'ce qui nous frappait le plus, c'était le nombre inoui de Boinas rouges qu'on rencontrait dans les rues. Les requetés [the Navarrese militia in General Franco's service] en avaient amené de pleins camions. Sans leur demander leur avis ni leurs opinions ils coiffaient de ces bérets tous les passants . . .'[2]

This picture of the Right contenting themselves with the imposition of paradoxically red berets on the Left was not inconsistent with the despatch of 3 July from Acting Vice-Consul Pears, which laid much more emphasis on 'red' atrocities during the period of Basque autonomy than on the mere 27 executions since the entry of General Franco's forces.[3] But the National Joint Committee, who regarded themselves – and were so regarded by the British Government – as responsible for the children, wanted to make sure. On 14 September 1937 they wrote to the Foreign Office asking whether two representatives of the Committee might visit Bilbao to ascertain whether or not it would be safe for the children to return. Thompson, then Chargé d'Affaires at Hendaye, made enquiries of General Franco's administration on the 16th, but had received no reply by the 30th and expected that any answer would be unfavourable.[4] The National Joint Committee were, after all, regarded by General Franco's supporters as politically motivated and Communist inspired. Even in London, Cardinal Hinsley, the Catholic Archbishop of Westminster, had told the Foreign Office on 17 August that he had always been opposed to the

[1] FO 369 2475. It later turned out that the Franco authorities were not prepared to give Pears full recognition as Vice-Consul before they were permitted representation in England. *The Times*, 10 July 1937.
[2] Georges Oudard, *Chemises Noires Brunes Vertes en Espagne* (Librairie Plon, Paris, 1938).   [3] FO 425 414.   [4] FO 371 21375.

children's evacuation, which 'took place from motives of a political nature'.[1]

His views were reflected within the National Joint Committee itself, whose Catholic members accepted the reassuring reports received from the Apostolic Delegate in Bilbao, while others wanted to be certain that the children would actually be reunited with their parents and not placed in orphanages for re-education as Fascists. Their spokesman was the Duchess of Atholl, who wrote a long letter to Eden on 2 October, in which (admirers of Nancy Mitford's *Love in a Cold Climate* will be pleased to note) she referred to her husband as 'Atholl'.[2]

Although these particular apprehensions fortunately proved to be unfounded, it was true enough that normality had yet to return to Bilbao, where Pears, still Acting Vice-Consul, painted a sombre picture in his report of 6 October of: '. . . the heavy hand of military justice overshadowing the inhabitants. The prisons are filled to overflowing with political offenders . . . estimates of the total shootings effected at Bilbao since its capture by General Franco vary between a minimum of 300 and a maximum of 1,000.'

In typically British fashion he deplored as characteristically Spanish 'this spirit of vengeance'.[3] It is scarcely surprising that the formation – by the Duke of Wellington at the request of General Franco's representative in London – of a Basque Children Repatriation Committee[4] attracted adverse comment in the columns of the *New Statesman*.[5] Nevertheless, there were parents asking for their children back, some weight had to be given to the assurances of the Apostolic Delegate and the National Joint Committee were short of funds. By the end of October 1937 the process of repatriation began with some 800 children.[6]

One of the first parties to make the return journey left Victoria Station at ten o'clock on the morning of 12 November.

---

[1] FO 371 21374.   [2] FO 371 21377.   [3] FO 425 414.
[4] FO 371 21376.   [5] *New Statesman and Nation*, 19 February 1938.
[6] Arnold J. Toynbee, *Survey of International Affairs 1937*, vol. 2 (R.I.I.A. and O.U.P., 1938), p. 393.

There were 160 children and they travelled via Newhaven and Dieppe to the Franco–Spanish frontier at Irún and thence to Bilbao. As usual the health of the children was in the forefront of British preoccupations and the party was accompanied by two doctors: the formidably qualified Dame Janet Campbell, who had been a Medical Officer of Health before serving various government departments as adviser on such varied subjects as liquor control, maternity and child welfare; and Dr Norman White. Dame Janet, who had retired from government service three years before, was also a Justice of the Peace, so every contingency was covered, but her greatest asset may have been her freedom, as a former civil servant, from the kind of political associations that made most members of the National Joint Committee unacceptable to the new régime in Bilbao.

The Duchess of Atholl, for her part, profited by the occasion to hold a press conference and to appeal for more funds for the maintenance of the children still in England. She explained that 140 of the children were returning at the request of their parents, but *The Times*, from which the foregoing account is taken, did not record any reasons she may have given for the departure of the remaining twenty. Could these, too, have been boys whose behaviour had made their continued presence in England undesirable?

Her Grace spoke, on this occasion, on behalf of the National Joint Committee for Spanish Relief, an organisation which seems to have been much the same as the Basque Children's Committee, from which Canon Craven had resigned on 15 October because of disagreement over the procedures for repatriating children. Certainly, by this time, the two bodies shared the same three Honorary Secretaries: Captain Macnamara, Mr Wilfrid Roberts and Mr David Grenfell, who were respectively, Conservative, Liberal and Labour Members of Parliament.

The Committee's decision had the full approval of the British Government. On 4 November the Home Secretary told the House of Commons: 'my own view is that the sooner the children go back to their families the better'.[1] Their only com-

---

[1] Hansard, vol. 328, col. 1112.

plaint was that the process was not fast enough and the Cabinet, on 15 December, endorsed the Prime Minister's view that 'everything possible should be done with a view to the repatriation of the Basque children'.[1] They were not alone in these views. After the French Government had unsuccessfully sought British financial assistance in the maintenance of their Spanish refugees (the Ambassador told the Foreign Office on 23 July 1937 that 30,000 of them were costing the French Government 10 francs a head per day), they announced on 14 September their intention of evacuating all refugees who were a charge on public funds.[2] In England, of course, the children received no financial assistance from the Government. This was a grievance to the National Joint Committee and a source of great practical difficulty, but it strengthened their position. As long as they had funds to maintain the children they wanted to keep it was difficult for the Government actually to expel these young refugees.

Fortunately the Spaniards, usually more indulgent than the English to children, showed no disposition to visit upon them the political sins of their fathers and, as more and more encouraging reports came in, the Committee were able to accelerate the process of repatriation. The Foreign Office followed the results carefully. Miss McClintock, who had accompanied a party to Bilbao and who was herself of Spanish origin, called on 3 January 1938 to report her satisfaction: food was plentiful, the local authorities were helpful, there had been no reprisals against children and no restriction had been placed on her interviewing parents privately in their own homes.[3] Graham, the new Consul at Bilbao, was equally reassuring in his report of 4 February.[4]

The only trouble, as the National Joint Committee explained to the Foreign Office on the same date, was that the 2,500 children still on their hands fell into three roughly equal categories: those whose parents, though known to be in Bilbao, had not asked for their return; those whose return had been declined

[1] CAB 29 90. [2] FO 371 21376.
[3] FO 371 22603. [4] FO 371 22604.

by a parent on the grounds that he was himself a refugee; and those with parents whose fate was unknown.[1]

Marcel Segurola, then still at Bray, was in the second category. His parents and his two brothers – one just too young, the other just too old for HABANA's voyage to England – had fled from Bilbao, before it fell, to Santander. When that town, too, was on the point of capture, they had made their way to France and thence to Barcelona. Four times refugees and – Marcel's father having learnt political foresight in the sad school of experience – uneasily conscious that their wanderings might be resumed, they had no desire to snatch Marcel away from the peace and safety of England to share their hardships and their uncertain fate.[2]

These were considerations which the nagging questioners in the House of Commons preferred to ignore. Month after month they demanded to know when the children would be gone. In April 1938 the Home Secretary was able to announce that 1,722 had left,[3] in July the figure had risen to 2,006,[4] by June 1939 only 1,100 remained.[5] To some extent this progress reflected the return of more normal conditions in Bilbao (only a handful of children joined their parents in Republican territory) but it was also hastened by the Committee's financial difficulties. In March 1938, for instance, they had begun sending children back even before their parents had asked for them.[6] They still tried to make sure that there were parents to receive the child, but, understandably enough, with varying degrees of success. Segurola, who remembers some of these departures, never heard of a serious lapse. Mr Bautista Lopez, on the other hand, remembers[7] an organised protest among his section of the children because one of their number (a leading member of the football team) had been sent back to Bilbao only to discover, on his arrival, that his father was dead. In all probability much depended on the individual zeal and efficiency of those in charge of each particular group of children. If they insisted on thorough

[1] FO 371 22606. [2] Segurola. [3] FO 371 22607.
[4] FO 371 22611. [5] FO 371 24148. [6] FO 371 22606.
[7] Information given to the author in 1971 by Mr Bautista Lopez (henceforth Lopez).

investigation, this would be done. If not, financial realism might lead to a degree of wishful thinking within the Joint Committee itself.

It was in this same month of March 1938 that the Consul at Bilbao was able to report the remarkable reception accorded to one party of repatriated Basque children. Señor Carrillo, President of the Junta Provincial de Protección de Menores, had made them a speech of welcome, in which he congratulated them on their good behaviour during the journey and remarked that children returning from England were always superior, both in physique and in conduct, to those from other countries. He asked the Consulate to convey his thanks to the National Joint Committee and called on the children for three cheers, both for Spain and for England.[1] Thus did Spanish courtesy, chivalry and courage – for Señor Carrillo's position was semi-official and he must have been well aware of the view taken by General Franco's administration of the National Joint Committee – offer some compensation for the sneers and snarls of the committee's British critics.

His thanks were also directed to the right address, for the British Government's assistance to the children had ended when FEARLESS parted company with HABANA at the Needles. Even the tents the Army provided for the camp at North Stoneham had, as a tactless question by Harold Nicolson revealed, to be paid for by the National Joint Committee. This did not prevent the Cabinet, on 6 April 1938, including the fact that some of these tents were still on loan among their excuses for refusing financial assistance to Spanish refugees.[2] Their attitude was, of course, consistent. It had repeatedly been stated before any of the children ever left Bilbao; it was amplified soon after their arrival in England: 'As financial responsibility for the Spanish refugee children has been undertaken by a number of voluntary bodies, my right hon. Friend is not prepared to sanction expenditure on their maintenance by local authorities from public funds.'[3]

[1] FO 371 22607.   [2] CAB 23 93.
[3] Hansard, vol. 324, col. 667.

That was Mr Bernays answering on behalf of the Minister of Health, but the denial of assistance knew no departmental boundaries. It was most felt by the children in the field of education. Admittedly a special effort – and special expenditure – would probably have been needed to accommodate these children in ordinary English schools. Although many of them learned English, their command of the language and their educational background were not easily reconciled with the ordinary curriculum. This effort was seldom made. Instead, Marcel Segurola remembers, the younger children at Bray were given elementary lessons, in Spanish, by the teachers and assistants who had accompanied them on the journey from Bilbao. For the older children, including Marcel himself, then thirteen, no systematic education was available. Much of their time, admittedly, was devoted to the domestic chores inseparable from their maintenance and that of their younger companions. But these duties neither filled the day, nor provided a satisfying outlet for youthful energies. Perhaps some of those officials, at once so careful to prohibit expenditure from public funds and so censorious of childish unruliness, should have recalled the well-known lines of Isaac Watts:

> For Satan finds some mischief still
> For idle hands to do.[1]

These older children did, however, receive sporadic lessons, mainly in the English language, from a succession of English volunteers, a practice which *The Times*, in a survey published on 11 August 1937, found to be fairly common in other parts of the country as well. These teachers came and went unpredictably. Many of them, so Segurola remembers, seemed to be sympathisers with the Republican cause, who were as much concerned to improve their own Spanish as to impart instruction. At least one who disappeared without notice was later reported as fighting with the International Brigade in Spain.[2]

Bautista Lopez has similar memories, but his circumstances were odder and less comfortable. He had been sent from North

---

[1] Isaac Watts, *Divine Songs for Children.*   [2] Segurola.

Stoneham to another camp in the depths of the Norfolk countryside, not many miles from Diss. Here they were caught by the autumn rains and, flooded out, had to seek temporary shelter in the church hall of a neighbouring village, where they pulled down the curtains from the windows to serve as blankets. Eventually they found more permanent lodging in a large, disused house (Rollesby Rectory) which they had themselves to put in order. Once again it was very remote and Lopez believes that his group of boys, being regarded as politically active, were deliberately accommodated as far as possible from inhabited places. Certainly his companions were politically conscious: they had an elaborate system of self-government, electing delegates (who were recognised as such by their British guardians and paid threepence a day for discharging their duties). The boys also appointed their own tribunals to maintain order and regulate disputes.[1]

The children – and the finances of the National Joint Committee (which had to make a further appeal for funds on 31 March 1938) – lived from hand to mouth. Groups of them were organised to sing and dance – and raised money by their performances. Collections were taken after football matches between teams of Basque boys and those of local English schools. These earnings supplemented the contributions of the charitable – or the political. The children were fed and accommodated, but they were neither educated nor employed. One of the reasons for the attitude – otherwise paradoxically counter-productive – adopted by the British Government emerges from the reports of July and December 1939, by the Cabinet Committee on Refugee Problems, of which Mr Malcolm Macdonald was Chairman. These reports pointed out that there were, altogether, 50,000 refugees in the United Kingdom. These must on no account, so the Committee argued, be allowed to become a permanent charge upon public funds. Not only were their absolute numbers, and the consequential expense, large, but the total of unemployed and otherwise

[1] Lopez.

distressed British subjects was considerably larger. Yet anything done for the refugees could scarcely be denied to British subjects.[1]

The harsh syllogism that resulted was not drawn by Ministers and officials alone. As early as 24 May 1937, the day after the children arrived, an otherwise sympathetic leading article in the *Daily Herald*, the organ of the Labour Party, made the point that the children of British unemployed workers had as much to suffer as these refugees from Bilbao and were more numerous. There is in the English character a tendency to combine cheeseparing and chauvinism that has always been a little puzzling to the Scots. Nevertheless it must, in all fairness, be recalled that, in September 1937, there were over 1,300,000 unemployed in the United Kingdom[2] and even the ardent Mrs Manning remarked that the *per capita* expenditure on Basque children was higher than the official allowance for the children of the British workless.[3] Dame Leah's argument that the British Government were unreasonable in demanding that the Committee should guarantee ten shillings a week for the maintenance of each child is not, however, borne out by *The Times* survey previously quoted. Their correspondent reckoned that, when overheads were included, this figure was often reached in practice. The conclusion, however, is inescapable: these refugees had been rescued by a stronger Navy, they had come to a more hospitable country, but they found themselves in a harsher environment than the Britain of 1970.

Throughout their stay, moreover, the political climate was changing to the children's disadvantage. When they sailed, on 20 May 1937, it was still possible for optimistic British sympathisers to suppose that Bilbao would hold out, as Madrid had. When the first children returned in October 1937, all northern Spain had fallen to the Nationalists, but there was a military stale-mate elsewhere and a Basque government in exile in Barcelona. The survival of Republican Spain and the possibility

[1] CAB 67 3.
[2] Butler and Freeman, *British Political Facts 1900–1968* (Macmillan, 1969).
[3] Manning, *A Life for Education*, p. 127.

of the children returning to its territory were still not inconceivable. By the end of March 1938, however, when the National
Joint Committee appealed for more funds, the Nationalists
were sweeping forward in Aragón, and Barcelona, already
threatened, had repeatedly been bombed. A fortnight later
the Nationalists reached the Mediterranean and Republican
territory was cut in two. The children now belonged all too
obviously in the camp of the defeated: they were an irritant to
the victors, an obstacle to the future of Anglo–Spanish relations.
Even the Republican successes of that summer suggested at
most the possibility of a negotiated peace. And that respite was
short-lived. The Nationalist advance was resumed in November
1938; Barcelona fell in January 1939; the French frontier was
reached in February and the Republican leaders began to sue for
peace. By the end of that month both Britain and France had
recognised the Nationalists as the Government of Spain; by the
end of March the last convulsions of Republican resistance had
finally subsided. The war was over and had left the children
behind.

Yet, when every allowance has been made for the climate of
the times, and every excuse explored for the grudging tolera-
tion of the British Government, there remains one awkward
statistic. Altogether, as Stevenson reported at the time, 3,805
children, 99 female teachers, 120 attendants and 15 priests made
the voyage from Bilbao to Southampton aboard HABANA.[1]
There were no other organised evacuations to England from
Bilbao and, although a steady trickle of Spanish refugees
reached England by various routes, their numbers were never
significant. The total of all refugees, whatever their nationality
or origin, in the United Kingdom in 1939 was, as we have
already seen, only 50,000,[2] or a little more than one tenth of
1% of the indigenous population. In France there were,
according to the International Commission for the Assistance
of Child Refugees, 250,000 – not refugees, not even Spanish
refugees, but only Spanish women and children – in April 1939.[3]

---

[1] FO 371 21371.   [2] CAB 67 3.   [3] FO 371 24137.

This is not a comparison which reflects much credit either on self-congratulatory British sympathisers with the Republican cause or on those Members of Parliament who bewailed the burden that this handful of children had imposed on the British body public. Once again the cool analysis of K. W. Watkins is an indispensable corrective to the more romantic illusions which other writers have propagated about this period.[1] Although the Spanish Civil War may have engendered more personal involvement and more constructive action in Britain than did, thirty years later, the war in Vietnam, the ratio of eloquence to effort was much the same in both cases. Nor, alas, was this a phenomenon which affected Spaniards alone. *The Times* of 14 June 1939 reported the official admission that only 29,000 refugees from Germany had been allowed into Britain during the six years between 1933 and 1939.

It is, however, an interesting indication of the widespread diffusion of ideological prejudice in the thirties, that the presence in England of this dwindling number of Basque children should have continued to command so much attention, even to excite actual animosity, among the officials of a Government whose avowed policy of Non-Intervention was interpreted to exclude assistance in their maintenance, but not opposition to their presence. In June 1939, for instance, Mr Walter Roberts, Head of the League of Nations and Western Department in the Foreign Office, had for some time been engaged in correspondence with the Home Office, whom he considered insufficiently ready to co-operate with General Franco's Representative in speeding the repatriation of the 1,100 children still remaining in the United Kingdom. Mr Roberts conceded that the parents of these children were either refugees themselves or else of unknown whereabouts. These misfortunes, however, scarcely seemed to him to constitute any obstacle to the children's repatriation. The siege of Bilbao was long over and they would be well looked after in Spain. Sending them back, moreover, would please General Franco's Representative, who was for

---

[1] K. W. Watkins, *Britain Divided* (Nelson, 1963), passim.

ever pestering the Foreign Office on the subject. He, incidentally, was the Duke of Alba; it was the destiny of the children, for good or ill, to preoccupy those of ducal rank: Alba, Atholl, Wellington. Even the Duke of Norfolk was impelled to write to *The Times* on 5 July 1937.

Finding the Home Office recalcitrant, Mr Roberts devised a new argument on 16 June 1939: 'Finally, as there exists evidence that some at least of the children are being educated in communist and atheist doctrines, it seems undesirable that the government of a country which maintains an established Christian Church should do nothing to bring such a state of affairs to an end.'

This remarkable letter – it was in the old official form, becoming rare even then – was approved by Sir George Mounsey and by the Parliamentary Under-Secretary of State, Mr R. A. Butler. A singular feature is that the so-called 'evidence' is specified neither in the draft nor in the minutes. Careful perusal of the file, however, reveals a letter written by a British subject to the Duke of Alba and forwarded by the latter to the Foreign Office. The allegations of the Duke's correspondent seem to constitute the evidence.[1] The Western Department, with the single exception of Montague Pollock's uncharacteristic tribute to the Basques (see Chapter 9) had managed to keep very cool heads – or hearts – throughout the entire course of the children's adventures. None of their minutes, incidentally, were more careful, more non-committal, more cautiously adherent to official policy, than those of the member of the Third Room particularly concerned with Spain (what the jargon of today would term the 'desk-officer'). His rôle there was self-effacing. Not for many years would an evil notoriety invest the name of D. D. Maclean. Against this background it is scarcely worth remarking that, in this same month of June 1939, H.M. Consul at Bilbao had reported an acute shortage of food throughout his Consular district, where the ration of meat was issued twice a week and, though few workers could afford it,

---

[1] FO 371 24148.

had to be queued for from three in the morning. Bread, the staple food, was brown and mostly stale.[1]

The Home Office, curiously enough, do not seem to have been particularly impressed and, in spite of this outburst, both they and the Foreign Office remained reluctant intermediaries in the ensuing correspondence between the Duke of Alba and the National Joint Committee, each deeply suspicious of the other's good faith. It took the altered circumstances produced by the outbreak of the Second World War to bring a really significant fall in the number of children remaining in England. When, on 6 September, the Duke of Alba proposed to the Foreign Office the repatriation of all Spanish children whose parents had not specifically objected,[2] it was possible to argue that the original motive of their evacuation – danger from aerial bombardment – should now prompt their return.

In fact a number did go, though some went to Mexico[3] (where Sir Richard Rees witnessed the arrival of the first contingent – there were Spanish refugees from other countries as well – on behalf of the National Joint Committee)[4] and a couple of hundred stayed in England. One of them was Marcel Segurola. The colony of children at Bray had broken up in July 1939, probably because of shortage of funds, and Dr Ellis, a staunch friend of the children ever since he had gone to Bilbao to carry out the first of their many medical inspections, had managed to get the rest of the Segurola family over to England. They were lucky indeed, for their wanderings had taken them from Barcelona back to France[5] and the generosity originally shown by the French towards Spanish refugees was not sustained after the collapse of the Republican cause. And the plight of those still stranded in France when that country was overtaken by the débâcle of 1940 was miserable. Their exiled President even preferred the desperate expedient of escaping, disguised as a South American neutral, to Germany,

---

[1] FO 371 24138.   [2] FO 371 24148.
[3] Manning, *A Life for Education*, p. 133.
[4] *The Times*, 22 June 1939.   [5] Segurola.

but few of his compatriots had his audacity, his resources or his contacts.[1]

The Segurola family then settled in a cottage in Suffolk, which belonged to a Dr Griffiths. The parents ran the house, which accommodated six Basque children, and some of the boys worked for neighbouring farmers, their earnings helping to maintain the little colony. By one of the ironical consequences of official British policy, their employment was actually illegal, foreigners not being allowed to compete for jobs with the army of British workless. But the outbreak of war, which the Duke of Alba had found so compelling a reason for repatriating such children as remained, was actually to prove their salvation. Before long there was work for all in Britain, without distinction of nationality, and Segurola was soon employed by English Electric in the Midlands. Altogether in this area there were some fifty Basque children and, at week-ends, they used to congregate at the house of a prosperous English sympathiser.[2] Did they sometimes reflect, as they relaxed in the luxury of gossiping in their own tongue about the eccentricities of their English hosts, that it had taken the fall of German bombs to complete the welcome which, years before, the descent of similar bombs upon Bilbao had somewhat grudgingly extorted?

[1] José Antonio Aguirre y Lecube, *De Guernica a Nueva York, Pasendo por Berlín* (Editorial Ekin, Buenos Aires).   [2] Segurola.

CHAPTER 13

Peterkin's question

'But what good came of it at last?'
Quoth little Peterkin.
'Why, that I cannot tell,' said he,
'But 't was a famous victory.'
                              Southey[1]

Peterkin's question is fissionable: it is a living cell that divides and multiplies beneath our scrutiny. However we restrict our assumptions, even if we arbitrarily select only three main lines of enquiry, each will display its own ramifications. Supposing we begin, as indicated at the outset, by considering whether the British Government achieved their objectives, we must first ask which of the many conflicting purposes pursued by British Ministers and officials represented the essential core of British policy. Having identified this and measured the results, we must then compare these with the cost and side-effects of their attainment. This will lead naturally to the second line of questioning: were the methods adopted the most appropriate or could the desired results have been more economically reached by other means? This enquiry could so easily expand into the consideration of innumerable hypotheses that it must be rigidly constrained: did warships provide a necessary and useful reinforcement of diplomatic representations?

Peterkin, however, would scarcely have been content with the aridity of political judgments or the abstract analysis of diplomatic techniques. Our story concerns children and it can not be completed without some indication of the repercussions on their adult lives. Did they, or did they not, have reason to be grateful for the efforts made on their account, if not always on their behalf? And what happened to the other characters involved,

[1] Robert Southey, 'The Battle of Blenheim'.

by chance or their own intention, in the saga of the children? Did they live happily ever afterwards?

This must be the subject of a further chapter, leaving to this one the comparison of intention and result and the analysis of technique.

The first is perhaps the most difficult task. Twelve chapters have so emphasised the conflicting motives of British politicians and officials, their disputes about facts and interpretation, the twists and turns of British policy, the extent to which one objective emerged from the collapse of arguments intended to support another, that it may now seem impossible to tease out from this tangled skein any single and illuminating thread of purpose.

This is partly because we have hitherto taken so close and detailed a view of our subject. Anyone who has examined a ship's course recorder graph will have observed the incessant zig-zags that denote the quartermaster's responses to the inconstant pressures of wind and wave. But the chart will bear a smooth, undeviating line pencilled across the breadth of the ocean. Unless, that is, navigational hazards have demanded actual alterations of course or, as in this case, the bridge has echoed with the conflicting orders of officers arguing among themselves as they peer into the fog that obscures their vision. Even then, if we stand back and take the oceanic view, there will emerge, perhaps not an unbroken track, but a series of curves that do not transcend certain bounds, that lead, however deviously, from one point to another.

British policy during the incidents described is best envisaged as a succession of adaptations to the exigencies of a developing situation. But its turns and twists were not entirely, even mainly, the fortuitous outcome of circumstances or of personal confrontations. There were always certain constraints, limits in either direction, which were no less real for being vaguely defined and susceptible of diverse interpretation. In terms of people we may see Eden as representing one school of thought, Chatfield as defending another. Yet the objectives of each were only divergent outcrops of the same common ground. The differences within the British Government and their administrative apparatus were always far smaller than those dividing them from their domestic, their foreign and, still more, their retrospective critics.

The negative constraints upon British policy are perhaps the easiest to identify and define. There was the fear of war and the accompanying anxiety to avoid embroilment in disputes carrying the risk of war. This was a factor always emphasised by Eden. Before the Spanish Civil War had even begun, he remarked, on 26 March 1936[1] that

. . . our neighbours may become involved in conflict and may call for help in a quarrel that is not ours. That I believe to be a general apprehension. The people of this country are determined that that shall not happen and that is the view of the Government. We agree with it entirely . . . we accept no obligation beyond those shared by the League except the obligations which devolve on us from Locarno.

He could scarcely have been more explicit – or more prophetic. On 6 June 1936, again before the Civil War began, he was vaguer, but no less emphatic: 'the objective of British foreign policy is the maintenance of peace'. On 14 October 1936 he was more specific. Having argued that 'The fighting that broke out in this comparatively isolated corner of Western Europe[2] threatened at a moment's notice to scatter strife far beyond the borders of Spain', he concluded that it was '. . . our duty to make every effort to confine that tragedy within the boundaries of the country wherein it is being enacted'.

This was to be his line throughout and, at the outset of our particular story, on 12 April 1937, he explained that Non-Intervention, whatever its imperfections in practice, was essential: 'unless we were ourselves prepared to intervene in Spain . . . and no one in this country advocates that course'.

Eden's pacific views did undoubtedly reflect those of his

[1] This and, unless otherwise indicated, the quotations that follow, are taken from Eden's own selection of his speeches in his *Foreign Affairs* (Faber, 1939).
[2] Compare Chamberlain's later, and, more famous, phrase: 'a far-away country of which we know nothing'.

politically conscious countrymen, most of whom either loathed the very idea of war or, as in Chatfield's case, were pre-occupied by the inadequacy of British armaments. These sentiments were reinforced by what, on 14 October 1936, Eden called 'a very general and widespread feeling in this country of distaste for these extreme political doctrines'. To his mind, 'Democracy came near to dictatorship when the will of the majority is imposed in a spirit of intolerance on the minority'.

Although, as Eden later commented, 'from the early months of 1937, if I had had to choose, I would have preferred a Government victory',[1] his preference was seldom strong enough to overcome his 'distaste' and never capable of out-weighing his aversion from the risk of war.

Moreover, whatever his personal views, Eden had always to reckon with the extent to which the Spanish Civil War had divided British public opinion in general. This was a factor of which the Prime Minister was particularly conscious: 'there was one thing more than anything that I was afraid of – party division on foreign policy'.[2] Its importance has been admirably analysed by Watkins in his *Britain Divided*. His arguments should be studied in detail, but may be summarised in his quotation from a contemporary article by Churchill: 'the division is so deep and balanced that no coherent action was at any time possible'.[3]

The natural result of these complementary constraints was the doctrine of Non-Intervention, a doctrine which became a dogma and acquired, in the eyes of the British Government, an intrinsic significance and value transcending its susceptibility to diverse interpretation and partial application. These side-effects of Non-Intervention – the inescapable fact that, as has earlier been emphasised, it was an internationally unattainable objective – have distracted some historians from its true nature

---

[1] Anthony Eden, *Facing the Dictators* (Cassell, 1962), p. 441.
[2] Keith Middlemas & John Barnes, *Baldwin* (Weidenfeld and Nicolson, 1969), p. 961.
[3] K. W. Watkins, *Britain Divided* (Nelson, 1963), p. 11.

and purpose. The doctrine was never intended to create the impossible ideal of maintaining strict British impartiality between the contending factions in Spain; it was not meant to hold the ring and ensure that the best man won. It served the domestic, not the foreign, purposes of the British Government.

This is a point that has to be emphasised, because so many historians have analysed the consequences of Non-Intervention in terms of its supposedly international purposes. They have pointed out that the dangers of a wider war were less than the British Government suggested; that Communist ascendancy among the Spanish Republicans was the result, and not the cause, of the British refusal to sell arms; that even the divisions of British public opinion might be ascribed to the absence of any clear lead from the British Government.

These are retrospective arguments and they are not addressed to the problem that then confronted the British Government, who neither accepted any obligation towards Spaniards, nor regarded the outcome of a purely Spanish conflict as being of fundamental importance to British interests. None of these arguments, moreover, takes account of the psychological, one might almost call it the neurotic, background to the Government's decision. Non-Intervention, to Baldwin and his Ministers, was the lesson they had learnt from the Abyssinian crisis. This had been, for the politicians of the thirties, almost as traumatic an experience as, twenty years later, the Suez affair was to prove for their successors. Indeed, there is a curious affinity between these two failures of British policy. In each case a British Government had attempted to impose on others their own conception of international law; in each case, finding their bluff called and the support of their allies inadequate, they had flinched at the final test and accepted humiliating defeat. It was on 18 June 1936, just one month before the outbreak of the Spanish Civil War, the anniversary, as Mowat points out, of the battle of Waterloo, that the British Government abandoned sanctions against Italy. Lloyd George's terrible comment could have been repeated twenty years later:

Peterkin's question

'This is a unique occasion . . . I have never before heard a British Minister . . . come down to the House of Commons and say that Britain was beaten, Britain and her Empire beaten, and that we must abandon an enterprise we had taken in hand.'[1]

The lesson was obvious – 'interfering in a dispute with which we have no concern' (Eden, 11 July 1935)[2] – was liable to prove nationally and politically disastrous. It was particularly taken to heart by two of those most closely involved: Hoare, whom Abyssinia brought crashing down from the Foreign Office, and Chatfield, whose naval concentration in the Mediterranean had not merely been exposed as bluff, but had painfully revealed the deficiencies of the Fleet, above all when Germany occupied the Rhineland on 7 March 1936. There were then only one cruiser, seventeen destroyers and nine submarines readily available in home waters and the British Chiefs of Staff had every reason to conclude that 'any question of war with Germany, while we are as at present heavily committed to the possibility of hostilities in the Mediterranean would be thoroughly dangerous'.[3]

It was this nightmare, that a forward policy in Spanish waters might again expose the inability of the Royal Navy to fight Germany and Italy simultaneously – to say nothing of the risk of Far Eastern complications with Japan – that understandably haunted Chatfield. He and Hoare thus excelled all others in the desire to carry Non-Intervention to the extremity of appeasement. But even Eden, in the speech he subsequently entitled 'The Failure of Sanctions', spoke on 18 June 1936 of 'the shortcomings, the weaknesses and even the dangers which have been revealed by the experience of the last few months'. As another Minister later described another débâcle, it had been 'no end of a lesson'.

---

[1] This quotation is taken from *Britain Between the Wars: 1918–1940* (p. 562) by Charles Loch Mowat (Methuen, 1955). He is one of the few writers to have appreciated the significance of this failure for British politicians. Others are Middlemas and Barnes in their biography of Baldwin, particularly pp. 897–99.

[2] He was arguing in the opposite sense, but what is significant is that he called this 'the first charge brought against us'. Eden, *Foreign Affairs*.

[3] Arthur Marder, 'The Royal Navy and The Ethiopian Crisis of 1935–36', *American Historical Review*, LXXV, 5 (June 1970).

If these sentiments of pacifism, of abstention, of retreat from the dangerous disputes of foreigners had been the only influences at work upon the British Government, there would have been no tale to tell. Britain – and the Royal Navy – might have remained entirely aloof from events in Spain and Hoare have secured his Order in Council prohibiting British merchant ships from carrying even food to that country.[1] Even the need to give some satisfaction to the Popular Front Government of France – it was a perpetual and, in retrospect, paradoxical nightmare of British politicians that the even more pacific French would drag them into war – might not sufficiently have reinforced the pressures exerted by the British Left or by those ardent advocates of humanitarianism to whose arguments Ministers were intermittently susceptible.

There was another, deeper, more potent undercurrent of emotion. Eden – it was in keeping with his entire career – was its most consistent exponent. 'Our country', he declared on 22 November 1935, 'has a great part to play'[2] and he returned to this theme again and again in the months that followed. On 14 December 1936, for instance, he expressed '. . . a profound conviction that in the restless and anxious state of present day Europe this country has an especial part to play' and concluded 'We must therefore be watchful at all times and in all places. We cannot disinterest ourselves from this or that part of the world . . .'

On 19 July 1937 he applied these general sentiments expressly to the Civil War in Spain: 'But disinterestedness in this matter [the internal affairs of Spain] must not be taken to mean disinterestedness where British interests are concerned on the land or the sea frontiers of Spain or the trade routes that pass her by.'

These, then, were the parameters of policy. The British Government wanted neither risks nor foreign entanglements nor courses of action abroad liable to exacerbate controversy at home. But Ministers had not forgotten that they were entrusted with the guidance of a Great Power. They would not have

---

[1] See Chapter 5.　　　[2] Eden, *Foreign Affairs.*

uttered[1] – they were not that kind of men and the times were out of joint – but there lurked in the depths of their subconscious a memory of those famous words:

But if a situation were to be forced upon us in which peace could only be preserved by the surrender of the great and beneficent position which Britain has won by centuries of heroism and achievement, by allowing Britain to be treated, where her interests were vitally affected, as if she were of no account in the Cabinet of Nations, then I say emphatically that peace at that price would be a humiliation intolerable for a great country like ours to endure.[2]

Such recollections were not often stirred in Mr Baldwin's Cabinet – even Eden could talk of 'peace at almost any price'[3] – but, when they were, HOOD was despatched to the northern coast of Spain.

Against this background, therefore, the cyclical movement of British policy during the spring and early summer of 1937 is best envisaged as an alternating current of appeasement and assertion. Commander Caslon was where he was, and acted as he did on 6 April, in the assertive phase: Britain had an interest in northern Spain and it was intolerable that foreigners should molest British ships upon the high seas. The sine curve dipped to its nadir and protection was withdrawn from British ships disregarding the Government's advice against proceeding to Bilbao. The cycle continued and ships were forced through the blockade; it attained its zenith and Spanish children in Spanish ships were protected from a Spanish cruiser.

These conflicting surges of emotion provide garish colours in which to depict the policy of His Majesty's Government, but other explanations are even less convincing. Ideological conspiracy, for instance, will scarcely serve. Even the luckless Samuel Hoare is hardly more plausible as a Fascist than Eden as a Communist sympathiser. Conspiracy, admittedly, was

---

[1] Though Baldwin had come near it in 1934. G. M. Young, *Stanley Baldwin* (Hart-Davis, 1952), p. 180.

[2] Mr Lloyd George's speech of 21 July 1911 on the occasion of the Agadir Crisis. David Lloyd George, *War Memoirs*, vol. 1 (Odhams, 1938), p. 26.

[3] On 25 June 1937, quoted in Arnold J. Toynbee, *Survey of International Affairs 1937*, vol. 2 (R.I.I.A. and O.U.P., 1938), pp. 152–3.

suspected at the time. Eden's Private Secretary, Oliver Harvey, recorded in his diary:

[17 April 1937]   It is very difficult to get facts out of Admiralty at all.

[21 April 1937]   He [Eden] is sure, as we all are, that Hoare and Admiralty have not been frank and have made much more of danger of mines than was justified by facts.[1]

But neither Harvey nor Eden suggested that Chatfield had ideological motives and there is no evidence to support such a theory. Hoare might intermittently complain that Britain was trying to stop Franco from winning, but Chatfield would probably have been just as opposed to breaking a Republican blockade of equal strength and with potential allies of similar power. As Harvey had commented at the outset (on 10 April 1937) 'The Admiralty as usual are for doing nothing.'[2]

But the Admiralty, as has earlier been noted, had their own, essentially pragmatic, reasons for inaction. Indeed, what has to be explained is not the negative, but the positive, element in British policy. Economic factors offer an inadequate answer, if the fantastic hypotheses so dear to General Franco are excluded (he told the German Ambassador that the British Government were only concerned to secure repayment of the large loans they had made to the Basque Government).[3] The one course of action that would have assured the safety of British investments in Spain – enough backing for one side to make certain that they won and had solid reasons for gratitude – was the one course everyone rejected. Imports of iron-ore, though often invoked in argument by Ministers and their critics alike, provided no more than the rationalisation of deeper motives. Attempts to promote them were fitful and, in the medium term, they declined no more than was the natural result of the disruption entailed by civil war:

[1] John Harvey (ed.), *The Diplomatic Diaries of Oliver Harvey 1937–1940* (Collins, 1970).   [2] Ibid.
[3] *Documents on German Foreign Policy*, series D, vol. 3 (H.M.S.O., 1951), no. 269.

Exports of iron-ore from Vizcaya to Britain[1]
Monthly average 1936 51,416 tons
Monthly average 1937 42,000 tons
March 1938 46,615 tons

The one undoubted economic achievement of British policy – the fat profits made by blockade running British shipowners – was the effect that no one defended and many strongly resented. It can, in any case, scarcely have been of much significance on the national scale.

Humanitarianism did provide a stronger incentive. There is little reason to impugn the sincerity of the Cabinet's response to the bombing of Guernica. This was an incident that stirred even more distant observers. 'The American Ambassador had informed him [Eden] that the latter event had been received with the utmost horror in America, where [a deeply significant comment] it was regarded as a practice for the bombing of London and Paris.'[2] But, if humanitarianism sufficed to protect Spanish ships for some weeks, it was, as we have seen, diluted almost beyond analysis by the passage of time and the pressure of events. As early as 19 May 1937, Ministers found their most compelling argument to be that Britain must keep up with the French Joneses.[3]

The pacifist intermission of mid-April excepted, therefore, the objective of British policy in this curious episode was not unfairly stated by Eden: 'Even if our naval action at Bilbao could be interpreted as inconsistent with non-intervention, a reminder of British strength could only be salutary.'[4]

The intention was, at minimum cost and without running undue risks, to reassure British public opinion and the Government of France, while reminding General Franco and the Governments of Germany and Italy, that Britain was still a Great Power, a nation endowed with the will and the capacity to impose upon others wishes which she, and she alone, had deliberately confined within the bounds of international law

[1] Brian Crozier, *Franco* (Eyre and Spottiswoode, 1967), p. 254.
[2] CAB 23 88 on 5 May 1937.   [3] FO 371 21371.
[4] Eden, *Facing the Dictators*, p. 448.

and the principles of humanity. This is the yard-stick by which the results must be measured and not by the conflicting claims of those concerned with events in Spain itself. General Franco, for instance, complained that the Royal Navy had so prolonged the endurance of Bilbao as to cost him an extra 20,000 casualties;[1] Major Attlee had an opposite grievance: that British endorsement of the Nationalist blockade had been a contributing cause of Bilbao's fall.[2] Perhaps the German Ambassador, who wrote on 9 July 1937 for the eyes of his own Government alone, was nearer the mark when, in his analysis of the Nationalist campaign against Bilbao, he altogether ignored both the blockade and the interventions of H.M. ships and attributed 'the exceptional slowness of the operations' to the incompetence of the attackers.[3]

All three arguments were equally irrelevant, as is any attempt to judge the success of British policy by its probably negligible impact upon the outcome of the Spanish Civil War. That was not its purpose. Nor were British actions intended to win foreign friends for Britain. Even the thousands of women and children who were actually rescued owed their protection primarily to the desire of the British Government to appease British public opinion and thus to facilitate the pursuit of Non-Intervention. The Basques, the Spanish Republicans and their supporters, whether in Britain or elsewhere, had all hoped for more and were probably as disappointed as they were grateful. The Spanish Nationalists, the Germans and the Italians were angry and indignant. Few foreigners, still fewer foreign officials and no foreign government liked Britain any better than before.

Admittedly she was more respected. The Captain of ALMIR-ANTE CERVERA may have had 'lágrimas de rabia en los ojos' when he reiterated 'hay que ser prudente', but he did conclude 'no podemos empeorar nuestras relaciones con Inglaterra'.[4] And the final accolade was bestowed)ʃ he coldly calculating

---

[1] FO 371 21295.   [2] FO 371 21296.
[3] German Documents no. 390.
[4] 'tears of rage in his eyes' . . . 'needs must be prudent' . . . 'we cannot worsen our relations with England'. Almirante Juan Cervera Valderrama, *Memorias de Guerra* (Editora Nacional, Madrid, 1968).

hand of Joseph Stalin. Nobody had less disposition to view the British Government with favour or indulgence, nobody – as the Nazi Soviet Pact of 1939 would prove – was less swayed by sentiment or ideology in the dispassionate reckoning of interest and advantage. When he instructed his Ambassador to seek, on 27 August 1937, British naval protection, it was simply and solely because he thought this was worth having.[1]

But was there any advantage in securing this reluctant tribute or in extorting the bitter respect of Captain Moreu? British diplomats and naval officers did not, as we have earlier noted, think so at the time. Nor does the record of British policy in the ensuing years suggest much conscious effort to exploit or develop any prestige that might have been acquired off Bilbao. Must the success of British policy be measured entirely in terms of its contribution to British self-esteem?

This would be too narrow a view. The exercise of limited naval force may serve to avert loss as well as to secure advantage.[2] This was a period when European rivalries found expression in a series of challenges and responses, each conducted largely on a basis of bluff by nations whose readiness for war bore little relation to their ostensible willingness to risk it. In this dangerous game of poker Britain had, before our story begins, sustained two recent and resounding defeats: Abyssinia and the Rhineland. Off Bilbao she had been challenged again and it is arguable that the consequences of a third surrender might have proved more substantial and enduring than the actual advantages of her petty triumph. If Hoare's preferences had prevailed and the presence of ALMIRANTE CERVERA and ESPAÑA had been allowed to exclude British merchantmen from the Biscayan ports of Spain, damaging conclusions would have been drawn in more capitals than Moscow.

The northern coast of Spain, after all, was a spot-lit stage holding the eyes of the world, in that spring of 1937. There was no chance of avoiding the issue, no hope that the decision of

---

[1] See Chapter 9.
[2] See James Cable, *Gunboat Diplomacy* (Chatto and Windus, 1971), p. 21.

the British Government would pass unregarded or be reckoned of little future account. It was a dilemma that was to afflict British Ministers and officials throughout the later thirties, as the rivalries of Europe pursued their centripetal course from quarrels of little concern towards that final contest which Britain foresaw and wished to postpone. It was obviously desirable to gain time, and to avoid complications, so that British strength might be restored. But it was equally obvious that Britain could not simply withdraw from the international arena and spend in undisturbed seclusion the years of her re-armament. The game was going on all the time and the other players would not suspend their bids while the British Government accumulated aces, a process they might, in any case, simultaneously be attempting for themselves. Each fresh challenge – and General Franco's had been clear and evident – demanded the same obnoxious choice between opposing dangers: the sudden disaster that bluffing too high might bring; the downward step of throwing in yet another hand.

This was one occasion when, perhaps mainly thanks to Blake on Saint George's Day, the British Government assessed and bid their cards correctly. It was a small show of resolution – there is little evidence to suggest that any real risks were run – but, for that very reason, the failure to make it might have proved disproportionately damaging. Whether or not it at all delayed the moment of actual war, it added something, perhaps something of more value than any merely logistic achievement, to the preparations of the Royal Navy. When that awful moment actually arrived, the speed, the guns, the armour, the technical characteristics of British men-of-war often seemed to have derived less benefit from the years of peace than had the ships of their adversaries. In terms of engineering the Royal Navy was often, and inexcusably, out-classed: there was really very little material justification for their complex of superiority. But it was rather a useful complex and, if Hoare had had his way in April 1937, perhaps it would not have been so highly developed in 1939.

Three successes, two positive and one negative, may thus

be claimed for British policy: public opinion at home was placated, the morale of the Royal Navy was fortified, foreigners were denied the spectacle of another British surrender. What did these gains cost? The calculations made at the time are not impressive. Of course General Franco's supporters, whether Spanish, Italian or German, were annoyed. But the Foreign Office argument, which was also Eden's, always lacked any foundation: 'When at last this terrible Spanish conflict is ended, is it not conceivable that the Spanish people will like best those who have fought least on their soil?'[1]

It was not conceivable and, if it had been, this Spanish preference would have gone to some distant country of the Americas. British men-of-war had, after all, been flaunting the White Ensign round the coasts of Spain ever since that conflict began. However benevolent and legitimate their motives, they had constantly interfered and intervened. To expect gratitude because this meddling had never had a specifically Spanish purpose was to expect more than human, and particularly Latin, nature could attain. General Franco's supporters were not the only Spaniards to deny the possibility, let alone the validity, of neutrality or impartiality in a war that, for them, over-rode all other issues. If the British Government had maintained the line originally adopted by the Cabinet on Sunday 11 April – asserting the right to protect British merchantmen but ordering them not to proceed – General Franco could only have ascribed their decision to fear, not friendship. If his regard was to be won at all – and the Spanish attitude towards Germany and Italy during the Second World War casts some doubt on this possibility – he was entitled to expect, if not outright support for his cause, at least full recognition of his status as a ruler and belligerent. The reports of the German Ambassador show how cynically General Franco interpreted British motives and, if Hoare had had his way, cynicism would have been almost obligatory. If the 'reminder of British strength' was too isolated an event to be quite as 'salutary' as Eden hoped,[2]

---

[1] Eden's speech of 12 April 1937. FO 425 414.
[2] Eden, *Facing the Dictators*, p. 448.

it is impossible to imagine any advantage being derived from a further confession of British weakness.

After all that historians have written and revealed during the last twenty-five years, it is scarcely necessary to labour similar arguments in the case of Germany and Italy. All that need be said – and that only because anxiety to conciliate those powers swayed so many British Ministers and officials at the time – is that neither Government had intervened in Spain from love of Spaniards and that the last thing either wanted was a better understanding between Britain and General Franco, whom both saw as a potential instrument in their existing rivalry with Britain and France. There was no pleasing them in this instance and – as the Nyon Agreement later showed – much less risk of provoking them to action than was supposed at the time in London. Whichever course the Royal Navy had followed off Bilbao, there was no useful friendship to be won for Britain and the advantages of boldness carried no penalty in international relations.

Indeed, if we exclude the administrative inconvenience to the Navy – a factor which impatient civilians may regard Admirals as always inclined to exaggerate – we must seek the true cost of this policy in an unexpected quarter, as indirectly revealed by the answer to our final question: did warships provide a necessary and useful reinforcement to diplomatic representations? At first sight this seems too obvious to deserve analysis. As the British Chargé d'Affaires at Hendaye told the Foreign Office on 28 August 1937: 'I am afraid that lectures on international law cut very little ice these days.'[1]

His words could be supported by a hundred instances of the fate of British requests, appeals, protests that were unsupported by British warships. In this particular case neither he nor Sir Billy could, by mere persuasion, have induced General Franco to let British food-ships into Bilbao or Basque children out. Even an ultimatum, if this could have been imagined by the British Government or endorsed by the British people, might

---

[1] ADM 116 3516.

not have sufficed. The blockade, as Admiral Backhouse reasonably remarked, 'would certainly have been effective for part of the time had none of H.M. Ships been there to interrupt it'.[1] In so far as the British Government wanted to feed, or to rescue, the women and children of Bilbao, British warships were the indispensable instruments of their purpose.

But the British Government, it was earlier argued, had a different purpose. They wished to preserve their prestige by responding, in a resolute and effective manner, to the challenge General Franco had offered to their international authority. Here, too, HOOD served their purpose well. But would this challenge have been seen as such, or this authority been called in question, 'had none of H.M. Ships been there'? Suppose no British destroyers had been patrolling the Cantabrian Sea on 6 April 1937, that all H.M. ships had been withdrawn from Spanish waters once British subjects had been evacuated, would the arrest, or the turning back, of THORPEHALL have demanded positive action to preserve British prestige?

No conclusive answer is possible to so hypothetical a question, but it would clearly not have taken much to alter the decisions of Ministers who wavered so long between appeasement and assertion. Just the difference between despatching warships and withdrawing, or reinforcing, those already there might have been enough to tip a trembling balance. Without Commander Caslon's destroyers the British Government might simply have sent a note of protest; without HOOD even the Opposition might merely have bewailed the sufferings of the Basques. Those grey ships were the instruments of policy, but they were also – and not just because of the initiatives of a Caslon or a Blake – one of its contributory impulses. A nation with warships on the spot had greater opportunities, but also greater demands to meet, higher standards to match, than one without.

This was perhaps the true cost of British policy, the price predicted, though rather late in the day, by Chatfield and

[1] ADM 116 3679.

Mounsey. Every British warship in Spanish waters was an asset that could be exploited, but also a stake that could be jeopardised. It was the attack on H.M.S. HAVOCK that pushed the Chamberlain Government into the Nyon Conference. Hoare's earlier notion that the presence of HOOD could give appeasement the colour of resolution was never really a starter. The British public not unreasonably expected value for their naval money. There may thus have been something of a circular tendency in the entire argument: British warships had to assert themselves in order to preserve British prestige, which was in issue because British warships were there – for the sake of British prestige. The trouble was – and it started many months before our story – that the British Government did not really know why they wanted warships in Spanish waters. They were making a catalytic use of naval force,[1] but the ships that were meant to extend their options could also force unforeseen choices.

If there is a lesson to be drawn from this story, it is surely that the end should be envisaged before the means are chosen. When the Admiralty rejoiced that, by 24 July 1936, they had 'ships at every major Spanish port',[2] when Eden proclaimed that 'we must therefore be watchful at all times and in all places',[3] both would have done well to bear in mind an ancient Spanish proverb, *tomalo que quieres, dice Dios, y pagalo*: take what you want, says God, and pay for it! Hindsight, unlike the recorded emotions of that apprehensive April, suggests that the price must always have been low, but anyone who follows the twists and turns of this phase of British policy may be inclined to ascribe its success to luck and not to judgment.

From this censure, which applies as much to the Admiralty as to the Foreign Office or Cabinet, British naval officers in the Cantabrian Sea must be excepted. In spite of confusing orders, inadequate communications and a general deficiency of political information and guidance, they displayed courage, coolness, foresight and tact, to such good effect that, in a series of con-

---

[1] See Cable, *Gunboat Diplomacy*, pp. 49–63.   [2] ADM 116 3677.
[3] Eden, *Foreign Affairs*.

frontations extending over half a year, the threat of force always sufficed and violence was averted. As a demonstration of the prolonged application of limited naval force for political ends, the operations off the northern coast of Spain during the spring and summer of 1937 must be reckoned a model of their kind. Credit, admittedly, must be given to the Government for the decision to send HOOD and, thereafter, to provide those capital ships which enabled the Senior Naval Officer North Spain to concentrate a superior force whenever one was needed. But the entire pattern of events would have been different, and far more dangerous, without the good sense and the calculated boldness of Commanders Taylor and Caslon or the 'superlative tact' later praised by Captain Caveda.[1]

In a sense this first incident of 6 April was the most interesting of all, for the advantage of superior force lay initially with the Spaniards, whom BRAZEN confronted alone for nearly five hours. It is a curious speculation how matters might have developed if Captain Moreu had delayed his first intervention until THORPEHALL was nearer the 3 mile limit and had then pressed it more vigorously, sending GALERNA to intercept THORPEHALL while keeping ALMIRANTE CERVERA to seaward and ready to bar BRAZEN's approach. As it was, he revealed his intentions prematurely, then allowed Commander Taylor's vigorous response – clearing BRAZEN for action and taking her between THORPEHALL and the cruiser – to remain unanswered. By the time Captain Moreu finally decided – if he ever did – to force the issue, it was too late: British reinforcements had arrived.

Whenever possible, the technique employed by British warships was simple: to interpose themselves between the victim and the potential assailant, thus daring the latter to fire the first shot. Its effectiveness may be contrasted with the sorry record of 1938, when twenty-two attacks were made on British ships in Spanish waters, mostly by Italian aircraft based in Majorca. Eleven ships were sunk or seriously damaged and

---

[1] His letter to Captain McGrigor in FO 425 414.

British protests were entirely unavailing. Thomas, in his account of these events, quotes a revealing comment by Chamberlain: 'I have been through every possible form of retaliation, and it is absolutely clear that none of them can be effective unless we are prepared to go to war with Franco.'[1]

If diplomatic representations alone had been attempted in 1937, it is scarcely conceivable that these would have secured entry to Bilbao for British merchant vessels or egress for Spanish refugee ships. And, if the aircraft that bombed Guernica and Durango were not then employed against ships in territorial waters, the reason may well be sought in the resolution displayed on the high seas by British men-of-war. The immediate application of local force is not only intrinsically more effective than a larger but more distant menace: it also constitutes the most convincing reminder of the strength (which must be moral as well as material) that lies behind it. Until the moment of its application power is only latent and hypothetical; the local use or threat of force is actual.

Regarded in isolation, therefore, we may reasonably conclude that British naval operations off the northern coast of Spain constituted 'a famous victory', if rather a minor one. For all their hesitations, their false starts, their needless fears, Ministers had fumbled their way to the right decisions: the Navy carried them out. The immediate objectives were economically attained: British food-ships entered Biscayan ports; Basque children found safety in England and France. Even the tarnished prestige of Britain acquired a new lustre, soon to reflect the larger success of Nyon. But that summer's rose had a worm in

---

[1] Hugh Thomas, *The Spanish Civil War* (Eyre and Spottiswoode), pp. 538–9. The futility of threats that are neither specific nor seriously intended may be illustrated by the following example. After the British ship ALCIRA was bombed and sunk 20 miles S.E. of Barcelona on 4 February 1938, Sir R. Hodgson, the British Representative at Burgos, was told: 'You should therefore let it be known to General Franco that H.M.G. reserve to themselves the right henceforth without any further notice to take such retaliatory action, in the event of any recurrence of these attacks, as may be required by and appropriate to the particular case.' Nevertheless, when STANWELL was attacked at Tarragona on 15 March, there followed only another protest. ADM 116 3532.

the bud, a worm that denied next spring its promise, a worm that grudged the children their English refuge. If little 'good came of it at last', the fault did not lie with those who devised or executed British policy in April and May 1937. The fatal moment, the engendering hour of the worm, came only on 2 June: Neville Chamberlain held his first Cabinet as Prime Minister.

H

CHAPTER 14

Happily ever after

Call no man happy till he dies, he is at best fortunate
Solon[1]

There is a book to be written one day, though this is not it, a
saga of the children who sailed, in their thousands and their
tens of thousands, from the Biscayan ports of Spain for France
and for England, for Belgium and the Soviet Union, for refuges
even more remote. For many this meant less than a year's
separation – though a year can be eternity for a child – from
parents, from brothers and sisters and from the familiar sights
and sounds and feel of home. For some it can even have been a
strange, wild holiday in camps and colonies of the very young.
For most it was a respite from bombs and sirens and shelters
and from that ultimate sense of insecurity that afflicts the child
who sees his parents' fear.

They were more fortunate than many of those left behind.
Less than a month after HABANA's departure for England there
began the final flight from Bilbao. Steer, who saw it, has left a
picture fit for Goya:

All along the riverside, for over six miles, women and children and
old men were filing uncontrollably into trawlers for Santander. The
night showed a moon, and the moon a restless ebb and flow of
people, dressed in black, with shining hair and pale faces, and men
with melancholy black berets who moved slowly over black docks and
under black cranes and tips and furnaces to a riverside shuddering
with motion and mirrored light.

. . .

In the city at the bridges of the Nervion the land evacuation
gathered speed. Lorries all night were rumbling through Bilbao,

---

[1] Solon, quoted in Herodotus, *Histories*, i. 32.

built high with chairs and bedsteads and sagging bundles, to which people clung and under which they cowered.

. . .

That night the enemy aviation came out in the soft moonlight and machine-gunned the length of the road to Santander, flying very low. They fired tracer bullets, which lit the lower sky with sudden strips of fire, delicate as silk and flicked the earth to either side of the terrified refugees. These were the whips which they had to travel under, till they reached haven at Castro Urdiales or Laredo or Santoña, and fell off their lorries to sleep heavily at the roadside, all sexes and ages rolled into one common grass bed. They were so worn out that they still went on sleeping when the planes returned to light, with their horrible subtle tracery, the towns where they lay before morning broke.[1]

Altogether, so Steer estimates, nearly 200,000 people thus fled from Bilbao before the entry of General Franco's troops. Many of them were children and for many months these had to trail uncomprehending from one imperfect sanctuary to another, escaping again from Santander, bombed once more in Barcelona, caught up in the final misery, the rotting despair of those camps – guarded by Senegalese – which the French Government established at Le Boulou, at Argèles, at Saint-Cyprien and at a dozen other places adapted to receive the final flight of 1939.[2] At least the children did not have to remain, with their fathers, in these camps. But the scattered sanctuaries found for them in France brought no end to their wanderings. When the German armour broke through into the plains of northern France a year later, there were still Basque children to join the files of frantic, plodding refugees that choked those long, straight, poplar-shaded roads.[3] The slow Biscayan waves did not advance and recede more aimlessly, more remorselessly, than the tides of war and politics that sucked these children to and fro, spilling them across Europe as the flotsam of statesmanship.

[1] G. L. Steer, *The Tree of Gernika* (Hodder and Stoughton, 1938), pp. 330–1.
[2] Hugh Thomas, *The Spanish Civil War* (Eyre and Spottiswoode, 1961), pp. 575–6.
[3] José Antonio de Aguirre, *Freedom was Flesh and Blood* (Gollancz, 1945).

The Royal Navy and the siege of Bilbao

Were those who stayed more fortunate or those who returned early to Bilbao or those who found new lives and, eventually, a different nationality in the countries where chance had cast them? 'What song the Syrens sang or what name Achilles assumed when he hid himself among women, though puzzling questions, are not beyond all conjecture',[1] but which historian will undertake to track down a hundredth of these scattered children and, by comparing their stories, decide whose parents chose best for them and why? He will have to begin soon, or too much will be forgotten, but he will be troubling painful memories, exploring controversies that still live and burn today. It is, after all, that majority of Basque children who either never left Bilbao at all or else, after an interval of months or years, resumed in Vizcaya or Guipúzcoa the interrupted pattern of their lives, that one would like to question. Without a substantial sample of their testimony no valid conclusions can be drawn from the reminiscences of a handful of exiles. But, whether it was better to go or to stay, to return or to start a new life, these are questions more readily answered in London than in Bilbao, where the events of 1937 are a wound it would still be rash to probe. Any fundamental enquiry must await a bolder historian and a more propitious time.

We shall do better to confine ourselves to the children who remained in England and to employ their impressions only as a wash of colour to enliven the sparse lines of conjecture. They were relatively few in number – two or three hundred is the usual estimate – many of them kept in touch with one another, they exchanged information. In this restricted field hearsay is a less inadequate guide and the reminiscences of a handful may offer some clue to the experiences and reactions of most. The question is a simple one. These children represent an extreme case – not so much of suffering, for fate had worse in store for some of the others – but in the finality with which embarkation in HABANA shaped their lives. What price did they pay for escaping the bombs of Bilbao, the frantic flight to Santander, the months and years of fearful wandering?

[1] Sir Thomas Browne, *Urn Burial.*

To be valid, any answer can only be attempted in terms of their more ordinary experiences. In 1938, for instance, the merchant vessel CANTABRIA, which still flew the Republican flag, was sunk in the North Sea by one of the auxiliary cruisers fitted out by the Nationalist navy. On board was a Basque boy – his name has not been preserved – who had once been evacuated from Bilbao to Southampton aboard HABANA. Perhaps he was afterwards deported as unruly, possibly his parents had asked for his return to Republican territory. Conceivably he just ran away and joined his ship in a British port. His story lies concealed behind a reference to documents since destroyed in volume 3 of the Foreign Office Index to General Correspondence for 1938 in the Public Record Office. That he had friends in England who persuaded the Foreign Office to seek his release is obvious. The outcome of their efforts is not recorded and, whatever his fate, it was neither typical nor a consequence of his original evacuation. An adventurous boy had no need to leave Spain before joining the crew of CANTABRIA.

On the other hand, a child remaining in Bilbao would undoubtedly have had a different education. One comment was universal among those who settled in England and were interviewed there: the handicap imposed on their adult lives by an interrupted education. Not one of the children questioned by the author had received any proper schooling in England, at most a little religious instruction or some sporadic lessons in English. One of them contrasted, a little sadly, his experience with that of a Basque acquaintance who had been evacuated not to England, but to the Soviet Union, where he had been trained, and had eventually qualified, as an architect. Even more remarkably he had thereafter been able to return to Spain and, as the result of protracted negotiation, had passed further examinations and settled down in his own country to a career in his chosen profession.[1]

It is easier to understand than to excuse this neglect of the children's education. Their stay was always regarded as temporary; they might be leaving at any moment; the Government

[1] Segurola.

would not help; the National Joint Committee lacked funds; it would, in any case, have been very difficult to organise schooling in England for foreign children scattered in small groups throughout the country. The obstacles were genuine enough: what is odd is that so little effort was made to overcome them. Education is one subject never mentioned in all the parliamentary questions, the Cabinet minutes, the newspaper articles that preoccupied themselves with so many aspects of the children's welfare and conduct. No one even seems to have suggested that regular lessons would at least keep them out of the mischief that received such disproportionate attention. One of the few exceptions to this general neglect seems to have been the group of children in the care of the London Teachers' Association, who attended either a village school or, in the case of the older boys, the West Essex Technical College. Teachers, obviously, would appreciate the value of education and would find it easier to overcome the administrative difficulties, but why, one wonders, was this example not more widely followed?[1]

Too many of the children were thus confined, when they grew up, to jobs below their obvious capacities. This mattered less during the war, when the factories, the land, the Merchant Navy and the Armed Forces, for which twenty-five of the boys volunteered and in which some were killed in action, inevitably claimed their services and would have, whatever their education. It was the wider opportunities of returning peace that revealed the extent of their handicap.

Nevertheless, most of the children consulted thought their parents had taken the right choice in the difficult circumstances that then confronted them. Pilar Ortiz de Zarate, who was thirteen when HABANA sailed, still remembers her father assuring her that their separation would, at most, be for three months. Fourteen years passed before he saw her again and he then declared that, had he known the length of the parting that lay in store, he would never have let her go. Miss Ortiz is less certain. The fear engendered by the bombing of Bilbao is still

---

[1] Leah Manning, *A Life for Education* (Gollancz, 1970), p. 133.

Happily ever after

vivid in her memory. It was, she emphasises, far worse than anything she experienced in London during the raids of 1940. These did not frighten her. But the sufferings of Bilbao were unprecedented and its inhabitants knew themselves to be defenceless. They had no comforting statistics of bombers shot down to reassure them, no savage music of anti-aircraft barrages to sustain their morale, not even the bitter satisfaction of knowing their enemies to be enduring an equal atrocity. In 1937 the Basques were helpless victims and Bilbao no place for a child to be.

Nor did even Pilar's father stay there long. When Bilbao fell he fled to Santander and, unluckier than some of his compatriots, was caught there by the Nationalists. The next six years he spent in prison. At the time, Pilar wanted to return to Spain nevertheless and she and her sister were bitterly disappointed, in September 1939, when they went to Victoria Station to bid farewell to one of the last parties of children returning to Spain. It included all their friends, indeed, the whole group of girls from Carshalton Beeches where Pilar had spent her last few months in England – she had begun her stay in a Catholic Convent. But her guardians had decided that, with the father in prison, the girls could not prudently return to Spain. Thirty years later they were still in England.[1]

The arguments for evacuation from Bilbao were of a different, and a sharper character than those which perplexed a handful of British parents in 1940, when they were considering the option of sending their children to Canada or the United States. But the case of the Ortiz sisters also illustrates the capriciously unpredictable consequences of even the most reasonable decisions in such agonising circumstances. They stayed in England because they happened to be in the charge of people who took a particular view of their responsibilities towards those children. It was by no means a universal view. Other children, as we have seen, were sent back in the absence of even a single parent to welcome them. And, in 1940, Mr Bautista Lopez, then already

[1] Information given to the author in 1971 from Miss Pilar Ortiz de Zarate.

working for the English Electric Company at Stafford, remembers that he and his Basque comrades at the factory were visited by an English sympathiser with very different advice. This lady urged on them the disadvantages of remaining in a country at war, the risks of discrimination as aliens, the dangers, even, of internment. She thought they ought to go back to Spain, even though the parents of Lopez were themselves refugees in France. The boys discussed this advice anxiously among themselves – they were already, in that apprehensive year, subject to special restrictions on their movements – and eventually decided to stay. Lopez, at least, has not regretted his decision.[1]

Nor did Marcel Segurola, who also thought that his parents had chosen rightly in sending him away aboard HABANA. Mrs Lopez, on the other hand, felt that she herself, in similar circumstances, would never part with her own children, knowing how uncertain their eventual return might be. Many parents would agree with her, when considering the question calmly on its abstract merits, yet reach a different decision if ever they were confronted with the choice so starkly posed in that bitter May of 1937. In Bilbao death fell daily from the skies; food dwindled as the queues for it lengthened; the sound of the enemy's guns was creeping nearer. In England there would be peace, safety, nourishment. The children's absence would be an agony, but perhaps less acute than the pain of a parent unable to protect his child. They made their option of immediate good or evil and more evidence would be needed than has yet been assembled to prove that, in the long term, their choice was wrong.

If the parents were right, then, it might be argued, so were the British organisers of the evacuation. No evidence concerning the children who came to England has so far emerged to justify that emotional outburst by the Secretary of the Save the Children Fund: 'he would sooner see them die in their own land than rot slowly in exile where they deteriorate physically, morally and mentally'.[2]

[1] Lopez.   [2] On 4 May 1937. FO 371 21370.

Happily ever after

These were predictions that events disproved, as they also falsified the expectation of the British organisers that the children would soon be able to return to a peacefully Republican Spain. The National Joint Committee were not, of course, alone in this error and they can scarcely be blamed for their initial mistake. As the months passed, however, as 1937 ended and 1938 gave way to 1939, there ought perhaps to have come a moment of fresh comprehension: that the problem had altered and that new responsibilities had arisen. Of course the Committee were short of funds and the Government were recalcitrant. The obstacles existed and have earlier been analysed and discussed. But were they insuperable: having brought these children to England and, finding that they would have to stay longer than expected, that some of them might have to remain indefinitely, could no new and better arrangements have been made to prevent the children suffering from altered circumstances beyond their control? It is a hypothetical question, but one which leaves a certain unease.

It is also a question without a single or a simple answer. Two and a half years after HABANA sailed from Bilbao, on 1 September 1939, there began the evacuation of British cities. Hundreds of thousands of school-children, of teachers, of mothers and infants descended on railway stations from Southampton to Dundee. In three days a succession of bulging trains deposited them up and down the countryside. This was an operation for which the Government assumed full responsibility, which they had begun to plan eighteen months before. These were British children entrusted to the care of their own countrymen. What happened? 'No organisation existed for dealing with them. Schools and other buildings were opened, but bedding and blankets did not exist. In some cases for four days they lived – teachers, mothers and children – on an official diet of milk, apples and cheese, sleeping on straw covered by grain bags.'[1]

Plans there were, but no money had been sanctioned, until the last moment, for their implementation. And even the plans

[1] This account is based on ch. 2 of *The People's War* by Angus Calder (Cape, 1969) which is also the source of the quotations.

197

covered only the immediate emergency: 'On August 29th [1939], the Board of Education sent out a circular to local authorities which blandly observed, "the extensive preparations for evacuation being well forward, it is time to consider what is to happen to children after evacuation".'

The authorship of this belated truism is significant, for 'the nation's education system had reached a consummation of chaos in the cities, over a million children were left to run wild . . . statistics for January 1940 showed that . . . 430,000 children in all – were still getting no teaching at all'.

If these were the results of an officially organised, nationally supported endeavour – admittedly for a thousand times the number of children – can we blame the National Joint Committee if their amateur efforts, their sparse finance, their handful of voluntary helpers sometimes achieved less for the Basque children than was altogether ideal?

One exceptionally well-qualified observer – and actor – who has never had any doubts concerning the correctness of the decision to evacuate the children is Mr Angel de Ojanguren. Indeed, he gave effect to his views at the time and not only in his official capacity. He saw to it that the family of his future wife – he was then a bachelor, but engaged to be married – were evacuated as well as his own family. He himself remained in Bilbao until the last moment, then left for Santander, having promised the Basque authorities to continue from that port his assistance in the organisation of evacuation. Before Santander fell he was able to escape to France, whence he accompanied Stevenson on a visit to Barcelona as the guests of President Aguirre, who had established something of a government in exile in that still Republican city.

Before the final collapse in Spain, Ojanguren was back in France, where he stayed to be with his fellow Basques, in whose politics of exile he was by now deeply immersed. He did not leave when war broke out and was still there when the Germans occupied France. This led to such harassment by the French police and even the Gestapo, that, in despair, he returned to Spain, was promptly arrested and sent for trial in

Happily ever after

Bilbao, where he was accused of being a British agent. Fortunately he had relations and friends, including a police officer who remembered how Ojanguren had arranged the evacuation of one of his family. Their influence and a little judicious bribery earned Ojanguren a suspended sentence. He then got in touch with the British Embassy in Madrid, who helped him escape to Gibraltar and thence to England, where he re-entered the service of His Majesty's Government. Not long after the war he was Pro-Consul at Trieste and soon found himself engaged in another of Stevenson's humanitarian enterprises, for Stevenson was by then Consul-General at Zagreb and wanted help in smuggling someone out of Yugoslavia.

Ojanguren eventually retired in England (he had been made M.B.E. for his services), but the lure of the sun and of Basque politics soon drew him southwards once more and, in 1970, he was established in Rome with the resounding titles of 'Ministro Plenipotenciario, Delegado Diplomático Oficioso del Gobierno de la República Española y Delegado Vasco'. But he still visited England, where one of his daughters lived, and was always happy to talk of those brave old days of 1937 before, as he put it, the clock stopped for him. His recollections and the introductions he effected have been of the utmost assistance in the telling of this story.[1]

He has had few rivals in his courageous survival of vicissitudes and in his longevity – he first entered the service of the British Consulate at Bilbao in 1919. Aguirre (who published the reminiscences of an equally adventurous life) and Joaquin Eguia are both dead, as are Blake (to whom ill-health denied the opportunity for command in the Second World War), Chilton, Mounsey and Ramsey. Only Ramsey, who was promoted the following year, seems to have derived any direct benefit from the part he played in this story. He retired in 1942 as an Admiral, a Commander-in-Chief and a Knight Commander of the Bath, only to take further service as a Commodore of Convoys.[2] Eden ended an outstanding career as Prime

[1] Ojanguren. [2] *Who's Who 1967*.

Minister and Earl of Avon and his books have been no less useful than the autobiography of Dame Leah Manning, who kindly consented to talk to the author in the retirement of her Suffolk cottage. Chatfield, though less successful as a politician than as First Sea Lord, also died ennobled and the researches of the indefatigably obliging Professor Temple Patterson should soon add perspective to the incomplete account of his activities in these pages.

Our attention, however, may more appropriately be directed to those lesser figures who have so far tempted no biographer, but who played such decisive rôles in our story. Commander Caslon, who began it all, received the promotion his conduct had deserved at the end of 1937 and, as Captain (D), successively commanded the Fourth, Eighteenth and Sixth destroyer flotillas during the Second World War, in which, incidentally, H.M.S. BLANCHE was sunk – the first British destroyer lost in that conflict – when she struck a mine in the Thames Estuary on 13 November 1939.[1] It was an ironic stroke of fate. Captain Caslon, however, no longer commanded her and survived the war to retire, as Vice-Admiral, C.B. and C.B.E., in 1950 and to afford the author invaluable assistance in 1970.[2]

HOOD and ROYAL OAK, for ships may interest us as well as men, were both lost in the Second World War, but their fate was perhaps more illustrious than that of most, which ended in the breaker's yard, certainly than that of J. L. DIEZ – that 'Non-Intervention Power'. But for a brief clash in August 1937, when she fired 200 shells at JUPITER and missed with every one, her conduct at Santander had been 'as supine as ever. When Santander fell, the J. L. DIEZ and 3 submarines escaped' to Gijón and thence, early in September, to Falmouth, where she put in for repairs and where 66 of her crew deserted their ship.[3] Her end was in keeping with her undistinguished career; she was caught trying to sneak through the Straits of Gibraltar on the night of 26 August 1938 by CANARIAS and three Nationalist

---

[1] Edgar J. March, *British Destroyers* (Seeley, Service, 1966), p. 265.
[2] Caslon and *Who's Who*.
[3] *Illustrated London News*, 25 September 1937.

destroyers. These were not deceived by the attempt of J. L. DIEZ to pass as a British destroyer and, as her feckless crew had not even charged their torpedoes, they could offer no defence. Driven damaged into Gibraltar she lingered there during months of diplomatic wrangling, made an incompetent sortie on 30 December, was attacked (while still in British territorial waters) by her old antagonist JUPITER and driven ashore. Though eventually refloated, that was the end of her career: the ship was interned and her crew repatriated.[1]

One ship mentioned in these pages was still afloat and in active service in 1970. This was CANARIAS, the cruiser which sank NABARA in the epic action of March 1937, subsequently flew the flag of Admiral Moreno and, in 1970, completed the last of many refits to equip her for the rôle of flagship of the Spanish Navy.[2] Of all our many characters, this ship and the Spanish Head of State, General Franco, survived longest in their leading rôles.

Nobody would have been more surprised by such an outcome than Steer, who devoted one of his most vivid – and most exploited – chapters to the action between CANARIAS and NABARA. Nobody's advice and comments could have better corrected the deficiencies of the present work. But that ardent spirit, at once so compassionate and so belligerent – he 'liked and accepted' war – was destined to see much fighting, yet not to find a soldier's death. After leaving the service of *The Times*, he had represented the *Daily Telegraph* in Africa, then went to Finland for the Winter War, his fate drawing him inevitably to share the doomed resistance of gallant peoples. Observation then gave place to action. He joined the British Army, was commissioned in the Intelligence Corps and, an altogether exceptional instance of official imagination and common sense, was selected in June 1940, on the strength of his previous Abyssinian experience, to accompany the Emperor Haile Selassie to the Sudan, *en route* for Ethiopia. Thompson, once Chargé d'Affaires at Hendaye, organised this journey and saw

---

[1] ADM 116 3518; ADM 116 3678; and ADM 116 3947.
[2] *Jane's Fighting Ships* (Sampson Low, Marston, 1970).

him off. Having worked under Wingate during the Ethiopian campaign, he naturally rejoined that leader, who was even more eccentric than himself, in Burma. By the time he met his death, in a motor accident, on Christmas Day 1944, he was a Lieutenant-Colonel. He was also the author of five books, of which *The Tree of Gernika* deserves to be read and not merely quarried by other writers.[1]

But Steer, the journalist, the soldier, even a little the artist, was also an adventurer. For personal and political reasons alike he had thrown himself deeper into the Basque drama than most, but it was still only one episode in a decade of violence and excitement. It did not shape his destiny as Abyssinia did.

On Stevenson, that quiet, self-contained official, the impact was deeper, more lasting and more obscure. He wrote no book and spoke little of his experiences, even to his wife. Prolonged exposure to the violent emotions of others seemed to have deepened his own reserve: his letters from Bilbao were fewer than usual and still more reticent.[2] Yet his service there was the outstanding and, with unintended irony, the climactic moment of his entire career. It should not have been. He had distinguished himself, he had attracted recognition: strangest of all he was rewarded, though not by the Treasury, who grudgingly paid him two thirds of the value of the personal effects he had lost in Bilbao.[3]

It was not simply that, in the Coronation Honours for 1937 and to the fury of the Italian Press, who called it 'an insolent reply to General Franco's protest' (which the Foreign Office never received) at his 'illicit interference', Stevenson was made C.B.E.[4] That was a decoration he might eventually have received, without any special distinction, as the reward of long and faithful service. The official letter addressed to him on 29 July 1937 was more important: 'I am to convey to you an expression of Mr Eden's high appreciation of the manner in

---

[1] *The Times*, 2 January 1945; and Sir Geoffrey Thompson, *Front Line Diplomat* (Hutchinson, 1959).   [2] Miss Stevenson.
[3] Foreign Office Index to General Correspondence for 1937, vol. 4, p. 218.
[4] FO 371 21292.

which you carried out the task of supervision of the evacuation
of refugees and in which you performed your other Consular
duties up to the last moment in circumstances of great difficulty
and of personal danger to yourself.'[1]

The language was stilted, but the commendation was real. An
even more striking recognition of Stevenson's services, of the
experience he had acquired and of what were evidently regarded
as his exceptional deserts, came a few months later when he
was selected for the 1938 course at the Imperial Defence
College. Even for officers of the armed services that was a
distinction (Caslon achieved it), but for a Consul it was an
unheard-of honour. Those were condescending and hierarchical
days and it was the settled conviction of senior members of the
Foreign Office that Providence, in its infinite wisdom, had early
marked out members of the Consular Service as specially
adapted by their nature for such distastefully necessary tasks
as trade promotion, the supervision of British shipping and
assistance to distressed, and generally distressing, British
subjects. To allow, indeed to encourage, one of them to interest
himself in the political and strategic mysteries of Imperial
Defence, was wantonly to fly in the face of all precedent and
privilege.

It may even have aroused greater hopes in Stevenson, for his
next post was Moscow, an appointment offering a minimum
of consular routine and fascinating opportunities for political
observation. Might this have been intended as the second step,
the Imperial Defence College having been the first, towards
eventual translation to a diplomatic appointment? No conclusions can be drawn from the fact that Stevenson was given
the local rank of First Secretary on the diplomatic list of the
Embassy; this was a necessary precaution in Moscow, where
even a Consul needed the protection of diplomatic immunity.
But the posting was deliberately made; because there was no
established and appropriate post at Moscow, Stevenson had
nominally to be appointed Consul first at Boston and then at
Valencia.[2] Was he being tried out in a capital where his unusual

---

[1] FO 371 21295.   [2] FO List 1939.

experience would be peculiarly relevant and in which his Consular origins would not – in the eyes of the Foreign Office – constitute quite their usual social impediment to diplomatic employment?

Stevenson may have thought so. Their supposed unsuitability for diplomacy was a standing grievance of Consuls in those days and the hope of being singled out as an exception the dream of the more ambitious among them. Not all the rare precedents, admittedly, were encouraging. The legend was whispered with awe in the Consular Service – and repeated with relish in the Diplomatic – of an oustanding Consul who had actually been appointed an Ambassador but, wilting beneath an honour to which he had not been born, had sickened and perished in his prime.

Whatever the Foreign Office may have contemplated, or Stevenson hoped, was not to be. The war that Steer had predicted, that he had almost wanted, that gave him fresh occasion for adventure and distinction, was drawing nearer. On 30 May 1939, nearly five months after Stevenson's arrival, the German Ambassador in Moscow was told 'we have now decided to undertake definite negotiations with the Soviet Union'. On 12 June the British Foreign Office despatched Mr Strang on a similar mission. The cryptic and ambiguous favours of the Kremlin were becoming the object of competition. For or against Germany: that was the question.

Stevenson had answered that question as finally as any man could: from 1915 to 1918 he had fought Germany as a soldier. In Bilbao he had qualified for the honourable distinction that was to brighten many a dossier otherwise less impeccable than his of 'premature anti-Fascist'. But he had a German wife and, in that ominous summer of 1939, this seemed to the Foreign Office, always apprehensive of the criticism by which they are usually unjustly afflicted, a disqualification for service in so sensitive a post. On 5 July he left Moscow and on 13 October he took up his new appointment at Rio de Janeiro.

The Foreign Office did what they could to soften the blow. Stevenson was given the local rank of Consul-General (he was not promoted until 1945). But it was the ruin of any hopes he may have entertained. No longer even a local, let alone a potential, diplomat, not at the centre of affairs, he had to stimulate the patriotism of the British community, assist the flow of volunteers for the armed forces, preside over committees of the benevolent, discharge the accustomed consular functions. In the busy tedium of his routine duties the arrival of Aguirre, once President of the Basque Autonomous Republic, now a refugee, escaping under an alias from a continent occupied by his enemies, must have been a welcome distraction. He received his old friend cordially and gave him all the assistance he could.[1]

Alas, this was not the only break in an otherwise tranquil existence. On a voyage to England Stevenson's ship was torpedoed and he spent three days in an open boat. After his return to Rio he contracted tuberculosis, to which his exposure to poison gas in the First World War had left him particularly vulnerable. The disease was less understood in those days and Stevenson never recovered his health. Eventually he had to have one lung removed.[2]

Again the Foreign Office did what they could for him. Having been promoted Consul-General on 9 May 1945 (was it a coincidence that this was the day after the end of the war with Germany?) he was transferred to Zagreb in 1947 and to Naples in 1952. His health deteriorated further, he suffered from severe bronchial attacks, but he served his full time, retiring only in 1955.[3]

He never forgot those two years in Bilbao or Ojanguren, with whom he maintained a regular correspondence and who saluted his death, on 10 December 1967, with an obituary in the *Boletín de Información* published in Paris by the Oficina Prensa Euzkadi, the organ in exile of the Basque Nationalists. This described him as 'un amigo de los Vascos' and correctly related how, in the discharge of his duties, he had overcome difficulties to do service to Great Britain and the cause of humanity by

[1] Aguirre, *Freedom was Flesh and Blood.*   [2] Miss Stevenson.
[3] FO List 1956.

saving the lives of those in peril. Many men of greater worldly distinction have had worse epitaphs.

Only Stevenson could have told us whether it was also appropriate, whether those hectic months, when destroyers ferried him to and fro, when the meetings of Basque Ministers were interrupted to receive him, when his telegrams were quoted to the Cabinet in London, were really the most memorable moments of his life. For it is the common fate of many men, perhaps particularly of those in official positions, to find that others arrange in a different order the relative importance of their achievements and their experiences. Was Bilbao the high point of his existence, the culmination of his career, or was it merely a natural topic of conversation and correspondence with Ojanguren, whom he happened to like?

It is too late to ask that reserved and reticent official, that Englishman of a type that made us famous and that we know no longer. He kept no diary, wrote no memoirs, confided no reminiscences of his public duties. Those who knew him mourned the man, but felt the Consul had gone, still a stranger, from their lives.

What has not gone out of the lives of any of us is the cry of children. Successive years have racked that sound from every continent. Today it reaches more ears than once it did. The screen can even show us the lips that utter it. Now we can all know, as in 1937 only a few could guess, how a child looks that war has broken. But which Consul has called, and with what success, for the rescue of foreign children? When did a government last send warships to protect them?

When we have weighed all that can be urged against Baldwin, his Ministers and the British bureaucracy they controlled – the mixed motives, the hesitations, the cheese-paring – one fact remains. They did save children. In spite of 'a very general and widespread feeling in this country of distaste for these extreme doctrines',[1] the Royal Navy escorted 'fervent little Reds'[2] and did so even when they were bound for the Soviet Union.[3] What later and more enlightened ruler can claim half as much?

---

[1] See Chapter 13.   [2] See Chapter 4.   [3] See Chapter 9.

Bibliography

Of all the books listed below, only Hansard and Steer's *The Tree of Gernika* deal at length with British naval operations off the northern coast of Spain during the spring and summer of 1937. Others make passing reference to these events, but most are included as the source of information on the background, on personalities, on facts and figures or on side-issues. A much longer list could be compiled of books about the period which surprisingly omit all useful reference to the subject of this story. Two successive First Lords of the Admiralty, Sir Samuel Hoare and Mr Duff Cooper, excluded it from their memoirs and Professor Thomas is one of the few historians to have admitted it to his pages. These are thus books to which the author is indebted, rather than alternative accounts.

Aguirre, José Antonio de. *Freedom was Flesh and Blood*. Gollancz, 1945.

Atholl, Duchess of. *Working Partnership*. Barker, 1958.

Azpilkoeta, Dr de. *Le Problème Basque*. Grasset, Paris, 1938.

Bolin, Luis. *Spain: The Vital Years*. Cassell, 1967.

Bowers, Claude G. *My Mission to Spain*. Gollancz, 1954.

Butler & Freeman. *British Political Facts 1900–1968*. Macmillan, 1969.

Cable, James. *Gunboat Diplomacy*. Chatto and Windus, 1971.

Calder, Angus. *The People's War*. Cape, 1969.

Cervera Valderrama, Almirante Juan. *Memorias de Guerra*. Editora Nacional, Madrid, 1968.

Chatfield, Lord. *It Might Happen Again*. Heinemann, 1947.

Churchill, Winston S. *The Gathering Storm*. Cassell, 1948.

Cleugh, James. *Spanish Fury*. Harrap, 1962.

Cloud, Yvonne. *The Basque Children in England*. Gollancz, 1937.

†Colvin, Ian. *The Chamberlain Cabinet*. Gollancz, 1971.

†Connell, John. *The 'Office'*. Wingate, 1958.

Crozier, Brian. *Franco*. Eyre and Spottiswoode, 1967.

† Useful on British politicians, but strangely silent on the Spanish Civil War.

Bibliography

Documents on German Foreign Policy, series D, vol. 3. H.M.S.O., 1951.

Eden, Anthony. *Facing the Dictators*. Cassell, 1962.

Foreign Affairs. Faber, 1939.

García, Durán, Juan. *Bibliografía de la Guerra Civil Española*. Editorial El Siglo Ilustrado, Montevideo, 1964.

Grenfell, Captain Russell. *The Bismarck Episode*. Faber, 1948.

Goya, Francisco. *Los Desastres de la Guerra*. Phaidon – Allen and Unwin, 1937.

Hansard.

Harvey, John (ed.). *The Diplomatic Diaries of Oliver Harvey 1937–1940*. Collins, 1970.

Hodgson, Sir Robert. *Spain Resurgent*. Hutchinson, 1953.

Jackson, Gabriel. *The Spanish Republic and The Civil War*. Princeton U.P., 1965.

Jane's Fighting Ships. Sampson Low, Marston, 1937 and later editions.

Lloyd George, David. *War Memoirs*. Odhams, 1938.

Lojendio, Luis Maria de. *Operaciones Militares de la Guerra de España 1936-1938*. Montaner y Simon S.A., Barcelona, 1940.

Maisky, Ivan. *Spanish Notebooks*, tr. Kisch. Hutchinson, 1966.

Manning, Leah. *A Life for Education*. Gollancz, 1970.

March, Edgar J. *British Destroyers*. Seeley, Service, 1966.

Merry del Val, Marquis. *Spanish Basques and Separatism*. Burnes, Oates, 1939.

Middlemas, Keith & Barnes, John. *Baldwin*. Weidenfeld and Nicolson, 1969.

Mitford, Jessica. *Hons and Rebels*. Gollancz, 1960.

Moreno Fernández, Almirante D. Francisco. *Le Guerra en el Mar*, ed. Moreno de Reyna. Editorial AHR, Barcelona, 1959.

Mowat, Charles Loch. *Britain Between The Wars: 1918-1940*. Methuen, 1955.

Oudard, Georges. *Chemises Noires Brunes Vertes en Espagne*. Librairie Plon, Paris, 1938.

Padelford, Norman J. *International Law and Diplomacy in the Spanish Civil Strife*. Macmillan, New York, 1939.

Puzzo, Dante A. *Spain and The Great Powers 1936-1941*. Columbia U.P., 1962.

Schwartzenberger, Georg (ed.). *The Law of Armed Conflict*. Stevens, 1968.

Smith, Peter. *Destroyer Leader*. William Kimber, 1968.

Bibliography

Steer, G. L. *The Tree of Gernika: A Field Study of Modern War.* Hodder and Stoughton, 1938.

Taylor, A. J. P. *English History 1914–1945.* O.U.P., 1965.

Thomas, Hugh. *The Spanish Civil War.* Eyre and Spottiswoode, 1961.

Thompson, Sir Geoffrey. *Front Line Diplomat.* Hutchinson, 1959.

Toynbee, Arnold J. *Survey of International Affairs 1937*, vol. 2. R.I.I.A. and O.U.P., 1938.

Trythall, J. W. D. *Franco.* Hart-Davis, 1970.

Watkins, K. W. *Britain Divided.* Nelson, 1963.

Who's Who and *Who Was Who.*

Young, G. M. *Stanley Baldwin.* Hart-Davis, 1952.

Index

Names of ships appear as in the text: thus HOOD.
Names of persons are given as they were at the time.

Index

Index

Index

Index